$1⁰⁰

HERITAGE OF FREEDOM

PUBLISHED IN COOPERATION WITH

THE AMERICAN HERITAGE FOUNDATION

HERITAGE OF FREEDOM

THE HISTORY & SIGNIFICANCE
OF THE
BASIC DOCUMENTS
OF AMERICAN LIBERTY

———◆———

BY FRANK MONAGHAN

HISTORICAL CONSULTANT
AMERICAN HERITAGE FOUNDATION

PRINCETON UNIVERSITY PRESS · PRINCETON, N. J.

1947

The photographs for the facsimile reproductions in this book were made by Peter A. Juley & Son of New York City.

TO THE READER

THIS is a book presenting and explaining the documents on the Freedom Train. This remarkable exhibition of the basic documents of the American Heritage has been made possible by the effective and generous co-operation of many institutions and individuals. That same spirit of co-operation has made the present book possible. The details of our gratitude are recorded in a special section of acknowledgments.

Experts have stated that the Freedom Train presents the finest collection of original documents on American history ever assembled for exhibition purposes. But the Freedom Train itself is chiefly a means of awakening the interest of all citizens in our heritage of freedom.

Here are the documents and the implications of those documents. They are generally grouped by subject and in the approximate order in which they are presented on the Freedom Train. Facsimiles frequently provide the full, legible text of many of the most significant documents. Where this is not possible the full text is, in most cases, given together with the historical introduction. The index provides further guidance for the consultation of the documents.

FRANK MONAGHAN

American Heritage Foundation
New York, New York

CONTENTS

HERITAGE OF FREEDOM

1. Christopher Columbus Describes His First Voyage to the New World (1493)

BEFORE the momentous voyages of Columbus, men had sailed from Europe to the shores of the unknown continent of North America. But their efforts were as ephemeral as their courage was great. They came for a brief moment and then disappeared without as much as footnoting a durable page in history. The appreciation of the significance of the discoveries of Columbus brought to the view of a crumbling feudal civilization in western Europe a new and glittering vista from beyond the horizon. Men were slow to realize what had actually been discovered as well as the implications of the new discoveries. Had these been quickly known the effect would have been greater than the discovery of atomic fission in our own age. Columbus himself, being a stubborn character, refused to the end of his days to believe that he had discovered a new world. A few men soon divined it and tried to persuade him, but he remained unconvinced. He *knew* that he had discovered the westward water route to the fabled wealth of Asia and that only a few obstructing islands had prevented him from reaching his ultimate objective.

It was early in 1493, while homeward bound, that Columbus wrote his famous letter on his first voyage. While this document is often called the letter to Sanchez or to Santangel, it was actually not written to any particular person. It was, if you may so term it, an early kind of publicity release; it was meant to be the announcement to the public of his voyage and discoveries. When it was received many manuscript copies were quickly made and circulated. One of these copies, endorsed to Louis de Santangel, was printed in the summer of 1493 as a four-page folio pamphlet in Barcelona. From a somewhat more accurate copy than that used in Barcelona one Leondro de Cosco made a Latin translation which went through nine various editions. This Latin translation was completed on April 29, 1493, and during that year it had three Roman editions. The original exhibited on the Freedom Train is the second edition, lent by Mrs. Marshall Ludington Brown and the Princeton University Library.

This eight-page pamphlet was a best seller of its day. An avid public was greatly interested in the descriptions of the naked savages—a phenomenon then much less common than in our own age. Europeans were astounded by the absence of religion (as understood by Europeans) among these strange natives and by their total ignorance

of the weapons of warfare devised by more civilized peoples. But the greatest good news was probably the statement that "most of the rivers" in Hispaniola "yield gold." This is the text of the letter in the translation of R. H. Major in Hakluyt Society *Publications* XII (1847).

(Note: It should be remarked that Columbus sailed from Palos rather than from Cadiz; this was probably a simple error in translation. The reader is reminded that Columbus employed certain geographical terms which have long since fallen into disuse. Clarification is made somewhat simpler if the reader will substitute the modern "North Caico" for the old "Santa Maria de la Concepción;" "Little Inagua" for "Fernandina;" "Great Inagua" for "Isabella;" "Cuba" for "Juana;" and "San Domingo" for "Española.")

A Letter addressed to the noble Lord Raphael Sanchez, Treasurer to their most invincible Majesties, Ferdinand and Isabella, King and Queen of Spain, by Christopher Columbus, to whom our age is greatly indebted, treating of the islands of India recently discovered beyond the Ganges, to explore which he had been sent eight months before under the auspices and at the expense of their said Majesties.

Knowing that it will afford you pleasure to learn that I have brought my undertaking to a successful termination, I have decided upon writing you this letter to acquaint you with all the events which have occurred in my voyage, and the discoveries which have resulted from it. Thirty-three days after my departure from Cadiz, I reached the Indian sea, where I discovered many islands, thickly peopled, of which I took possession without resistance in the name of our most illustrious Monarch, by public proclamation and with unfurled banners. To the first of these islands, which is called by the Indians Guanahani, I gave the name of the blessed Saviour (San Salvador), relying upon whose protection I had reached this as well as the other islands; to each of these I also gave a name, ordering that one should be called Santa Maria de la Concepción, another Fernandina, the third Isabella, the fourth Juana, and so with all the rest respectively. As soon as we arrived at that, which as I have said was named Juana, I proceeded along its coast a short distance westward, and found it to be so large and apparently without termination, that I could not suppose it to be an island, but the continental province of Cathay. Seeing, however, no towns or populous places on the sea coast, but only a few detached houses and cottages, with whose inhabitants I was unable to communicate, because they fled as soon as they saw us, I went further on, thinking that in my progress I should certainly find some city or village. At length, after proceeding a great way and finding that nothing new presented itself, and that the line of coast was leading us northwards (which I wished to avoid, because it was winter, and it was my intention to move southwards; and because moreover the winds were contrary), I resolved not to attempt any further progress, but rather to turn back and retrace my course to a certain bay that I had observed, and from which I afterwards dispatched two of our men to ascertain whether there were a king or any cities in that province. These men reconnoitred the country for three days, and found a most numerous population, and great numbers of houses, though small, and built without any regard to order: with which information they returned to us. In the mean time I had learned from some Indians whom I had seized, that that country was certainly an island: and therefore I sailed towards the east, coasting to the distance of three hundred and twenty-two miles, which brought us to the extremity of it; from this point I saw lying eastwards another island, fifty-four miles distant from Juana, to which I gave the name of Española: I went thither, and steered my course eastward as I had done at Juana, even to the distance of five hundred and sixty-four miles along the north coast. This said island of Juana is exceedingly fertile, as indeed are all the others; it is surrounded with many bays, spacious, very secure, and surpassing any that I have ever seen; numerous large and healthful rivers intersect it, and it also contains many very lofty mountains. All these islands are very beautiful, and distinguished by a diversity of scenery; they are filled with a great variety of trees of immense height, and which I believe to retain their foliage in all season; for when I saw them they were as verdant and luxuriant as they usually are in Spain in the month of May,—some of them were blossoming, some bearing fruit, and all flourishing in the greatest perfection, according to their respective stages of growth, and the nature and quality of each: yet the islands are not so thickly wooded as to be impassable. The nightingale and various birds were singing in countless numbers, and that in November, the month in which I arrived there. There are besides in the same island of Juana seven or eight kinds of palm trees, which, like all the other trees, herbs, and fruits, considerably surpass ours in height and beauty. The pines also are very handsome, and there are very extensive fields and meadows, a variety of birds, different kinds of honey, and many sorts of metals, but no iron. In that island also which I have before said we named Española, there are mountains of very great size and beauty, vast plains, groves, and very fruitful fields, admirably adapted for tillage, pasture, and habitation. The convenience and excellence of the harbours in this island, and the abundance of the rivers, so indispensable to the health of man, surpass anything that would be believed by one who had

not seen it. The trees, herbage, and fruits of Española are very different from those of Juana, and moreover it abounds in various kinds of spices, gold, and other metals. The inhabitants of both sexes in this island, and in all the others which I have seen, or of which I have received information, go always naked as they were born, with the exception of some of the women, who use the covering of a leaf, or small bough, or an apron of cotton which they prepare for that purpose. None of them, as I have already said, are possessed of any iron, neither have they weapons, being unacquainted with, and indeed incompetent to use them, not from any deformity of body (for they are well-formed), but because they are timid and full of fear. They carry however in lieu of arms, canes dried in the sun, on the ends of which they fix heads of dried wood sharpened to a point, and even these they dare not use habitually; for it has often occurred when I have sent two or three of my men to any of the villages to speak with the natives, that they have come out in a disorderly troop, and have fled in such haste at the approach of our men, that the fathers forsook their children and the children their fathers. This timidity did not arise from any loss or injury that they had received from us; for, on the contrary, I gave to all I approached whatever articles I had about me, such as cloth and many other things, taking nothing of theirs in return: but they are naturally timid and fearful. As soon however as they see that they are safe, and have laid aside all fear, they are very simple and honest, and exceedingly liberal with all they have; none of them refusing any thing he may possess when he is asked for it, but on the contrary inviting us to ask them. They exhibit great love towards all others in preference to themselves: they also give objects of great value for trifles, and content themselves with very little or nothing in return. I however forbad that these trifles and articles of no value (such as pieces of dishes, plates, and glass, keys, and leather straps) should be given to them, although if they could obtain them, they imagined themselves to be possessed of the most beautiful trinkets in the world. It even happened that a sailor received for a leather strap as much gold as was worth three golden nobles, and for things of more trifling value offered by our men, especially newly coined blancas, or any gold coins, the Indians would give whatever the seller required; as, for instance, an ounce and a half or two ounces of gold, or thirty or forty pounds of cotton, with which commodity they were already acquainted. Thus they bartered, like idiots, cotton and gold for fragments of bows, glasses, bottles, and jars; which I forbad as being unjust, and myself gave them many beautiful and acceptable articles which I had brought with me, taking nothing from them in return; I did this in order that I might the more easily conciliate them, that they might be led to become Christians, and be inclined to entertain a regard for the King

¶ Epistola Christofori Colom: cui etas nostra multū debet: de Insulis Indie supra Gangem nuper inuētis. Ad quas pergrendas octauo antea mense auspiciis τ ere inuictissimoᵽ Fernādi τ Helisabet Hispaniaᵽ Regū missus fuerat: ad magnificum dñm Gabrielem Sanchis eorundē serenissimoᵽ Regum Tesaurariū missa: quā nobilis ac litteratus vir Leander de Cosco ab Hispano idiomate in latinum cōuertit tertio kal's Maii. M·cccc·rciii Pontificatus Alexandri Sexti Anno primo.

Quoniam suscepte prouintie rem perfectam me ᵽsecutum fuisse gratum tibi fore scio: has constitui erarare: que te vniuscuiusᵱ rei in hoc nostro itinere geste inuenteᵱ admoneant: Tricesimotertio die postᵱ Gadibus discessi in mare Indicū perueni: vbi plurimas insulas innumeris habitatas hominibus repperi: quarum omnium pro felicissimo Rege nostro preconio celebrato τ verillis extensis contradicente nemine possessionem accepi: primeᵱ earum diui Saluatoris nomen imposui: cuius fretus auxilio tam ad hanc: ᵱ ad ceteras alias peruenimus. Eam vo Indi Guanabanin vocant. Aliarū etiam vnam quanᵱ nouo nomine nuncupaui: quippe aliā insulam Sancte Marie Conceptionis. aliam Fernandinam. aliam Hysabellam. aliam Joanam. τ sic de reliquis appellari iussi. Cum primum in eam insulam quam dudum Joanam vocari dixi appulimus: iurta eius littus occidentem versus aliquantulum processi: tamᵱ eam magnam nullo reperto fine inueni: vt non insulā: sed continentem Chatai prouinciam esse crediderim: nulla tñ videns oppida municipiaue in maritimis sita confinib° preter aliquos vicos τ predia rustica: cum quoᵱ incolis loqui nequibam. quare simul ac nos videbant surripiebant fugam. Progrediebar vltra: existimans aliquā me vrbem villasue inuenturū. Deniᵱ videns ᵱ longe admodum progressis nihil noui emergebat: τ hñoi via nos ad Septentrionem deferebat: ᵱ ipse fugere exoptabā: terris etenim regnabat bruma: ad Austrumᵱ erat in voto cōtendere:

Columbus Describes the Discovery of America. This Page is from the Second Latin Edition, Printed in Rome in 1493 and Queen, our Princes and all Spaniards, and that I might induce them to take an interest in seeking out, and collecting, and delivering to us such things as they possessed in abundance, but which we greatly needed. They practise no kind of idolatry, but have a firm belief that all strength and power, and indeed all good things, are in heaven, and that I had descended from thence with these ships and sailors, and under this impression was I received after they had thrown aside their fears. Nor are they slow or stupid, but of very clear understanding; and those men who have crossed to the neighbouring islands give an admirable description of everything they observed; but they never saw any people clothed, nor any ships like ours. On my arrival at that sea, I had taken some Indians by force from the first island that I came to, in order that they might learn our language, and communicate to us what they knew respecting the country; which plan succeeded excellently, and was a great advantage to us, for in a short time, either by gestures and signs, or by words, we were enabled to understand each other. These men are still travelling with me, and although they have been with us now a long time, they continue to entertain the idea that I have descended from heaven; and on our arrival at any new place they published this, crying out immediately with a loud voice to the other Indians, "Come, come and look upon beings of a celestial race": upon which both women and men, children and adults, young men and old, when they got rid of the fear they at first entertained, would come out in throngs, crowding the roads to see us, some bringing food, others drink, with astonishing affection and kindness. Each of these islands has a great number of canoes, built of solid wood, narrow and not unlike our double-banked boats in length and shape, but swifter in their motion: they steer them only by the oar. These canoes are of various sizes, but the greater number are constructed with eighteen banks of oars, and with these they cross to the other islands, which are of countless number, to carry on traffic with the people. I saw some of these canoes that held as many as seventy-eight rowers. In all these islands there is no difference of physiognomy, of manners, or of language, but they all clearly understand each other, a circumstance very propitious for the realization of what I conceive to be the principal wish of our most serene King, namely, the conversion of these people to the holy faith of Christ, to which indeed, as far as I can judge, they are very favourable and well-disposed. I said before, that I went three hundred and twenty-two miles in a direct line from west to east, along the coast of the island of Juana; judging by which voyage, and the length of the passage, I can assert that it is larger than England and Scotland united; for independent of the said three hundred and twenty-two miles, there are in the western part of the island two provinces which I did not visit; one of these

is called by the Indians Anam, and its inhabitants are born with tails. These provinces extend to a hundred and fifty-three miles in length, as I have learnt from the Indians whom I have brought with me, and who are well acquainted with the country. But the extent of Española is greater than all Spain from Catalonia to Fontarabia, which is easily proved, because one of its four sides which I myself coasted in a direct line, from west to east, measures five hundred and forty miles. This island is to be regarded with especial interest, and not to be slighted; for although as I have said I took possession of all these islands in the name of our invincible King, and the government of them is unreservedly committed to his said Majesty, yet there was one large town in Española of which especially I took possession, situated in a remarkably favourable spot, and in every way convenient for the purposes of gain and commerce. To this town I gave the name of Navidad del Señor, and ordered a fortress to be built there, which must by this time be completed, in which I left as many men as I thought necessary, with all sorts of arms, and enough provisions for more than a year. I also left them one caravel, and skilful workmen both in ship-building and other arts, and engaged the favor and friendship of the King of the island in their behalf, to a degree that would not be believed, for these people are so amiable and friendly that even the King took a pride in calling me his brother. But supposing their feelings should become changed, and they should wish to injure those who have remained in the fortress, they could not do so, for they have no arms, they go naked, and are moreover too cowardly; so that those who hold the said fortress, can easily keep the whole island in check, without any pressing danger to themselves, provided they do not transgress the directions and regulations which I have given them. As far as I have learned, every man throughout these islands is united to but one wife, with the exception of the kings and princes, who are allowed to have twenty: the women seem to work more than the men. I could not clearly understand whether the people possess any private property, for I observed that one man had the charge of distributing various things to the rest, but especially meat and provisions and the like. I did not find, as some of us had expected, any cannibals amongst them, but on the contrary men of great deference and kindness. Neither are they black, like the Ethiopians: their hair is smooth and straight: for they do not dwell where the rays of the sun strike most vividly,—and the sun has intense power there, the distance from the equinoctial line being, it appears, but six-and-twenty degrees. On the tops of the mountains the cold is very great, but the effect of this upon the Indians is lessened by their being accustomed to the climate, and by their frequently indulging in the use of very hot meats and drinks. Thus, as I have already said, I saw no cannibals, nor did I hear of any, except in a certain island called Charis, which is the second from Española on the side towards India, where dwell a people who are considered by the neighbouring islanders as most ferocious: and these feed upon human flesh. The same people have many kinds of canoes, in which they cross to all the surrounding islands and rob and plunder wherever they can; they are not different from the other islanders, except that they wear their hair long, like women, and make use of the bows and javelins of cane, with sharpened spear-points fixed on the thickest end, which I have before described, and therefore they are looked upon as ferocious, and regarded by the other Indians with unbounded fear; but I think no more of them than the rest. These are the men who form unions with certain women, who dwell alone in the island Matenin, which lies next to Española on the side towards India; these latter employ themselves in no labour suitable to their own sex, for they use bows and javelins as I have already described their paramours as doing, and for defensive armour have plates of brass, of which metal they possess great abundance. They assure me that there is another island larger than Española, whose inhabitants have no hair, and which abounds in gold more than any of the rest. I bring with me individuals of this island and of the others that I have seen, who are proofs of the facts which I state. Finally, to compress into few words the entire summary of my voyage and speedy return, and of the advantages derivable therefrom, I promise, that with a little assistance afforded me by our most invincible sovereigns, I will procure them as much gold as they need, as great a quantity of spices, of cotton, and of mastic (which is only found in Chios), and as many men for the service of the navy as their Majesties may require. I promise also rhubarb and other sorts of drugs, which I am persuaded the men whom I have left in the aforesaid fortress have found already and will continue to find; for I myself have tarried no where longer than I was compelled to do by the winds, except in the city of Navidad, while I provided for the building of the fortress, and took the necessary precautions for the perfect security of the men I left there. Although all I have related may appear to be wonderful and unheard of, yet the results of my voyage would have been more astonishing if I had had at my disposal such ships as I required. But these great and marvellous results are not to be attributed to any merit of mine, but to the holy Christian faith, and to the piety and religion of our Sovereigns; for that which the unaided intellect of man could not compass, the spirit of God has granted to human exertions, for God is wont to hear the prayers of his servants who love his precepts even to the performance of apparent impossibilities. Thus it has happened to me in the present instance, who have accomplished a task to which the powers of mortal men had never hitherto attained; for if there have been those who have anywhere written

or spoken of these islands, they have done so with doubts and conjectures, and no one has ever asserted that he has seen them, on which account their writings have been looked upon as little else than fables. Therefore let the king and queen, our princes and their most happy kingdoms, and all the other provinces of Christendom, render thanks to our Lord and Saviour Jesus Christ, who has granted us so great a victory and such prosperity. Let processions be made, and sacred feasts be held, and the temples be adorned with festive boughs. Let Christ rejoice on earth, as he rejoices in heaven in the prospect of the salvation of the souls of so many nations hitherto lost. Let us also rejoice, as well on account of the exaltation of our faith, as on account of the increase of our temporal prosperity, of which not only Spain, but all Christendom will be partakers.

Such are the events which I have briefly described. Farewell.

Lisbon, the 14th of March.

Christopher Columbus,
Admiral of the Fleet of the Ocean.

2. Magna Carta Becomes a Landmark in the History of Constitutional Liberties

THE world of mesne lords and fiefs, mortmain and scutage seems long ago and far away. It is. And if the complexities of that world sometimes seem unintelligible and confusing to us, it might be a measure of solace to realize that even the men of that day did not always have the clearest understanding of the things about them. The details of feudal contracts and the intricacies of feudal law were of such stuff as only lawyers understand. With or without lawyers, there remained always the resort to armed force for the settlement of difficulties.

Magna Carta has been variously described as a formally enacted law, a treaty, the royal answer to a petition, and a declaration of rights. It was the result of a bargain between King John and his rebellious barons. It originally had 63 clauses, but when it was first confirmed by the Earl of Pembroke on behalf of the boy-king Henry III these had been reduced to 42. By 1217 it again had 47. When it received its fifth confirmation in 1225 it had 37 clauses and these proved to be the final and accepted legal version.

It has been denounced as a reactionary feudal document. In some respects this is correct. It did not pretend to introduce any new or revolutionary concept of government. It is likewise true that the vast majority of the people of England were excluded from its privileges, because they were not free men but serfs. It was mainly a statement of ancient customs which were now described as rights. The chief concern of the barons was to retain their privileges and properties, including the serfs, against spoliation by a rapacious king. A modern historian thus summarizes Magna Carta: the King had not played the game; in the future he must; and here were the rules for all to read.

It has been extolled as the basis of all our modern constitutional liberties, the source of "no taxation without representation," etc. This, too, is an exaggeration.

The truth is somewhere between these conflicting views. The nobles, in acting to preserve their own interests, established principles which were later to be applied in ways of which they had never dreamed. It is the foundation of modern liberties in the sense that it marked the first successful limitation of the royal authority and gave to posterity a symbol of the triumph of law over the personal authority of the king. Henceforth the law was to bind the king as well as the chief vassals of the king. In the 17th century the Magna Carta was interpreted by legal-minded reformers, who sought to curb the powers of the throne, into something it had never been before. They translated Magna Carta into a statement of the liberties of the whole English people and of the privileges of a parliament which had not even been dreamed of in 1215. Happily for posterity the lawyers of the 17th century twisted meanings in favor of an enlargement of English freedoms.

In spite of varying interpretations there are certain sections of Magna Carta which permit of no misunderstanding and have never lost their vibrant challenge: "To no man will we sell, to no man will we deny or delay right or justice." King John unwittingly contributed to the growth of English freedom by provoking the barons to the point where they forced him to sign Magna Carta; and in their turn, the barons unwittingly contributed to that growth, even though their own objectives were narrow and selfish. Magna Carta, with all its vicissitudes, remains one of the great landmarks in the development of constitutional liberties.

Only four copies of the Magna Carta of 1215 have survived, and even the later manuscript versions with amendments, statutes, and omissions are extremely rare. The copy of *Magna Carta cum aliis statuis*, lent to the Freedom Train exhibit by the John H. Scheide Library, seems to belong to the early fourteenth century. It was almost certainly written after 1301, for it contains the Charter of the Forest of that year, and before 1306, when Edward I, "the English Justinian," revoked the disafforestations made in 1301. Written in legal Latin and in French in Gothic characters, its 95 parchment leaves contain three large historiated initials executed in gold and colors. These initials represent, first, Edward I (apparently a contemporary attempt at portraiture; Edward is shown pointing to his own name in the accompanying text); second, a huntsman armed with a

bow and blowing his horn, with dogs and stags in the background; and, third, a monk reading a book to two men. There are also six large initials in gold and colors decorated with leafy arabesques or strapwork, and other initials in red and blue, together with nineteen coats-of-arms in color, some with their bearers' names added. The manuscript is in its original binding, pink-stained doe-skin over boards, with painted foredge. Some of the marginal grotesques have unusual interest. In addition to Magna Carta, the Scheide copy contains the Provisions of Merton (1236), the Statutes of Marlborough (1267), the Statutes of Westminster I and II (1275 and 1285), and other state documents. Additions were made on 21 leaves in handwriting of the fourteenth and fifteenth centuries, beginning with the Statutes of Winchester (1285). An entry on the last two leaves, in a later handwriting, is dated 1471. Exhibited is the first page, which contains the portraiture of Edward I.

3. The "Mayflower" Pilgrims Form a Compact (1620)

THE group which history knows as the Pilgrims left England in 1608 to avoid religious persecution. They went first to the Netherlands, but after twelve years there decided to migrate to America, where they hoped they could maintain their chosen way of life but under English laws. In September 1620, after two false starts, they sailed for the western world in the *Mayflower*. The ship made a rough crossing, and was blown by storms far north of its destination. The Pilgrims intended to settle in the territory under the jurisdiction of the Virginia Company which had granted them certain rights to the soil and to local self-government. By storms and faulty navigation they were driven far northward to bleak Cape Cod. Finally it was decided to land at Plymouth.

But all the rights which the Pilgrim leaders had obtained from the Virginia Company had no validity if they were to settle in New England. The settlers would have possessed no legal status in New England until a new patent could be secured from the Council for New England.

When the implications of this changed situation were grasped, some of the more restless spirits threatened to strike out for themselves. In the cabin of the *Mayflower*, as she rode at anchor in the harbor at Plymouth, were heard "discontented and mutinous speeches" by those who declared that they "would use their own liberty" once they had landed. Here, then, was an ominous invitation to disorder, even anarchy, within the weary and troubled band of pioneers.

William Bradford, the leader of the colony, explains in his *History of Plymouth Plantation*, that it was this

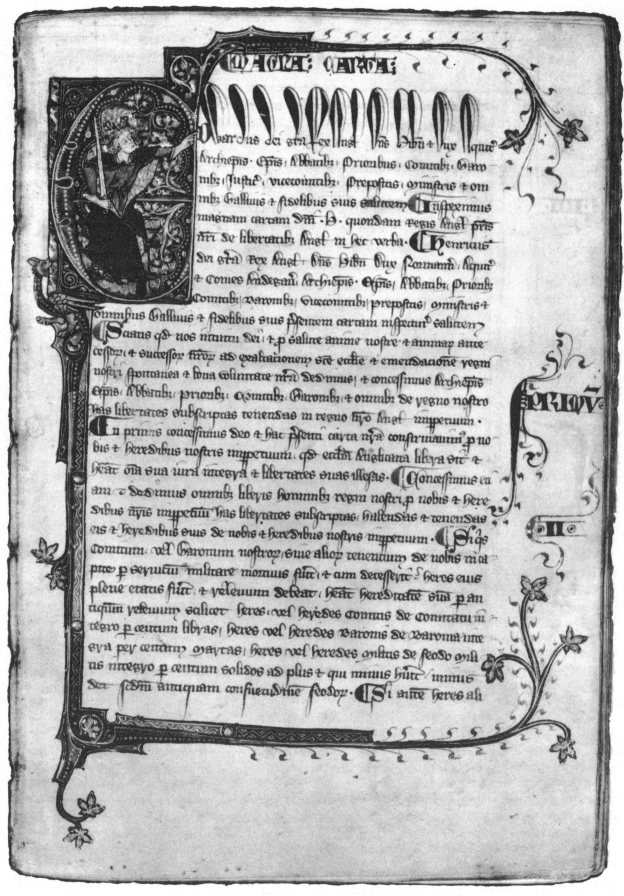

An Early Fourteenth Century Manuscript of Magna Carta

situation that led to the drawing up of the famous *May-flower Compact*. All male passengers signed an agreement that they would, in Bradford's words, submit to "such government and governors as [they] should by common consent agree to make and choose." It was not intended as a constitution, but was an extension to civil circumstances of the customary church covenant. It was a temporary device to meet a threatened crisis. The signers had come to Plymouth not to create a "democracy" or to change any government but to exercise and enjoy their own particular version of what they were pleased to term religious freedom. It would be a serious mistake to confuse their meaning of religious freedom with the modern conception of freedom of religion. They wanted the opportunity to exercise their own religious beliefs. But for anyone who did not agree with them, there was neither toleration nor liberty.

The authors of the Mayflower Compact had no conception of and no desire to promulgate any new philosophy of democratic government. They met a threatened crisis with a necessary temporary measure: the establishment of a local government which, having no recognized legal sanction, would at least be bolstered by the strength of common consent. Plymouth Colony was always more theocratic than democratic.

The document exhibited on the Freedom Train is the account as printed in John Mourt's *Relation* (1622), lent by the Library of Congress.

The following is the text:

In the name of God, Amen. We whose names are underwritten, the loyall Subjects of our dread soveraigne Lord King James, by the grace of God of Great *Britaine*, *France* and *Ireland* King, Defender of the Faith &c.

Having under-taken for the glory of God, and advancement of the Christian Faith, and honour of our King and Countrey, a Voyage to plant the first Colony in the Northerne parts of VIRGINIA, doe by these presents solemnly & mutually in the presence of God and one of another, covenant, and combine our selves together into a civill body politike, for our better ordering and preservation, and furtherance of the ends aforesaid; and by vertue hereof to enact, constitute, and frame such just and equall Lawes, Ordinances, acts, constitutions, offices from time to time, as shall be thought most meet and convenient for the generall good of the Colony: unto which we promise all due submission and obedience. In witnesse whereof we have here-under subscribed our names. *Cape Cod* 11. of *November*, in the yeare of the raigne of our soveraigne Lord King James, of *England*, *France*, and *Ireland* 18. and of *Scotland* 54. *Anno Domino* 1620.

| John Carver | Samuel Fuller | Edward Tilly |
| William Bradford | Christopher Martin | John Tilly |

Edward Winslow	William Mullins	Francis Cooke
William Brewster	William White	Thomas Rogers
Isaac Allerton	Richard Warren	Thomas Tinker
Miles Standish	John Howland	John Ridgdale
John Alden	Steven Hopkins	Edward Fuller
John Turner	Digery Priest	Richard Clark
Francis Eaton	Thomas Williams	Richard Gardiner
James Chilton	Gilbert Winslow	John Allerton
John Craxton	Edmund Margesson	Thomas English
John Billington	Peter Brown	Edward Doten
Joses Fletcher	Richard Bitteridge	Edward Liester
John Goodman	George Soule	

4. William Penn Grants Liberal Privileges to the Inhabitants of Pennsylvania (1701)

THE Pennsylvania Charter of Privileges of 1701 was clearly one of the most important of all grants of colonial liberties. This original signed and sealed document, one of the most precious of all the Freedom Train exhibits, was lent by the American Philosophical Society. Down to the second decade of the 19th century the Charter was in private hands. It was then that a number of civic-minded members of the American Philosophical Society became impressed with the possibility of loss or damage to the document. They acquired it early in 1812 for safekeeping in the vaults of the Library of the Society and since that time it has been preserved with their other most precious documents. During World War II it was temporarily transferred to the vaults of a Philadelphia bank for protection against the possible hazards of air raids. Otherwise, since 1812, it has been kept in the Hall of the Society on Independence Square, Philadelphia. The records indicate that it has never been exhibited elsewhere and has never been outside the city of Philadelphia since it was first acquired by the Society. Thus it is a double honor that the Freedom Train is permitted to bring this cherished document directly to the people of the United States.

Of the document itself we cannot do better than to quote the words of Dr. William E. Lingelbach, the distinguished Librarian of the Society:

"First among the Penn materials in the Library is the original of the Charter of Privileges granted by William Penn, Esq., to the Inhabitants of Pennsylvania and territories, in 1701. Engrossed on parchment, signed and sealed with the Great Seal . . . it is, with Jefferson's draft of the Declaration of Independence, one of the most highly prized documentary possessions of the Society.

"The first paragraphs review the grant to Penn by Letters Patent of 4th March, 1680, by Charles II, and to that of 24th August, 1682, by James, Duke of York and Albany, of 'all that tract of land, now called the Territories of Pennsylvania, together with power, and jurisdiction for the good government thereof.' Then, referring to the second charter and the 'Frame' of government, it states the reasons for the new Charter. 'The Frame of the Government of the Province of Pennsylvania and Territories thereunto belonging, in America, being found in some parts of it not so suitable to the present circumstances of the inhabitants, was . . . delivered up to me, by six parts of seven of the freemen of this province and territories in General Assembly met. . . .'

"'And whereas I was then pleased to promise, that I would restore the said Charter to them again, with necessary alterations, or in lieu thereof, give them another better adapted to answer the present circumstances and conditions of the said inhabitants; which they have now through their representatives in General Assembly met in Philadelphia, requested of me to grant.'

"'Know ye, therefore, that . . . I the said William Penn, do declare, grant and confirm, unto all the freemen, planters and adventurers, and other inhabitants of this province and territories, these following liberties, franchises and privileges . . . forever.'

"Then follow the eight provisions of the Charter, the account of its reception and approval by the Assembly, and the Founder's signature and great seal.

"The statement of approval by the Assembly has an historical interest all its own, because of the definite recognition of the principle that government is based on the consent of the governed. . . .

"Here we have a clear indication that the assembly, as Logan points out in a letter to Penn four years later, considered the privileges 'No more than their due, and, therefore, these are not so much to be accounted acts of grace as performance of a covenant.' It is the contract idea of government some years before Penn met John Locke, and decades before Rousseau's *Social Contract*. So far as Pennsylvania is concerned, the Charter served as the basis of government of the colony till the Revolution, and its principles have been continued in the successive constitutions and fundamental laws of the state to the present day."

Charter of Privileges for Pennsylvania

WILLIAM PENN, Proprietary and Governor of the Province of *Pensilvania* and Territories thereunto belonging, To all to whom these Presents shall come, sendeth Greeting. WHEREAS King CHARLES the *Second*, by His Letters Patents, under the Great Seal of *England*, bearing Date the *Fourth* Day of *March*, in the Year *One Thousand Six Hundred and Eighty-one,* was graciously pleased to give and grant unto me, and my Heirs and

Assigns for ever, this Province of *Pensilvania*, with divers great Powers and Jurisdictions for the well Government thereof.

AND WHEREAS the King's dearest Brother, JAMES *Duke of* YORK *and* ALBANY, &c. by his Deeds of Feoffment, under his Hand and Seal duly perfected, bearing Date the *Twenty-Fourth* Day of *August, One Thousand Six Hundred Eighty and Two,* did grant unto me, my Heirs and Assigns, all that Tract of Land, now called the Territories of *Pensilvania,* together with Powers and Jurisdictions for the good Government thereof.

AND WHEREAS for the Encouragement of all the Freemen and Planters, that might be concerned in the said Province and Territories, and for the good Government thereof, I the said WILLIAM PENN, in the Year *One Thousand Six Hundred Eighty and Three,* for me, my Heirs and Assigns, did grant and confirm unto all the Freemen, Planters and Adventurers therein, divers Liberties, Franchises and Properties, as by the said Grant, entitled, *The* FRAME *of the Government of the Province of* Pensilvania, *and Territories thereunto belonging, in* America, may appear; which Charter or Frame being found in some Parts of it, not so suitable to the present Circumstances of the Inhabitants, was in the *Third* Month, in the Year *One Thousand Seven Hundred,* delivered up to me, by *Six* Parts of *Seven* of the Freemen of this Province and Territories, in General Assembly met, Provision being made in the said Charter, for that End and Purpose.

AND WHEREAS I was then pleased to promise, That I would restore the said Charter to them again, with necessary Alterations, or in lieu thereof, give them another, better adapted to answer the present Circumstances and Conditions of the said Inhabitants; which they have now, by their Representatives in General Assembly met at *Philadelphia,* requested me to grant.

KNOW YE THEREFORE, That for the further Well-being and good Government of the said Province, and Territories; and in Pursuance of the Rights and Powers before-mentioned, I the said *William Penn* do declare, grant and confirm, unto all the Freemen, Planters and Adventurers, and other Inhabitants of this Province and Territories, these following Liberties, Franchises and Privileges, so far as in me lieth, to be held, enjoyed and kept, by the Freemen, Planters and Adventurers, and other Inhabitants of and in the said Province and Territories thereunto annexed, for ever.

FIRST. Because no People can be truly happy, though under the greatest Enjoyment of Civil Liberties, if abridged of the Freedom of their Consciences, as to their Religious Profession and Worship: And Almighty God being the only Lord of Conscience, Father of Lights and Spirits; and the Author as well as Object of all divine Knowledge, Faith and Worship, who only doth enlighten the Minds, and persuade and convince the

Understandings of People, I do hereby grant and declare, That no Person or Persons, inhabiting in this Province or Territories, who shall confess and acknowledge *One* almighty God, the Creator, Upholder and Ruler of the World; and profess him or themselves obliged to live quietly under the Civil Government, shall be in any Case molested or prejudiced, in his or their Person or Estate, because of his or their conscientious Persuasion or Practice, nor be compelled to frequent or maintain any religious Worship, Place or Ministry, contrary to his or their Mind, or to do or suffer any other Act or Thing, contrary to their religious Persuasion.

AND that all Persons who also profess to believe in *Jesus Christ*, the Saviour of the World, shall be capable (notwithstanding their other Persuasions and Practices in Point of Conscience and Religion) to serve this Government in any Capacity, both legislatively and executively, he or they solemnly promising, when lawfully required, Allegiance to the King as Sovereign, and Fidelity to the Proprietary and Governor, and taking the Attests as now established by the Law made at *New-Castle,* in the Year *One Thousand and Seven Hundred,* entitled, *An Act directing the Attests of several Officers and Ministers,* as now amended and confirmed this present Assembly.

II. For the well governing of this Province and Territories, there shall be an Assembly yearly chosen, by the Freemen thereof, to consist of *Four* Persons out of each County, of most Note for Virtue, Wisdom and Ability, (or of a greater number at any Time, as the Governor and Assembly shall agree) upon the *First* Day of *October* for ever; and shall sit on the *Fourteenth* Day of the same Month, at *Philadelphia,* unless the Governor and Council for the Time being, shall see Cause to appoint another Place within the said Province or Territories: Which Assembly shall have Power to chuse a Speaker and other their Officers; and shall be Judges of the Qualifications and Elections of their own Members; sit upon their own Adjournments; appoint Committees; prepare Bills in order to pass into Laws; impeach Criminals, and redress Grievances; and shall have all other Powers and Privileges of an Assembly, according to the Rights of the free-born Subjects of *England,* and as is usual in any of the King's Plantations in *America.*

AND if any County or Counties, shall refuse or neglect to chuse their respective Representatives as aforesaid, or if chosen, do not meet to serve in Assembly, those who are so chosen and met, shall have the full Power of an Assembly, in as ample Manner as if all the Representatives had been chosen and met, provided they are not less than *Two Thirds* of the whole Number that ought to meet.

AND that the Qualifications of Electors and Elected, and all other Matters and Things relating to Elections of Representatives to serve in Assemblies, though not herein particularly expressed, shall be and remain as by a Law of this Government, made at *New-Castle* in the Year *One Thousand Seven Hundred,* entitled, *An Act to ascertain the Number of Members of Assembly, and to regulate the Elections.*

III. That the Freemen in each respective County, at the Time and Place of Meeting for Electing their Representatives to serve in Assembly, may as often as there shall be Occasion, chuse a double Number of Persons to present to the Governor for Sheriffs and Coroners to serve for *Three* Years, if so long they behave themselves well; out of which respective Elections and Presentments, the Governor shall nominate and commissionate one for each of the said Offices, the *Third* Day after such Presentment, or else the *First* named in such Presentment, for each Office as aforesaid, shall stand and serve in that Office for the Time before respectively limited; and in Case of Death or Default, such Vacancies shall be supplied by the Governor, to serve to the End of the said Term.

PROVIDED ALWAYS, That if the said Freemen shall at any Time neglect or decline to chuse a Person or Persons for either or both the aforesaid Offices, then and in such Case, the Persons that are or shall be in the respective Offices of Sheriffs or Coroners, at the Time of Election, shall remain therein, until they shall be removed by another Election as aforesaid.

AND that the Justices of the respective Counties shall or may nominate and present to the Governor *Three* Persons, to serve for Clerk of the Peace for the said County, when there is a Vacancy, one of which the Governor shall commissionate within *Ten* Days after such Presentment, or else the *First* nominated shall serve in said Office during good Behavior.

IV. That the Laws of this Government shall be in this Stile, viz. *By the Governor, with the Consent and Approbation of the Freemen in General Assembly met;* and shall be, after Confirmation by the Governor, forthwith recorded in the Rolls Office, and kept at *Philadelphia,* unless the Governor and Assembly shall agree to appoint another Place.

V. That all Criminals shall have the same Privileges of Witnesses and Council as their Prosecutors.

VI. That no Person or Persons shall or may, at any Time hereafter, be obliged to answer any Complaint, Matter or Thing whatsoever, relating to Property, before the Governor and Council, or in any other Place, but in ordinary Course of Justice, unless Appeals thereunto shall be hereafter by Law appointed.

VII. That no Person within this Government, shall be licensed by the Governor to keep an Ordinary, Tavern or House of Publick Entertainment, but such who are first recommended to him, under the Hands of the Justices of the respective Counties, signed in open Court; which Justices are and shall be hereby impowered, to suppress and forbid any Person, keeping such Publick-

House as aforesaid, upon their Misbehaviour, on such Penalties as the Law doth or shall direct; and to recommend others from time to time, as they shall see Occasion.

VIII. If any person, through Temptation or Melancholy, shall destroy himself; his Estate, real and personal, shall notwithstanding descend to his Wife and Children, or Relations, as if he had died a natural Death; and if any Person shall be destroyed or killed by Casualty or Accident, there shall be no Forfeiture to the Governor by reason thereof.

And no Act, Law or Ordinance whatsoever, shall at any Time hereafter, be made or done, to alter, change or diminish the Form or Effect of this Charter, or of any Part or Clause therein, contrary to the true Intent and Meaning thereof, without the Consent of the Governor for the Time being, and *Six* Parts of *Seven* of the Assembly met.

But because the Happiness of Mankind depends so much upon the Enjoying of Liberty of their Consciences as aforesaid, I do hereby solemnly declare, promise and grant, for me, my Heirs and Assigns, That the *First* Article of this Charter relating to Liberty of Conscience, and every Part and Clause therein, according to the true Intent and Meaning thereof, shall be kept and remain, without any Alteration, inviolably for ever.

And Lastly, I the said *William Penn*, Proprietary and Governor of the Province of *Pensilvania*, and Territories thereunto belonging, for myself, my Heirs and Assigns, have solemnly declared, granted and confirmed, and do hereby solemnly declare, grant and confirm, That neither I, my Heirs or Assigns, shall procure or do any Thing or Things whereby the Liberties in this Charter contained and expressed, nor any Part thereof, shall be infringed or broken: And if any thing shall be procured or done, by any Person or Persons, contrary to these Presents, it shall be held of no Force or Effect.

In Witness whereof, I the said *William Penn*, at *Philadelphia* in *Pensilvania*, have unto this present Charter of Liberties, set my Hand and broad Seal, this *Twenty-Eighth* Day of *October*, in the Year of Our Lord *One Thousand Seven Hundred and One*, being the Thirteenth Year of the Reign of King William *the Third*, over *England, Scotland, France* and *Ireland*, &c. and the *Twenty-First* Year of my Government.

And notwithstanding the Closure and Test of this present Charter as aforesaid, I think fit to add this following Proviso thereunto, as Part of the same, *That is to say*, That notwithstanding any Clause or Clauses in the above-mentioned Charter, obliging the Province and Territories to join together in Legislation, I am content, and do hereby declare, that if the Representatives of the Province and Territories shall not hereafter agree to join together in Legislation, and that the same shall be signified unto me, or my Deputy, in open Assembly, or

otherwise from under the Hands and Seals of the Representatives, for the Time being, of the Province and Territories, or the major Part of either of them, at any Time within *Three* Years from the Date hereof, that in such Case, the Inhabitants of each of the *Three* Counties of this Province, shall not have less than *Eight* Persons to represent them in Assembly, for the Province; and the Inhabitants of the Town of *Philadelphia* (when the said Town is incorporated) *Two* Persons to represent them in Assembly; and the Inhabitants of each County in the Territories, shall have as many Persons to represent them in a distinct Assembly for the Territories, as shall be by them requested as aforesaid.

Notwithstanding which Separation of the Province and Territories, in Respect of Legislation, I do hereby promise, grant and declare, That the Inhabitants of both Province and Territories, shall separately enjoy all other Liberties, Privileges and Benefits, granted jointly to them in this Charter, any Law, Usage or Custom of this Government heretofore made and practised, or any Law made and passed by this General Assembly, to the Contrary hereof, notwithstanding.

William Penn

This Charter of Privileges being distinctly read in Assembly; and the whole and every Part thereof, being approved of and agreed to, by us, we do thankfully receive the same from our Proprietary and Governor, at Philadelphia, this Twenty-Eighth Day of October, One Thousand Seven Hundred and One. Signed on Behalf, and by Order of the Assembly,

per Joseph Growdon, Speaker.

Edward Shippen	Griffith Owen
Phineas Pemberton	Caleb Pusey
Samuel Carpenter	Thomas Story
	Proprietary and
	Governor's Council.

5. The Colonies Protest against "Taxation without Representation" (1765)

The French and Indian War (1755–1763) was a clear victory for the British against their ancient enemies; it was also a heavy burden for British taxpayers. The protracted war had doubled the national debt of Great Britain. Much of this increase had been incurred in defending the American colonies. With the increase of empire came new responsibilities. Now it would be necessary to station a permanent garrison of British soldiers in the colonies to protect the frontier settlements against threatening Indians. The colonies had demonstrated that they themselves could not provide adequate military protection; they had also demonstrated that they could not be counted upon voluntarily to defray the expenses of a necessary military establishment. British taxpayers were in no mood to foot the entire bill themselves. A military establishment was necessary; and money was necessary for that establishment. How find the money? In the past, the British Parliament had not taxed the colonies for revenue purposes, but now the British ministry, under the leadership of Sir George Grenville, decided to levy a parliamentary tax upon the colonies in order to provide some relief for British taxpayers.

The Sugar Act of 1764 was passed as a first step. The revenues from this tax were judged to be less than the colonial share, so Grenville proposed a stamp tax upon the colonies. Grenville deferred the passage of the proposed Stamp Act for a year in order to give the colonies time in which to produce a better plan of raising money or one more to their liking. The colonies proposed nothing as a substitute; instead they chose to ignore the whole problem. Parliament, without much ado, passed the Stamp Act in March 1765. The use of stamps was to be required on papers used in legal transactions, such as deeds, mortgages, and inventories, on licenses to practice law or sell liquor, on college diplomas, playing cards, dice, pamphlets, newspapers, calendars and advertisements. Stamp duties were heavy and penalties were imposed for violations of the law.

When news of the Stamp Act reached the colonies there was an immediate storm of protest. There was a sudden realization that this act affected every section and nearly every class in America. Societies known as the "Sons of Liberty" were formed by artisans and laborers and enterprising politicians; the young maidens of Providence pledged themselves to favor no suitors who approved the Stamp Act; the offices of stamp agents were pillaged; and stamps were burned in the streets.

Protests from colonial assemblies came forth in the form of resolutions. In the Virginia House of Burgesses the fiery orator, Patrick Henry, forced through the Virginia resolutions, one of which declared that attempts to tax Virginians, except through the local assembly, were "illegal, unconstitutional, and unjust." In the heat of the debate on the resolutions, Henry uttered his oft-quoted defiance of King George III: "Caesar had his Brutus, Charles the First his Cromwell, and George the Third . . ." and when at this point there were cries of "Treason!" from the House he continued, "may profit by their experience. If this be treason, make the most of it." In Massachusetts the colonial legislature resolved that a meeting of delegates from the various colonial assemblies would be the best body to draw up a united protest against the Stamp Act. The Massachusetts legislature in June sent out a circular letter inviting the legislatures of all the colonies to send delegates to an October conference in New York City to consider a general plan for relief.

The Stamp Act Congress, as this conference became known, met in New York City Hall for the first time on October 7, 1765, with a total of twenty-seven delegates from nine colonies. Four colonies—Georgia, North Carolina, Virginia and New Hampshire—were not represented because the early date set for the conference made it impossible for their assemblies to select delegates.

On October 19, a declaration in the form of a number of resolutions, originally drafted by John Dickinson of Pennsylvania, was adopted by the Congress. After the customary expressions of affection for "his Majesty's person and government," the Declaration proceeded to assert that the colonists owed the same allegiance and had the same inherent rights as Englishmen born within the realm. Then followed the three noted resolutions concerning "taxation without representation":

"III. That it is inseparably essential to the freedom of a people, and the undoubted right of Englishmen, that no taxes be imposed on them but with their own consent, given personally, or by their representatives.

"IV. That the people of these colonies are not, and, from their local circumstances, cannot be, represented in the House of Commons in Great-Britain.

"V. That the only representatives of the people of these colonies are persons chosen therein by themselves, and that no taxes ever have been, or can be constitutionally imposed on them, but by their respective legislatures."

The Stamp Act Congress and the Declaration were significant in that they were the first evidence of united colonial action against parliamentary threats to colonial self-government. For the first time in colonial history the initiative for concerted colonial action came, not from Crown officers, but from the provincial assemblies themselves. The actions of the Stamp Act Congress and the resolutions of the Declaration were loyal in character, but they fostered the movement which gradually brought to maturity the spirit and agencies of American unity and independence.

This early printed copy of the proceedings of the Congress is from the collections of the Library of Congress.

6. Thomas Jefferson Defends the Rights of the Colonists (1774)

THE misunderstanding and ill-feeling between Great Britain and the colonies arising from the controversies from 1764 to 1770 had largely subsided by 1773. Prosperity was increasing and with it a feeling of satisfaction; most colonial leaders seemed content to let the future take care of itself.

The brief calm was broken by the celebrated Boston Tea Party in December 1773. To aid the powerful East ment these acts threw the thirteen colonies into a mighty ferment which led to the assembling of the first Continental Congress.

The Intolerable Acts provoked a flood of resolutions and tracts. The most noteworthy was one by a young Virginia lawyer, *A Summary View of the Rights of British America*. Its author, Thomas Jefferson, had been elected to represent Albemarle at the Virginia Convention of 1774, which, among its other duties, was to select delegates to the forthcoming Continental Congress. Before leaving his home at Monticello, he had prepared a set of instructions for these delegates. Late in July 1774, Jefferson started for Williamsburg one hundred and fifty miles away, but had to turn back because of illness. Copies of his paper were sent on to Peyton Randolph, chairman of the Convention, and to Patrick Henry. Commenting on the latter's inaction concerning the paper, Jefferson wrote, "Whether Mr. Henry disapproved the ground taken, or was too lazy to read it (for he was the laziest man in reading I ever knew) I never learned, but he communicated it to nobody." Randolph offered Jefferson's statement to the Convention but it was "thought too bold for the present state of things." The Convention finally approved a milder series of instructions which were drawn up by Henry himself.

Thereupon, friends of Jefferson sent his manuscript to a printer, Clementia Rind, who published it in Williamsburg in 1774. The volume on exhibit, one of the original pamphlets printed in 1774, is lent by the Library of Congress.

India Company, which was in financial distress, Parliament had passed the Tea Act of 1773 granting that company a monopoly on all tea exported to the colonies. Colonial reaction to the Tea Act was swift and immediate, but it was in Boston that it erupted most violently. On the night of December 16, a band of Bostonians in the war-paint of Mohawk Indians boarded the three tea ships and dumped the tea overboard with the cry of "Boston harbor a tea-pot this night."

Parliament reacted by passing a series of five acts between March and June 1774, the so-called Intolerable Acts, which were intended to serve as a punishment and a cure for the unrest in America. The first four acts were designed to punish Boston alone. By these acts the port of Boston was to be closed to commerce until the destroyed tea was paid for; the form of government in Massachusetts was radically changed; certain alleged offenders were to be transported to England for trial; and the quartering of troops in Massachusetts towns was legalized. The fifth Act, the Quebec Act, extended the boundaries of the province of Quebec south to the Ohio and west to the Mississippi River. While this was not meant to be a punitive act, it was so regarded by Virginia, Connecticut, and Massachusetts, for they possessed claims to this land. To the dismay of the British govern-

Jefferson's *Summary View* has been described as "the boldest declaration of American rights that had yet been written." He openly denied that Parliament had any control over the colonies, and looked upon any acts passed by that body for the colonies as encroachments of Parliament "upon those rights which God and the laws have given equally and independently to all. . . ." Jefferson went on and listed specific acts as examples. He then enumerated the grievances against King George III himself which were to appear later in the Declaration of Independence. He admonished George III not to allow his name to "be a blot on the page of history. . . ." In polite but unmistakable terms he warned the king that unless the repressive acts of Parliament were revoked and unless the grievances were removed, the American colonies might be lost to him. Then Jefferson voiced the noble sentiment which he later expressed in the Declaration of Independence: "The God who gave us life gave us liberty at the same time; the hand of force may destroy, but cannot disjoin them."

Next to the Declaration of Independence itself the *Summary View* was Jefferson's greatest literary contribution to the American Revolution.

7. Nathaniel Bacon Leads a Revolt against Royal Tyranny in Virginia (1676)

AN eminent American historian has declared that "Nathaniel Bacon was the greatest figure of the first century of American history." This extreme praise can be questioned, but there is no question that he ranks among the greatest of colonial Americans. It is likewise true that this extraordinary figure is too little known to the American public.

Bacon was well educated and well placed in England when he suddenly determined to migrate to Virginia. From the time he arrived in the colonies he found that his sympathies were with the people and he grew restless under Sir William Berkeley, a tyrannical and obstinate figure who had then served as the royal Governor of Virginia for more than thirty years. Berkeley disliked both Quakers and Puritans and savagely persecuted any who were unfortunate enough to settle there. He disliked newspapers and he disliked schools; he was happy to render thanks to God that Virginia had neither. He kept all branches of the government under his fat thumb; he refused to tolerate any opinions that differed from his own.

When the Governor failed to take adequate measures to protect the frontiers against the warring Indians, the people of Virginia, led by Bacon, rose up in armed rebellion. Bacon several times forced the Governor to flee the capital, and for a time Bacon became the real ruler

The Declaration of the People, against Sr.
Wm Berkeley, and Present Governors of
Virginia

For having upon specious Pretences of publick Works
raised unjust Taxes upon the Commonaltie. For
advancing of Private Favourites. And other
sinister Ends, but noe visible Effect, in any measure adequate.

For having not during the Long time of his Government,
In any measure advanced this hopefull Colonie,
either by Fortifications, Towns, or Trade.

For having abused and rendered Contemptable,
his Maties Justice, by advancing to Places of Judi-
cature, scandalous and ignorant Favourites.

For having wronged his maties Prerogative, and
Interest, by assuming the monopolie of the Bever
Trade.

For having in that unjust Gaine, betrayed and
sold His Matie Countrie, and the Liberties of his
loyall Subjects to the Barbarous Heathen.

For having Protected, favoured, and Emboldned, the
Indians against his Maties most Loyall Subjects;
due or proper Meanes of Satisfaction; for theire
many Incursions, Murthers, and Robberies, Committed upon Us.

For having when the Armie of the English, was
upon the Tract of the Indians, which now in all
Places, burne spoile, and Murder And when Wee
might with ease, haue destroyed them, Who were
in open hostilitie.

For having expresslie, countermanded, and sent
back, our Armie, by Passing his word, for the
Peaceable demeanours of the said Indians, who
Immediatly prosecuted theire Evill Intentions
Committing horrid Murders and Robberies, in all
Places, being Protected by the said Engagement, and
word passed by Him the said Sr Wm Berkeley
having Ruined and made desolate a greate Part
of his Maties Countrie, having now drawn Themselues
into such obscure and remote places, and are by
theire Success soe Emboldned, and Confirmed, and
by theire Confederates strengthned, That the Cryes
of Blood, are in all Places, and the Terror and Consternation of the People soe greate, That They are
not only become difficult, but a very formidable Enemie
Who might with ease haue bin destroyed.

Nathaniel Bacon's Manifesto against Governor Berkeley during "Bacon's Rebellion" (See No. 7)

When upon the loud outcries of Blood the Assemblie had with all care, raised, and framed an Armie, for the Prevention of future Mischeifs, and safeguard of his Ma:ties Colonie.

For having only with the Privacie of a fewe favourites, without the acquainting of the People, only by Alteration of a Figure forged a Commission, by I know not what hand, not only without, but against the consent of the People, for the Raising and Effecting of Civill Warr, and destruction, which being happilie and without Bloodshed prevented.

For having the second time attempted the same, thereby calling downe our forces from the Defence of the frontiers, and most weakened and Exposed Places, for the prevention of Civill Mischeife, and Ruine amongst our selves; whilest the Barborous Enemie in all places did Invade murder and Spoile us. his Ma:ties Loyall Subjects.

Of these the aforesaid Articles, Wee accuse Sr Wm Berkeley as guiltie of Each and Everie of the same. As one Who hath Traiterouslie, attempted Violated and Injured, his Ma:ties Interest here, by the loss of a greate Part of his Ma:ties Colonie, and many of his faithfull and Loyall Subjects, by Him betrayed in a Barbarous and shamefull Manner Exposed to the Incursion, and murder of the Heathen.

And Wee farther declare the Ensueing Persons in this List to have bin his wicked and Pernicious Councellors, and Confederates, Aiders and Asistants against the Commonaltie in these our Civill Commotions.

Sr Henrie Chickely	Wm Cole	Jon Page: Clerk
Coll: Christop: Wormly	Rich: Whitecar:	Jon Cuffe: Clerk
Phillip Ludwell:	Rich: Spencer	Hub: Farrill
Robert Beverlie	Joseph: Bridges	John: West
Richard Lee	Wm Claybourne	Tho: Readmuch
Thomas Ballard	Thom: Hawkins	
Wm Sherwood.	Math: Kemp	

And we farther Command that the said Sr Wm Berkeley with all the Persons in this List bee forthwith delivered upp or Surrender Themselves, within foure dayes after the notice hereof, or otherwise Wee declare as followeth.

Nathaniel Bacon's Manifesto, second page

That in whatsoever place, House, or Shipp, any of the said Persons shall Reside, bee hid, or protected, Wee doe declare the Owners, Masters and Inhabitants of the said Parties, to bee Confederates Traytors to the People and ye Estates, of them; as allsoe the aforesaid Persons, to be Confiscated, this Wee the Commons of Virginia doe declare.

Desiring a firme union amongst our Selves, that Wee may Joyntly and with one accord defend our selves against the Common Enimie, and lett not the faults of the Guiltie, bee the Reproach of the Innocent, or the faults and Crimes of the Oppressors, devide and sepperate us who have suffered, by theire oppressions.

These are therefore in his Ma:ties Name to Command you forthwith to seize the Persons above mentioned, as Traytors to the King and Countrie, and them to bring to the Middle Plantations; and there to secure them till further Order and in Case of opposition, if yu want any farther Assistance, you are forthwith to demaund It, In the Name of the People, in all the Counties of Virginia.

Nathaniell Bacon
Generall, by the Consent
of the People.

Nathaniel Bacon's Manifesto, third page

of Virginia. During a brief period of restored authority Governor Berkeley executed so many leaders of the rebellion that the King of England replaced him in disgust. Charles II declared that "the old fool has killed more people in that naked country than I have done for the murder of my father." Bacon was not one of those executed by the savagery of Berkeley, for in the midst of the struggle he fell ill and died. Bacon was a statesman as well as an able military leader. Had he lived he might well have changed the whole subsequent history of the southern colonies.

The Freedom Train exhibit displays a contemporary manuscript statement of their grievances—one authorized by Bacon and to which is appended the eloquent phrase, "Generall, by the Consent of the People." The document is from the collections of Colonial Williamsburg and the Institute of Early American History and Culture.

8. Caesar Rodney Writes, on a Memorable Day, about the Voting of the Declaration of Independence

THIS famous letter of Caesar Rodney, apparently the only surviving letter on July 4, 1776, written by a signer of the Declaration of Independence, refers to one of the most famous rides in American history. "Rodney's Ride," though not celebrated in poetry like those of Paul Revere and General Sheridan, was one of crucial importance. On the critical vote on the Resolution of Independence, Delaware's delegates were divided: Thomas McKean was in favor of independence, George Read voted against it, and Caesar Rodney was absent in Delaware on official business. In his old age McKean remembered that he had sent a messenger to Rodney urging him to hasten to Philadelphia in order to break the tie. During the night of July 1-2 Rodney covered the eighty miles to Philadelphia, "tho detained by Thunder and Rain." It was because of this heroic effort that the Richard Henry Lee Resolution of Independence was adopted on July 2, 1776 "without even one decenting Colony." This document is from the collections of Dr. A. S. W. Rosenbach.

Philada. July the 4th 1776

Sir

I have inclosed you a Summons directed to the Sheriff to Summon the Member for our County to meet in assembly at Newcastle on the 22nd day of this Instant which I hope you will have put into his hands as soon as possible after it Comes to Yours — I arrived in Congress tho detained by Thunder and Rain time Enough to give my Voice in the matter of Independence — It is now determined by the Thirteen United Colonies without even one decenting Colony — We have now Got through with the Whole of the declaration and Ordered it to be printed so that you will soon have the pleasure of seeing it — Handbills of it will be printed and sent to the Armies, Cities, County, Towns, etc. — to be published or rather proclaimed in form. Don't neglect to attend Closely and Carefully to my Harvest and You'll oblige,

Yours, etc.

Caesar Rodney

9. James Iredell Defends the Rights of the Colonists (1776)

IN 1774, James Iredell, 23-year-old native of England, resigned his post as Collector of the Crown Revenue at the port of Edenton, North Carolina. Thenceforth he devoted his pen so wholeheartedly to the American cause that he was disinherited by his uncle, a wealthy Jamaican planter. But he gained the esteem of George Washington, who as President appointed him in 1790 to the Supreme Court of the United States.

This manuscript essay, written in June 1776, held out hope of reconciliation with Great Britain even at that late date, but only on terms consistent with the preservation of American rights. Iredell stated: "In political affairs we are not always at liberty to choose what is best in the *abstract;* but what may be found so in practice. I can see no establishment in America . . . that is likely to arise of a happier nature than such a *re-union.* But if a re-union is not practicable but upon terms of dishonour, if one essential point is required as a sacrifice to obtain it, I should spurn the idea as scandalous and disgraceful; and in such an event, or on any occasion whatever, if *Independency* should become necessary to our safety, I should not hesitate an instant in giving my assent to it."

The Freedom Train exhibit displays the last two pages of the original manuscript essay which is a part of the collections of the Princeton University Library.

10. Thomas Jefferson's "Rough Draft" of the Declaration of Independence

THOMAS JEFFERSON's "Rough Draft" of the Declaration of Independence is one of the most precious state papers in all history. As the great charter of American freedom it ranks with Magna Carta, the Declaration of Rights, and other great documents in the long struggle to achieve liberty. In its second paragraph Jefferson compressed a whole system of philosophy and an entire theory of government, giving expression to these in language which Condorcet and many others have regarded as both simple and sublime. Its philosophy of government is that of the theory of natural rights which was commonly accepted in the eighteenth century. This theory is based on the self-evident truth that all men, being created equal, were endowed under the laws of nature and of nature's God with certain inalienable rights. Among these rights were those of life, liberty, and the pursuit of happiness. Since individuals possessed these inalienable rights but were unable in all cases to hold them inviolable, they had associated themselves together in societies and formed governments for the securing and protection of their rights. This being so, government depended upon the consent of the governed. Should *any* form of government—monarchy, oligarchy, or democracy—destroy or violate these inalienable rights and the ends for which government was formed, it was "the right of the people to alter or to abolish it, and to institute new government, laying its foundation on such principles and organizing its powers in such form, as to them shall seem most likely to effect their safety and happiness."

The idea of government by consent, based upon rights derived from natural law, was an ancient one. But the sublime statement of this theory of government in the Declaration of Independence was the first example in history in which a new nation erected its government "of the people, by the people, and for the people" with a formal declaration to the world that these were the principles on which it would rest.

In addition to this statement of a theory of government which made it legitimate under the "Higher Law" or the "law of nature and of nature's God" to revolt, the Declaration lists specific acts on the part of the King which the colonists viewed as tyrannical and which made independence from Great Britain necessary.

Strictly speaking it is improper to refer to this document as the "Declaration of Independence." The engrossed parchment copy of the Declaration which was signed on August 2, 1776, by the Delegates to the Continental Congress does not bear the title "Declaration of Independence" but has this caption: "The Unanimous Declaration of the Thirteen United States of America." Nor was it the decisive act by which independence was declared. The act of independence was the adoption of the Richard Henry Lee Resolution on July 2 that "these United Colonies are, and of right ought to be, free and independent states, . . . and that all political connection between them and the State of Great Britain is, and of right ought to be, totally dissolved." Thomas Jefferson's famous state paper was not, therefore, the actual declaration of independence, but was a document setting forth the reasons which made independence necessary and proclaiming also the theory of government which made a secession from the British Empire lawful. This great charter of freedom was promulgated because Congress

felt that "a decent respect to the opinions of mankind requires that they should declare the causes which impel them to the separation"—a separation which had already taken place on July 2.

Jefferson was living at the southwest corner of Seventh and Market Streets in Philadelphia in the home of a German bricklayer when, on June 10, 1776, he was designated one of a committee of five to "prepare a declaration" in support of the Richard Henry Lee Resolution of Independence. The other members of the committee were John Adams, Benjamin Franklin, Roger Sherman, and Robert R. Livingston. This "Rough Draft" was written between June 10 and June 28 when the Committee reported to Congress the draft of a declaration entitled "A Declaration by the Representatives of the United States of America in Congress Assembled." Jefferson, though he was only thirty-three years of age, was given the post of honor on this most important of all committees. The reason for his selection was obvious—he had come to Congress with "a reputation for literature, science, and a happy talent of composition." In 1774 he had written a famous pamphlet entitled *A Summary View of the Rights of the British Parliament*," which anticipated the Declaration of Independence in its theory of natural law and government. These and other writings were, according to John Adams, "remarkable for the peculiar felicity of expression."

Early in the nineteenth century Federalist partisans, and later the admirers of Thomas Paine, endeavored to disprove the fact of Jefferson's authorship of this immortal Declaration. Their efforts have been totally unsuccessful. Late in life, Jefferson wrote that Richard Henry Lee had charged him with copying the Declaration from Locke's *Treatise on Government*. To this he replied that he had turned to neither book nor pamphlet while writing it and added: "I did not consider it as any part of my charge to invent new ideas altogether and to offer no sentiment which had ever been expressed before." The important object, as Jefferson stated on another occasion, was "not to find out new principles, or new arguments, never before thought of, not merely to say things which had never been said before; but to place before mankind the common sense of the subject . . . All its authority rests then on the harmonizing sentiments of the day, whether expressed in conversation, in letters, printed essays, or the elementary books of public right, as Aristotle, Cicero, Locke, Sidney, etc., etc." Among these harmonizing sentiments of the day were Jefferson's own draft of a constitution for Virginia, which he had completed only a few weeks earlier, and George Mason's draft of a "Declaration of Rights . . . recommended to posterity as the Basis and Foundation of their Government." The first of these Jefferson indubitably used as the basis for his indictment against George III and the second paralleled the Declaration in its theory of natural law and the nature of government so closely that many historians have felt that Jefferson must have made use of this first Bill of Rights.

Strictly speaking, it is also incorrect to refer to this document as the "Rough Draft", if by that phrase is meant the original composition. The title "Rough Draft" was not given to this document by Jefferson until late in life. Internal evidence in the document itself led some historians to suppose that it was originally a fair copy of an earlier text of the Declaration. This supposition has proved to be well founded by the recent discovery of a fragment of the composition draft from which the "Rough Draft" was copied. The more correct designation of this document would be to call it the "Committee Draft" or the "Committee Report." For, after he had made the fair copy of the text which later became known as the "Rough Draft" Jefferson submitted it to Adams and Franklin, each of whom made alterations in the document. Jefferson himself undoubtedly made subsequent changes. The draft was then, according to Jefferson, submitted to the Committee and reported by the Committee unaltered to Congress. So far as is known, neither Sherman nor Livingston suggested any alterations in Jefferson's draft. Jefferson and his colleagues on the Committee made a total of forty-seven alterations in the text and there were thirty-nine additional changes made by Congress after the Committee had reported the draft.

It is a remarkable fact that Congress reduced the length of the Declaration, chiefly by striking out what John Adams described as some of its more "oratorical" passages. The most important excision made by Congress was that of the passage pertaining to the slave trade. This, according to Jefferson, was "struck out in complaisance to S. Carolina & Georgia, who had never attempted to restrain the importation of slaves & who on the contrary still wished to continue it. Our northern brethren also, I believe, felt a little tender under those censures; for tho' their people have very few slaves themselves, yet they have been pretty considerable carriers of them to others." Congress also struck out "those passages which conveyed censures on the people of England" lest this give needless offense. Jefferson thought that "the pusillanimous idea that we had friends in England worth keeping terms with still haunted the minds of many." While these changes were being made by Congress, Jefferson noted them on the "Rough Draft."

Thus this extraordinarily interesting document is at once the fair copy that Jefferson made from his composition draft, the text on which Adams and Franklin in their own handwriting made the changes that occurred to them, the text as reported by the Committee to Congress, and the final text as amended by Congress.

The following is the text not of the "Rough Draft" discussed above but of the official text:

In Congress, July 4, 1776,

The unanimous Declaration of the thirteen united States of America,

When in the Course of human events, it becomes necessary for one people to dissolve the political bands which have connected them with another, and to assume among the Powers of the earth, the separate and equal station to which the Laws of Nature and of Nature's God entitle them, a decent respect to the opinions of mankind requires that they should declare the causes which impel them to the separation.

We hold these truths to be self-evident, that all men are created equal, that they are endowed by their Creator with certain unalienable Rights, that among these are Life, Liberty and the pursuit of Happiness. That to secure these rights, Governments are instituted among Men, deriving their just powers from the consent of the governed, That whenever any Form of Government becomes destructive of these ends, it is the Right of the People to alter or to abolish it, and to institute new Government, laying its foundation on such principles and organizing its powers in such form, as to them shall seem most likely to effect their Safety and Happiness. Prudence, indeed, will dictate that Governments long established should not be changed for light and transient causes; and accordingly all experience hath shown, that mankind are more disposed to suffer, while evils are sufferable, than to right themselves by abolishing the forms to which they are accustomed. But when a long train of abuses and usurpations, pursuing invariably the same Object evinces a design to reduce them under absolute Despotism, it is their right, it is their duty, to throw off such Government, and to provide new Guards for their future security.—Such has been the patient sufferance of these Colonies; and such is now the necessity which constrains them to alter their former Systems of Government. The history of the present King of Great Britain is a history of repeated injuries and usurpations, all having in direct object the establishment of an absolute Tyranny over these States. To prove this, let Facts be submitted to candid world.

He has refused his Assent to Laws, the most wholesome and necessary for the public good.

He has forbidden his Governors to pass Laws of immediate and pressing importance, unless suspended in their operation till his Assent should be obtained; and when so suspended, he has utterly neglected to attend to them.

He has refused to pass other Laws for the accommodation of large districts of people, unless those people would relinquish the right of Representation in the Legislature, a right inestimable to them and formidable to tyrants only.

He has called together legislative bodies at places un-usual, uncomfortable, and distant from the depository of their Public Records, for the sole purpose of fatiguing them into compliance with his measures.

He has dissolved Representative Houses repeatedly, for opposing with manly firmness his invasions on the rights of the people.

He has refused for a long time, after such dissolutions, to cause others to be elected; whereby the Legislative Powers, incapable of Annihilation, have returned to the People at large for their exercise; the State remaining in the mean time exposed to all the dangers of invasion from without, and convulsions within.

He has endeavoured to prevent the population of these States; for that purpose obstructing the Laws of Naturalization of Foreigners; refusing to pass others to encourage their migration hither, and raising the condi-tions of new Appropriations of Lands.

He has obstructed the Administration of Justice, by refusing his Assent to Laws for establishing Judiciary Powers.

He has made Judges dependent on his Will alone, for the tenure of their offices, and the amount and payment of their salaries.

He has erected a multitude of New Offices, and sent hither swarms of Officers to harass our People, and eat out their substance.

He has kept among us, in times of peace, Standing Armies without the Consent of our legislature.

He has affected to render the Military independent of and superior to the Civil Power.

He has combined with others to subject us to a juris-diction foreign to our constitution, and unacknowledged by our laws; giving his Assent to their acts of pretended legislation:

For quartering large bodies of armed troops among us:

For protecting them, by a mock Trial, from Punish-ment for any Murders which they should commit on the Inhabitants of these States:

For cutting off our Trade with all parts of the world:

For imposing taxes on us without our Consent:

For depriving us in many cases, of the benefits of Trial by Jury:

For transporting us beyond Seas to be tried for pre-tended offences:

For abolishing the free System of English Laws in a neighbouring Province, establishing therein an Arbitrary government, and enlarging its Boundaries so as to render it at once an example and fit instrument for introducing the same absolute rule into these Colonies:

For taking away our Charters, abolishing our most valuable Laws, and altering fundamentally the Forms of our Governments:

For suspending our own Legislature, and declaring themselves invested with Power to legislate for us in all cases whatsoever.

He has abdicated Government here, by declaring us out of his Protection and waging War against us.

He has plundered our seas, ravaged our Coasts, burnt our towns, and destroyed the lives of our people.

He is at this time transporting large armies of foreign mercenaries to compleat the works of death, desolation and tyranny, already begun with circumstances of Cru-elty & perfidy scarcely paralleled in the most barbarous ages, and totally unworthy the Head of a civilized na-tion.

He has constrained our fellow Citizens taken Captive on the high Seas to bear Arms against their Country, to become the executioners of their friends and Brethren, or to fall themselves by their Hands.

He has excited domestic insurrections amongst us, and has endeavoured to bring on the inhabitants of our frontiers, the merciless Indian Savages, whose known rule of warfare, is an undistinguished destruction of all ages, sexes and conditions.

In every stage of these Oppressions We have Peti-tioned for Redress in the most humble terms: Our re-peated Petitions have been answered only by repeated injury. A Prince, whose character is thus marked by every act which may define a Tyrant, is unfit to be the ruler of a free People.

Nor have We been wanting in attention to our British brethren. We have warned them from time to time of attempts by their legislature to extend an unwarrantable jurisdiction over us. We have reminded them of the cir-cumstances of our emigration and settlement here. We have appealed to their native justice and magnanimity, and we have conjured them by the ties of our common kindred to disavow these usurpations, which, would in-evitably interrupt our connections and correspondence. They too have been deaf to the voice of justice and of consanguinity. We must, therefore, acquiesce in the ne-cessity, which denounces our Separation, and hold them, as we hold the rest of mankind, Enemies in War, in Peace Friends.

We, therefore, the Representatives of the united States of America, in General Congress, Assembled, appealing to the Supreme Judge of the world for the rectitude of our intentions, do, in the Name, and by Authority of the good People of these Colonies, solemnly publish and de-clare, That these United Colonies are, and of Right ought to be Free and Independent States; that they are Absolved from all Allegiance to the British Crown, and that all political connection between them and the State of Great Britain, is and ought to be totally dissolved; and that as Free and Independent States, they have full Power to levy War, conclude Peace, contract Alliances, establish Commerce, and to do all other Acts and Things

A Declaration by the Representatives of the UNITED STATES
OF AMERICA, in General Congress assembled.

When in the course of human events it becomes necessary for one people to
dissolve the political bands which have connected them with another, and to
~~take among the powers of the earth the~~ as-
-sume among the powers of the earth the separate and equal ~~~~ station to
which the laws of nature & of nature's god entitle them, a decent respect
to the opinions of mankind requires that they should declare the causes
which impel them to ~~the~~ the separation.

We hold these truths to be self-evident; ~~sacred & undeniable~~ that all men are
created equal ~~& independent~~ that ~~from that equal creation they derive~~ they are endowed by their creator with
~~~~ ~~~~ inherent & inalienable rights; that among ~~which~~ these are the ~~~~
life, & liberty, & the pursuit of happiness; that to secure these rights, go-
-vernments are instituted among men, deriving their just powers from
the consent of the governed; that whenever any form of government
~~shall~~ becomes destructive of these ends, it is the right of the people to alter
or to abolish it, & to institute new government, laying it's foundation on
such principles & organising it's powers in such form, as to them shall
seem most likely to effect their safety & happiness. prudence indeed
will dictate that governments long established should not be changed for
light & transient causes: and accordingly all experience hath shewn that
mankind are more disposed to suffer while evils are sufferable, than to
right themselves by abolishing the forms to which they are accustomed. but
when a long train of abuses & usurpations [begun at a distinguished period,
&] pursuing invariably the same object, evinces a design to ~~subject~~ reduce
them under absolute Despotism, it is their right, it is their duty, to throw off such
~~government~~ & to provide new guards for their future security. such has
been the patient sufferance of these colonies; & such is now the necessity
which constrains them to expunge their former systems of government.
the history of the present king of Great Britain is a history of [unremitting] injuries and
usurpations, [among which appears no solitary fact ~~~~] to contra-
-dict the uniform tenor of the rest, [all of which have] in direct object the
establishment of an absolute tyranny over these states. to prove this, let facts be
submitted to a candid world, [for the truth of which we pledge a faith
yet unsullied by falsehood]

Thomas Jefferson's "Rough Draft" of the Declaration of Independence (See No. 10) which Independent States may of right do. And for the support of this Declaration, with a firm reliance on the Protection of Divine Providence, we mutually pledge to each other our Lives, our Fortunes and our sacred Honor.

JOHN HANCOCK.

New Hampshire
JOSIAH BARTLETT,
WM. WHIPPLE,
MATTHEW THORNTON.

Massachusetts-Bay
SAML. ADAMS,
JOHN ADAMS,
ROBT. TREAT PAINE,
ELBRIDGE GERRY.

Rhode Island
STEP. HOPKINS,
WILLIAM ELLERY.

Connecticut
ROGER SHERMAN,
SAM'EL HUNTINGTON,
WM. WILLIAMS,
OLIVER WOLCOTT.

Georgia
BUTTON GWINNETT,
LYMAN HALL,
GEO. WALTON.

Maryland
SAMUEL CHASE,
WM. PACA,
THOS. STONE,
CHARLES CARROLL
of Carrollton.

Virginia
GEORGE WYTHE,
RICHARD HENRY LEE,
TH. JEFFERSON,
BENJA. HARRISON,
THOS. NELSON, JR.,
FRANCIS LIGHTFOOT LEE,
CARTER BRAXTON.

New York
WM. FLOYD,
PHIL. LIVINGSTON,
FRANS. LEWIS,
LEWIS MORRIS.

Pennsylvania
ROBT. MORRIS,
BENJAMIN RUSH,
BENJA. FRANKLIN,
JOHN MORTON,
GEO. CLYMER,
JAS. SMITH,
GEO. TAYLOR,
JAMES WILSON,
GEO. ROSS.

Delaware
CAESAR RODNEY,
GEO. READ,
THO. M'KEAN.

North Carolina
WM. HOOPER,
JOSEPH HEWES,
JOHN PENN.

South Carolina
EDWARD RUTLEDGE,
THOS. HEYWARD, JUNR.,
THOMAS LYNCH, JUNR.,
ARTHUR MIDDLETON.

New Jersey
RICHD. STOCKTON,
JNO. WITHERSPOON,
FRAS. HOPKINSON,
JOHN HART,
ABRA. CLARK.

11. The United States Seeks Aid from Frederick the Great of Prussia (1777)

THE embattled colonists early recognized their pressing need of men, money and the munitions of war from abroad, and they took steps to secure them. The first American to represent the united colonies in Europe was Silas Deane, a prosperous lawyer who had distinguished himself in revolutionary circles in Connecticut. In 1776, when he was selected to go to France, he was serving as a member of the Continental Congress. His authority stemmed from two secret committees of Congress—one commercial and the other diplomatic. In Paris he met Caron de Beaumarchais and soon became deeply involved in sending many critical supplies to America. The arrival of these materials may have played the decisive part in the American victory at Saratoga, which did much to persuade the French government to enter into the alliance with the United States in February 1778. Deane also sent Lafayette, Pulaski, De Kalb and Steuben to America with a host of far less desirable soldiers of fortune.

In September 1776 Congress determined to enlarge the mission in Paris and named Dr. Benjamin Franklin and Thomas Jefferson to join Deane. Jefferson declined the post and Arthur Lee of Virginia, a sour and conniving character, was appointed in his place. This embittered egotist, to whom intrigue was the breath of life, proved to be the undoing of Silas Deane. Shortly after Lee arrived in Paris he determined that there was nothing to occupy his vast talents, so, in February 1777, he went off on a mission to Spain where he obtained several unimportant successes. From May through July 1777 he was off on a mission to Berlin, where he was denied formal recognition and had all his diplomatic papers filched. Lee had many political connections in Congress, and to these friends he poured a steady flow of criticism and abuse of his colleagues, suspicions and suggestions. He wished to become the sole ambassador to France and to this end he suggested that both Dr. Franklin and Deane be sent off elsewhere where their "petty talents" would find more appropriate employment. In this he was unsuccessful, but he was able to cast unfair and damaging suspicions upon Deane. Deane had been doing an honest and able job, but Lee kept charging him with incompetency and peculation. Shortly after the signing of the French Alliance, Congress suddenly recalled Deane, who left Paris in such haste that he did not take with him the records and vouchers necessary for his vindication. This was the beginning of a series of misunderstandings and misfortunes during which poor Deane lost his peace of mind, his fortune and his health. It mattered but little that Congress, belatedly in 1842, vindicated him and made partial financial restitution, for Deane had died an embittered exile in 1789.

The present original manuscript letter, lent to the Freedom Train exhibit by Mr. Philip H. Rosenbach, was an attempt on the part of the American commissioners to enlist the aid of Frederick the Great of Prussia in a treaty of friendship and commerce with the United States. It does not bear the signature of Lee, who was

May it please Your Excellency   Paris Feby 14th 1777

We have the honor of enclosing the Declaration of the Indepen-
dancy of the United States of North America, with the
Articles of their Confederation, which we desire You To
take the earliest Opportunity, of laying before his
Majesty, the King of Prussia; At the same Time We
wish he may be Assured, of the earnest desire, of the
United States, to obtain his Freindship; & by a free
Commerce, to establish an intercourse between their
distant Countries, which they are Confident must
be mutually beneficial. The state of the Commerce
of the United States, and the Advantages which must
result to both Countries, from the Establishment of
a Commercial intercourse; We shall if agreeable
to his Majesty, lay before him.   Meantime We
take the Liberty of assuring Your Excellency that
the Reports of the Advantages gained by his

Brittannic

Letter of Benjamin Franklin and Silas Deane Transmitting the Declaration of Independence and Articles of Confederation (See No. 11)

Majesty's Troops, or or those of the United States are greatly exaggerated, and many of them without Foundation, especially those which assert that an Accommodation is about to take place, there being no probability of such an Event, by the latest intelligence, We have received from America.

— We have the honor to be with the most profound respect Your Excellency's

Most Obedient &
Very Hum: Serv:ts

B Franklin

Silas Deane

Commissioners Plenipotentiary
for the United States of
North America

then absent on his Spanish mission. With the letter went two enclosures (see items Nos. 12 and 13). The letter produced no tangible results in time to assist the colonies in their struggle for independence, but years later Dr. Franklin had the pleasure, as one of his last official acts before returning to the United States, of signing a treaty with the King of Prussia.

12. Dr. Franklin and Mr. Deane Send a Certified Copy of the Declaration to Frederick the Great (1777)

THE exhibited manuscript, lent to the Freedom Train by Mr. Philip H. Rosenbach, is a contemporary manuscript copy of the Declaration of Independence signed by Dr. Benjamin Franklin and Silas Deane and enclosed in their joint letter of February 14, 1777, to the Baron de Scolenberg, Minister of Frederick the Great, King of Prussia (see the preceding item, No. 11). Arthur Lee of Virginia was one of the three-man commission representing the United States in Paris. But at the time of this certification he, ostensibly finding nothing in Paris worthy of his vast talents, had gone off on a journey into Spain. Consequently his signature does not appear on this document. The original engrossed copy of the Declaration with all the signatures is, of course, on permanent display in the Library of Congress and Thomas Jefferson's "Rough Draft" is one of the most precious exhibits on the Freedom Train. The present manuscript is said to be the only official certified copy of the Declaration of Independence in existence.

13. Dr. Franklin and Mr. Deane Send a Certified Copy of the Articles of Confederation to Frederick the Great (1777)

THE exhibited document, lent to the Freedom Train by Mr. Philip H. Rosenbach, is a contemporary manuscript copy of the Articles of Confederation, which served as the framework of the government of the United States until the adoption and ratification of the Federal Constitution. It was enclosed in the letter from Dr. Benjamin Franklin and Silas Deane to the Baron de Scolenberg, Minister of Frederick the Great, King of Prussia (see the previous item No. 11). Here, as with the certified copy of the Declaration of Independence (item No. 12) it does not bear the signature of the third member of the United States commission, Arthur Lee of Virginia, who was then absent from Paris on a mission to Spain.

This contemporary manuscript copy, signed by both Franklin and Deane, is said to be the only certified official copy of the Articles of Confederation known to be in existence. It has several highly interesting features. Since Franklin and Deane were attempting to interest Frederick the Great in entering into a treaty of friendship and commerce they did not hesitate to take advantage of any opportunity they might seize upon. The King of Prussia possessed no detailed and accurate information on the progress of the American Revolution, and the American commissioners chose not to explain that the Articles of Confederation were merely a set of proposals for a confederation of the American states. This document was enclosed in their letter of February 14, 1777, to Baron de Scolenberg. But the Continental Congress did not formally approve a draft of the Articles of Confederation to be sent to each of the states for ratification until November 15 of that year. And since it required the approval of each of the states it did not become law until March 1, 1781, more than four years after the present copy was sent to the King of Prussia. The present manuscript is a copy of an early draft of the Articles and differs from the final Articles which were approved by Congress and ratified by each of the states.

14. "Common Sense" Rallies the Colonies to the Idea of Independence (1776)

AT the age of 37 Thomas Paine, after a long series of frustrations and defeats, found himself on his way to America. The world had treated him shabbily, and not a little roughly. His native England gave no prospect for anything better. Nor did the new world glow with bright promise. He arrived in Philadelphia in November 1774 a rather uninviting figure—sick and unkempt, low in purse and low in spirits. But he had not lost everything; he still had those old, unrealized hopes—and, more important, he had a letter of introduction from Dr. Benjamin Franklin referring to him as "this ingenious, worthy young man." Having recovered his health and worked at a few odd jobs he finally found himself a promising post as editor of the new *Pennsylvania Magazine*. But Paine could not long remain ensconced in such an easy position. He was caught up in the ferment of revolutionary ideas. He felt that he glimpsed America's future greatness, but he was puzzled and impatient that Americans were blind to the vision. Independence for the colonies was then only an infrequent suggestion. The majority talked of compromise and reconciliation.

With only a few shillings in his purse Paine left his good job and began to write a pamphlet to fit the great problem of the times. On January 10, 1776, there came from the small printing shop of Robert Bell an anonymous, two-shilling pamphlet of 47 pages entitled *Common Sense*. It was an immediate success and soon attained the phenomenal sale of more than 100,000 copies. It was a battle cry for immediate independence. Many who had wavered now became firm; many of the sluggish cast off their timidity. No single speech, no single publication was more instrumental in swaying public opinion. Paine urged immediate independence not merely as a practical gesture, but as the fulfillment of America's moral obligation to the world. In ringing terms he declared that the cause of liberty in America was the cause of liberty for all mankind. Paine was the first publicist to discover and articulate America's destiny and her high mission in an unfree world.

The present first edition of *Common Sense*, lent to the Freedom Train by the New-York Historical Society, is opened to display the last page of the preface and the first page of the main text. Since many editors fail to include Paine's preface in republishing *Common Sense* its two concluding paragraphs follow:

"In the following Sheets, the Author hath studiously avoided every Thing which is personal among ourselves. Compliments as well as censure to Individuals make no Part thereof. The wise, and the worthy, need not the Triumph of a Pamphlet; and those whose Sentiments are injudicious, or unfriendly, will cease of themselves unless too much Pains are bestowed upon their Conversion.

"The Cause of America is in a great Measure the Cause of all Mankind. Many Circumstances hath, and will arise, which are not local, but universal, and through which the Principles of all Lovers of Mankind are affected, and in the Event of which, their Affections are interested. The laying a Country desolate with Fire and Sword, declaring War against the natural Rights of all Mankind, and extirpating the Defenders thereof from the Face of the Earth, is the Concern of every Man to whom Nature hath given the Power of feeling; of which Class, regardless of Party Censure, is the

Author."

15. Tom Paine Inspirits Washington's "Poor, Ragged Continentals"

PAINE was astonished at the success of his pamphlet (see item No. 14) which, in the words of a discerning contemporary, "changed opinion overnight." But from this best seller of the day Paine derived no income, for he had refused to accept any royalties. He was now in the midst of the fray. After the voting of independence he joined up with a group of volunteers from Philadelphia and served as secretary to their commander. At Amboy the volunteers repented of their hasty enthusiasm and, following the example of so many others, in the

early days of the war, deserted and went back home. Paine then went on to Fort Lee where he joined Washington and the bewildered remnants of his army. He stuck with them through the weary retreat to the Delaware. In this hopeless hour Washington asked Paine if he could write something for the shattered morale of the troops—something that might do in this hour what *Common Sense* had done for the cause of independence. Paine scribbled away and when the general read the hasty sheets he was delighted. He ordered it to be read to the dispirited troops. Even Cheetham, later one of Paine's bitterest enemies, declared that "the number was read in the camp, to every corporal's guard, and in the army and out of it had more than the intended effect."

Certainly *The Crisis* itself did not win for the Americans the impending Battle of Trenton, but its eloquence did inspirit many who otherwise would have lacked the necessary will to victory.

The Crisis appeared first in the *Pennsylvania Journal* of December 19, 1776, and was published in pamphlet form on December 23. The first edition exhibited on the Freedom Train is from the collections of Colonel Richard Gimbel.

Paine's vigorous eloquence never found better expression than in the opening pages of *The Crisis*:

"These are the times that try men's souls. The summer soldier and the sunshine patriot will in this crisis, shrink from the service of his country; but he that stands it NOW, deserves the love and thanks of man and woman. Tyranny, like hell, is not easily conquered; yet we have this consolation with us, that the harder the conflict, the more glorious the triumph. What we obtain too cheap, we esteem too lightly; 'tis dearness only that gives everything its value. Heaven knows how to put a proper price upon its goods; and it would be strange indeed, if so celestial an article as FREEDOM should not be highly rated. Britain, with an army to enforce her tyranny, has declared that she has a right (*not only* to TAX) but "to BIND us in ALL CASES WHATSOEVER," and if being *bound in that manner*, is not slavery, then is there not such a thing as slavery upon earth. Even the expression is impious, for so unlimited a power can belong only to God.

"Whether the independence of the continent was declared too soon, or delayed too long, I will not now enter into as an argument; my own simple opinion is, that had it been eight months earlier, it would have been much better. We did not make a proper use of last winter, neither could we, while we were in a dependent state. However, the fault, if it were one, was all our own; we have none to blame but ourselves. But no great deal is lost yet; all that Howe has been doing for this month past, is rather a ravage than a conquest, which the spirit of the Jerseys a year ago would have quickly repulsed, and which time and a little resolution will soon recover.

"I have as little superstition in me as any man living,

The *American* CRISIS.

NUMBER I.

By the Author of COMMON SENSE.

THESE are the times that try men's souls: The summer soldier and the sunshine patriot will, in this crisis, shrink from the service of his country; but he that stands it NOW, deserves the love and thanks of man and woman. Tyranny, like hell, is not easily conquered; yet we have this consolation with us, that the harder the conflict, the more glorious the triumph. What we obtain too cheap, we esteem too lightly:---'Tis dearness only that gives every thing its value. Heaven knows how to set a proper price upon its goods; and it would be strange, indeed, if so celestial an article as FREEDOM should not be highly rated. Britain, with an army to enforce her tyranny, has declared, that she has a right (*not only to* TAX, but) " to " BIND *us in* ALL CASES WHATSOEVER," and if being *bound in that manner* is not slavery, then is there not such a thing as slavery upon earth. Even the expression is impious, for so unlimited a power can belong only to GOD.

WHETHER the Independence of the Continent was declared too soon, or delayed too long, I will not now enter into as an argument; my own simple opinion is, that had it been eight months earlier, it would have been much better. We did not make a proper use of last winter, neither could we, while we were in a dependent state. However, the fault, if it were one, was all our own; we have none to blame but ourselves*. But no great deal is lost yet; all that Howe has been doing for this month past is rather a ravage than a conquest, which the spirit of the Jersies a year ago would have quickly repulsed, and which time and a little resolution will soon recover.

I have as little superstition in me as any man living, but

my

---

* " The present winter" (meaning the last) " is worth an " age if rightly employed, but if lost, or neglected, the whole " Continent will partake of the evil; and there is no punish- " ment that man does not deserve, be he who, or what, or " where he will, that may be the means of sacrificing a season " so precious and useful." COMMON SENSE.

but my secret opinion has ever been, and still is, that God Almighty will not give up a people to military destruction, or leave them unsupportedly to perish, who have so earnestly and so repeatedly sought to avoid the calamities of war, by every decent method which wisdom could invent. Neither have I so much of the infidel in me, as to suppose that he has relinquished the government of the world, and given us up to the care of devils; and as I do not, I cannot see on what grounds the king of Britain can look up to heaven for help against us: a common murderer, a highwayman, or a house-breaker, has as good a pretence as he."

16. General Joseph Warren Certifies that Paul Revere is an Official Messenger of the Committee of Safety

THIS original manuscript, lent to the Freedom Train Exhibit by Dr. A. S. W. Rosenbach, unites two of the most famous names in the history of the American Revolution. Warren, burning with an intense patriotism, had been far more active in politics than in his medical practice for some ten years before the fateful morning at Lexington. It was he who, the evening of April 18, 1775, sent for Paul Revere and begged him to set off at once for Lexington to alert John Hancock and Samuel Adams to the fact that the British troops were on the march to seize them and to destroy the military stores at Concord. Although William Dawes, the other messenger, left Boston before Revere, it was Revere who first arrived at the parsonage of the Rev. Jonas Clark to alert the two hunted patriots. On his way from Lexington to Concord Revere was seized by a party of British soldiers and, in his own words, the British officer in command told him that he was "in a d—m—d critical situation." But he escaped and returned to serve again. Several weeks after issuing the present certificate General Warren was killed at the Battle of Bunker Hill and became, in the words of Daniel Webster, "the first great martyr to this great cause."

17. The Continental Congress Increases the Powers of General Washington (December 1776)

LESS than six months after the Declaration of Independence the Continental Congress conferred a large measure of dictatorial powers upon General Washington as Commander-in-Chief of the patriot army. This enlargement of Washington's authority was more significant of the efforts of an almost powerless government to solve its seemingly insurmountable problems of survival than it was a practical measure of conducting war against a powerful enemy. This grant of augmented power to Washington was a frank recognition of the melancholy and desperate circumstances which confronted the American cause.

In July 1776, the British fleet had landed in New York a force clearly superior in numbers, training and equipment. Washington was compelled to abandon first New York and then his defensive positions north of the city; and then to retreat ignominiously across New Jersey. He found refuge on the Pennsylvania side of the Delaware River across from Trenton only because of the approach of winter, the lackadaisical pursuit by the British, and his inspired seizure of all the boats from the New Jersey shore.

The continuous retreat and the apparent hopelessness of their cause were discouraging enough; the lack of pay and miserably inadequate clothing and supply depressed the morale of the American troops and further strengthened the inclination to desert the army and return home. Where the Continental Army had been denied much-needed produce, flour, and horses, the advancing British found that payment in gold put every facility of the countryside at their disposal. These were truly "the times that try men's souls," wrote Tom Paine in December 1776. "The summer soldier and the sunshine patriot" were "shrinking from the service." Washington, who had led an army of 18,000 in July, found barely 5,000 serving under him in December. The rest had simply gone home.

At this ebb in the patriot cause, the Continental Congress attempted to bolster the waning strength of its army by granting extraordinary powers to General Washington. Although Congress did not possess sufficient authority to requisition the men and money and supplies necessary to conduct a war, the granting of great arbitrary powers to General Washington was most remarkable because the war itself was being fought for the purpose of overthrowing the arbitrary and often despotic rule of the colonies by the British King. Washington was now vested with full and complete powers to raise additional troops and to take whatever he might need for the use of the army. To support the already inflated Continental currency he was given authority to arrest and imprison any who refused to accept the money.

Congress had no intention of appointing a dictator, no matter how great the emergency, and limited Washington's new authority to six months. But regardless of how complete his authority had become, Washington was not one to seek personal power. He replied to Congress that all his "faculties shall be employed, to direct properly the powers they have been pleased to vest me with, and to advance those objects and only those, which gave rise to this honorable mark of distinction." Recognizing that there must have been some misgivings in granting him

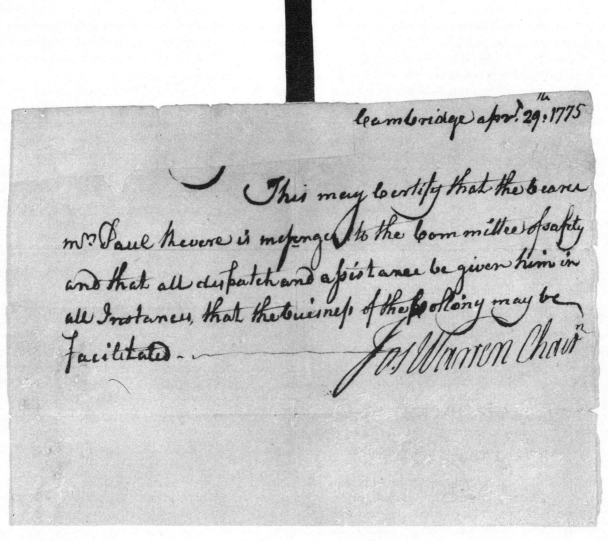

Paul Revere's Commission as Official Messenger (See No. 16)

powers "of the highest nature and almost unlimited in extent," he wrote: ". . . I shall constantly bear in mind, that as the sword was the last resort for the preservation of our liberties, so it ought to be the first thing laid aside, when those liberties are firmly established."

This original manuscript signed by John Hancock as President of the Continental Congress is lent to the Freedom Train exhibit by Dr. A. S. W. Rosenbach.

In Congress Dec'r. 27th, 1776

Resolved, That Genl. Washington be empowered to use every Endeavor, by giving Bounties and otherwise, to prevail upon the Troops whose Time of Enlistment shall expire at the End of the Month to stay with the Army so long after that Period as its Situation shall render their Stay necessary.

That the new Levies in Virginia, Maryland, the Delaware State, Pennsylvania & New Jersey, be ordered to march by Companies, and Parts of Companies, as fast as they shall be raised, and join the Army under Genl. Washington, with the utmost Dispatch.

That the foregoing Resolution be transmitted by the President to the executive Powers of the States before mentioned, who are requested to carry it into Execution; to appoint Commissaries to precede the Troops, and procure Provisions for them on their March; and that they be empowered to draw Money for this Purpose from the nearest Continental Paymaster.

That Genl. Washington be empowered to appoint a Commissary of Prisoners, and a Cloathier General for supplying the Army, to fix their Salaries, and return their Names to Congress.

That Genl. Washington be requested to fix upon that System of Promotion in the Continental Army, which in his Opinion, and that of the general officers with him will produce most general Satisfaction; that it be suggested to him whether a Promotion of Field Officers in the Colonial Line, and of Captains & Subalterns in the Regimental Line, would not be the most proper.

That the Committee of Congress at Philadelphia be desired to contract with proper Persons for creating at Carlisle in Pennsylvania, a Magazine sufficient to contain ten Thousand Stand of Arms and two Hundred Tons of Gun-Powder, and also for creating an Elaboratory adjacent to such Magazine.

That the Council of Massachusetts Bay be desired to contract with proper Persons for erecting in the Town of Brookfield in that State, a Magazine sufficient to contain Ten Thousand Stand of Arms, and two Hundred Tons of Gun-Powder, and also for erecting an Elaboratory adjacent to such Magazine.

That Congress approve of Genl. Washington's directing the Quarter Master General to provide Teams for each Regiment, and for other necessary Purposes.

That the Committee of Secret Correspondence be desired to direct the Commissioners at the Court of France to procure if possible from that Court, an Hundred Thousand Stand of Small Arms.

That the second and seventh Virginia Regiments, with all the Convalescents from the other Corps left in that State and now fit for Duty be ordered to march and join the Army under Genl. Washington with the utmost Dispatch, leaving the Arms that they have at present with the Governor and Council of that State, as they will be provided with others at the Head of Elk.

That three of the Regiments upon the new Establishment in North Carolina be ordered to march immediately to join Genl. Washington. That the State of Virginia be empowered to call into Service at the Continental Expense three Regiments of Militia or Minute Men if such a Measure shall be by that State judged necessary.

The unjust but determined Purpose of the British Court to enslave these free States, obvious through every delusive Insinuation to the contrary, having placed Things in such a Situation that the very Existence of Civil Liberty now depends on the right Execution of military Powers; and the vigorous decisive conduct of these being impossible to distant, numerous, and deliberative Bodies, This Congress having maturely considered the present Crisis, and having perfect Reliance on the Wisdom, Vigour, and Uprightness of Genl. Washington, do hereby—

Resolve, That Genl. Washington shall be, and he is hereby vested, with full, ample, and compleat Powers to raise and collect together in the most speedy and effectual Manner from any, or all these United States, sixteen Battalions of Infantry, in Addition to those already voted by Congress; to appoint Officers for the said Battalions; to raise, officer, and equip, three Thousand Light Horse;

three Regiments of Artillery, and a Corps of Engineers and establish their Pay; to apply to any of the States for such Aid of the Militia as he shall judge necessary; to form such Magazines of Provisions, and in such Places as he shall think proper; to displace and appoint all officers under the Rank of Brigadier General; and to fill up all Vacancies in every other department in the American Armies; to take wherever he may be, whatever he may want for the Use of the Army, if the Inhabitants will not sell it, allowing a reasonable Price for the same, to arrest and confine Persons who refuse to take the Continental Currency, or are otherwise disaffected to the American Cause, and turn to the States of which they are Citizens, their Names, and the Nature of their offences, together with the Witnesses to prove them.

That the foregoing Powers be vested in Genl. Washington for and during the Term of six Months from the date hereof, unless sooner determined by Congress.

Resolved, That the Council of Safety of Pennsylvania be requested to take the most vigorous and speedy Measures for punishing all such as shall refuse Continental Currency, and that the General be directed to give all necessary Aid to the Council of Safety for carrying their Measures on this Subject into effectual Execution.

By order of Congress
John Hancock President

18. General Washington Describes the Crisis of the Winter of 1780

VALLEY FORGE is fixed in the popular mind as the greatest of the sufferings endured by Washington and his ragged Continentals, but actually it was only the first of several bitter winters before the final victory was achieved. At Valley Forge the young republic stood alone, but after February 1778 we had the invaluable assistance of France. In some respects this foreign aid tended to diminish patriot efforts, for not a few were willing to shift much of the burden to our new allies. Nor can it be said that the Continental Congress attacked with conspicuous success the grim and ever-present problems of men, money and supplies. However, the dream life of some members of the Congress was both rich and bizarre. They sat around and concocted dazzling plans for military campaigns while they were oblivious to the fact that what little army Washington had was falling apart because of their neglect of the simple needs of money and supplies. Washington was often a man of great patience, but there were times when he felt compelled to speak out plainly. And when he did his language became vigorous and trenchant. He sat down in his winter quarters at New Windsor, a few miles north of West Point, and

New Windsor 10th Decr 1780.

Dear Sir,

Your letter of the 28th Ulto
I met with on my way to these quarters,
where I arrived on the 6th Inst. — The
suggestions contained in it required no
apology, as it gives me pleasure at all
times to know the sentiments of others
upon matters of public utility — Those
however which you have delivered
relative to an enterprize against the
enemy in New York, exhibit strong evi
dence how little the world is acquain
ted with the circumstances, and strength
of our Army. —

A small second embarka
tion took place about the middle of last
month — if another is in contemplation
to take effect at the reduction of our force
(which I think exceedingly probable)
it is too much in embryo to form more
than conjectural opinions of it at
this time. — But I will suppose it larger,
and that not more than 6000 regular
Troops will be left behind — Where are
the Men — where are the Provisions —
where are the Cloaths — the every thing
necessary to warrant the attempt you
propose, in an inclement Season? —

Yur.

George Washington's Letter Describing Conditions at His Winter Headquarters in 1780 (See No. 18)

Our numbers, never equal to those of the enemy in New York — Our State lines, never half compleat in Men, but perfectly so in every species of want, were diminished in the _Field_ so soon as the weather began to grow cold — near 2000 Men, on account of Cloaths which I had not to give, nor ought to have given (supposing a surplusage) to the levies, whose dismission was near at hand. — And now to prevent the Man who is a permanent Soldier from starving, I am obliged, in place of calling in the aid of Militia for new enterprizes, to dismiss the levies on acc[t] of the Provision. —

Under this description of our circumstances (which is not high coloured) — and when to it, is added, that instead of getting Lumber from Albany for building Barracks on York Island in the manner, & for the purposes you mention, that we have neither money nor credit adequate to the purchase of a few boards for doors to our log Huts. — When every species of Forage that has been used all the latter part of the Campaign — and a good deal of the Provision has been taken at the point of the Bayonet — When we were from the Month of May to the month of September assembling Militia that ought to have been in the Field by the middle of July, and then

obliged

George Washington's Letter, _second page_

obliged to dismiss them for want of
supplies — When we cannot dispatch
an Officer or a common Express upon the
most urgent occasion for want of the
means of support. — and when I add,
but this is a matter of trivial concern,
because it is merely personal, that I have not
been able to obtain a farthing of public
money, for the support of my Table for
near two months, you can be at no loss,
as I have before observed, to discover
the impracticability of executing the
measure you suggested, even supposing the enemy's numbers were reduced to your Standard, but which by the
way, neither is nor will be the case
till the reduction of our Army takes
place — the period for which they know
as well as we do, & will, I have a little doubt
govern themselves accordingly. —

An earnest desire however
of closing the Campaign with some degree of eclat, led me to investigate the
means, most thoroughly, of doing it, &
my wishes had so far got the better of
my judgment, that I had actually made
some pretty considerable advances in
the prosecution of a plan for this
purpose when alas! I found the means
inadequate to the end, & that it was
with difficulty I could remove the Army to its respective places of Cantonment, where it would be week for
the

George Washington's Letter, third page

the Troops if like Chamelions they cd.
live upon Air — or like the Bear suck
their paws for sustenance during the
rigour of the approaching season. —
I am D. Sir
Y. most Obed. Serv.
G. Washington

Gouvr. Morris Esq.
Philad.

10 Dec. 1790
G. Washington

George Washington's Letter, fourth page

phrased a reply to Gouverneur Morris with great care, making numerous corrections and revisions. When at last satisfied he himself made a fair copy of the manuscript and that is the four-page signed autograph letter which Morris received. This original manuscript was lent by Dr. Frank Monaghan. The early draft, with manuscript corrections and revisions, is in the Washington Papers in the Library of Congress.

New Windsor 10th Dec. 1780

Dear Sir,

Your letter of the 28th ulto. I met with on my way to these quarters where I arrived on the 6th Inst.—The suggestions contained in it required no apology, as it gives me pleasure at all times to know the sentiments of others upon matters of public utility—Those however which you have delivered relative to an enterprize against the enemy in New York, exhibit strong evidence how little the World is acquainted with the circumstances, and strength of our army.

A *small* second embarkation took place about the middle of last month—if another is in contemplation to take effect at the reduction of our force (which I think *exceedingly* probable) it is too much in embryo to form more than conjectural opinion of it at this time.—But I will suppose it large and that not more than 6,000 regular Troops will be left behind. Where are the men—where are the Provisions—where are the cloaths—the everything necessary to warrant the attempt you propose, in an inclement season?

Our numbers, never equal to those of the enemy in New York—our state lines, never half compleat in Men, but perfectly so in every species of want, were diminished in the *Field* so soon as the weather began to grow cold—near 2,000 Men, on account of Cloaths which I had not to give, nor ought to have given (supposing a surplusage) to the levies, whose dismission was near at hand.—And now, to prevent the man who is a permanent Soldier from starving, I am obliged in place of calling in the aid of Militia for new enterprizes, to dismiss the levies on acct. of the Provision.

Under this description of our circumstances (which is not high coloured) and when to it, is added; that instead of getting Lumber from Albany for building Barracks on York Island in the manner; & for the purposes you mention, that we have neither money nor credit adequate to the purchase of a few boards for doors to our log Huts—when every ounce of forage that has been used all the latter part of the Campaign—and a good deal of the Provision has been taken at the point of the Bayonet—when we were from the Month of May to the month of September assembling Militia that ought to have been in the Field by the middle of July, and then obliged to dismiss them for want of supplies—when we cannot dispatch an officer or a common Express upon the most urgent occa-

sion for want of the Means of support—and when further I add, but this is a matter of trivial concern because it is of a personal nature that I have not been able to obtain a farthing of public Money for the support of my Table for near two Months, you can be at no loss, as I have before observed, to discover the impracticability of executing the Measure you suggested, even supposing the enemy's numbers were reduced to your standard, but which by the way, neither is nor will be the case till the reduction of our Army takes place.—The period for which they know as well as we do, and will, I have little doubt, govern themselves accordingly.

An earnest desire however of closing the Campaign with some degree of eclat, led me to investigate the means, most thoroughly, of doing it and my wishes had so far got the better of my judgment that I had actually made some pretty considerable advances in the prosecution of a plan for this purpose when alas! I found the means inadequate to the end, and that it was with difficulty I could remove the Army to its respective places of Cantonment, where it would be well for the Troops if like Chameleons they could live upon Air—or like the Bear suck their paws for sustenance during the rigour of the approaching season.

I am D. Sir
Yr. Most Obedt. Serv.
Go. Washington

Govourn. Morris Esq
Philada.

19. News of the Battle of Lexington Spreads through the Colonies (1775)

THE Battle of Lexington, the first military engagement of the American Revolution, is so well known that it needs not an explanation, but merely a reminder. It was on the evening of April 18, 1775, that the British military governor of Boston sent forth some 700 regular troops to seize and destroy various munitions of war which his military intelligence had indicated were stored at Concord. The patriots, who had been watching closely the movements of the British, dispatched Paul Revere and William Dawes with warnings to the provincial leaders at Lexington and Concord. In the early hours of April 19 the approaching British found a part of a company of Minutemen drawn up on the Green at Lexington. The British Major Pitcairn ordered them to disband, but while they were reluctantly breaking ranks the British regulars fired a volley and cleared the ground. Eight provincials were killed and ten were wounded. The war had begun.

Committees of Correspondence had earlier been carefully organized in the various colonies and had played a most active part in the agitation for colonial rights. They

GLORIOUS NEWS.

PROVIDĒCE, October 25, 1781.

Three o'Clock, P. M.

THIS MOMENT an EXPRESS arrived at his Honour the Deputy-Governor's, from Col. Christopher Olney, Commandant on Rhode-Island, announcing the important Intelligence of the Surrender of Lord Cornwallis and his Army, an Account of which was printed This Morning at Newport, and is as follows, viz.

Newport, October 25, 1781.

YESTERDAY afternoon arrived in this Harbour Capt. Lovett, of the Schooner Adventure, from York-River, in Chesapeak-Bay (which he left the 20th Instant) and brought us the glorious News of the Surrender of Lord CORNWALLIS and his Army Prisoners of War to the allied Army, under the Command of our illustrious General, and the French Fleet, under the Command of his Excellency the Count de GRASSE.

A Cessation of Arms took Place on Thursday the 18th Instant, in Consequence of Proposals from Lord Cornwallis for a Capitulation. His Lordship proposed a Cessation of Twenty-four Hours, but Two only were granted by His Excellency General WASHINGTON. The Articles were completed the same Day, and the next Day the allied Army took Possession of York-Town.

By this glorious Conquest, NINE THOUSAND of the Enemy, including Seamen, fell into our Hands, with an immense Quantity of Warlike Stores, a forty Gun Ship, a Frigate, an armed Vessel, and about One Hundred Sail of Transports.

PRINTED BY EDWARD E. POWARS, in STATE-STREET.

"Glorious News" of Cornwallis's Surrender at Yorktown is Printed at Providence (See No. 20) had long since been in close communication with each other and it was through them that the electrifying news of "The Lexington Alarm" was spread through the colonies. The original signed manuscript, lent to the Freedom Train by the John H. Scheide Library of Titusville, Pennsylvania, is the manuscript copy of the message which was first carried beyond the immediate vicinity of Boston. The text is known in two other forms: one in a document in the Historical Society of Pennsylvania and the other in an unlocated copy of which the New York Public Library possesses a reproduction. But the Scheide copy is the oldest known copy of this historic document describing the first engagement of the Revolution. It was sent out by the Committee of Safety of Watertown, Massachusetts, to spread the alarm in New England. From New England the alarm was carried in manuscript form until it reached Philadelphia, where W. and T. Bradford printed it in a broadside and in this form the news was carried to the southern colonies.

> Watertown Wednesday Morning near 10 oClock To all the Friends of American Liberty—Be it Known that this Morning before Break of Day a Brigade Consist[in]g of about 1000 or 1200 Men Landed at Phips's Farm at Cambridge & marched to Lexington—where they found a Company of our Colony Militia in Arms, upon whom they fir'd without any Provocation & killed 6 Men and wounded 4 others—by an Express—from Boston this Moment we find another Brigade are now upon the March from Boston—supposed to be about 1000   the Bearer Mr Israel Bissel is Charged to alarm the Country quite to Connecticut & all Persons are Desired to furnish him with fresh Horses as they may be needed. I have spoken with several persons who have seen the Dead & wounded—Pray let the Delagates from this Colony to Connecticut see this they know—
> Jos Palmer, one of the Committe
> Colo. Foster of Brookfield—one of the Delagates
> A true Coppy taken from the Original p[er] Order of Committee of Correspondence for Worcester Worcester, April 19th 1775
> Attest Nathan Balding T[own] Clerk
> Brooklyne Thursday 11 oClock—The above is a true Coppy as rec[eived] here p[er] Express forwarded from Worcester—
> Test Daniel Tyler Junr

20. "Glorious News" Arrives from Yorktown

LEXINGTON marked the beginning of hostilities in the American Revolution; Yorktown, the end. Lord Cornwallis, with more than 7,000 seasoned troops, had been harassing the Americans in the southern colonies.

Lafayette, commanding a small untrained American force, had played a wary and a watchful game. Under mounting pressure, made possible by the arrival of French troops and the fleet of Admiral De Grasse, Cornwallis took up a strong position on the peninsula of Yorktown. This, in his mind, was a vantage point; here he might receive the expected reinforcements from the British garrison in New York or from here he might embark his troops and return to New York. All this was predicated upon British control of the seas. But this control was temporarily lost by the British; succor could not reach Cornwallis, nor could he escape the besieging allied forces. General Washington, with brilliant deception, added his own forces to the fray and on October 17, 1781, Cornwallis asked for surrender terms and on the 19th the surrender was completed. The vanquished laid down their arms to the tune of "The World Turned Upside Down." And so it was. While a formal peace was many months in the future, the surrender at Yorktown ended all fighting of consequence.

The electrifying news of the V-E and the V-J days of its time sped through the colonies as rapidly as courier and horse and boat could hasten it. The present original broadside, lent by Mrs. Frank Monaghan to the Freedom Train exhibit, indicates how the news was spread among the people of Providence after it had come by ship from Yorktown to Newport, Rhode Island, and thence to Providence. The printer was in such haste to get his broadside to the public that he spelled Providence incorrectly.

21. Great Britain Recognizes the Independence of the United States in the Treaty of Paris (1783)

THIS original signed copy of the Treaty of 1783 by which England recognized American independence is one of the two or three duplicate signed copies that were sent to America; each was sent by a different ship in order to decrease the possibility of loss. The booklet containing the Treaty consists of twenty-four pages, 9 by 15 inches, bound with a ribbon. The document is written in a careful, completely legible hand and is signed by D. Hartley for Great Britain; and John Adams, Benjamin Franklin and John Jay for America. The seal of each accompanies his signature.

The chief provisions of the Definitive Treaty of Peace were: Recognition of the independence of the United States; evacuation "with all convenient speed" of British troops in America; guaranty against legal obstacles to the collection of pre-war debts owed to British creditors; boundary settlement, especially granting the new nation land west to the Mississippi; and fishing rights in British North American waters.

The Treaty of Paris, in which Great Britain Recognized U. S. Independence (See No. 21) without Difficulty and without requiring any Compensation.

Article 10th..

The solemn Ratifications of the present Treaty expedited in good & due Form shall be exchanged between the contracting Parties in the Space of Six Months or sooner if possible to be computed from the Day of the Signature of the present Treaty. In Witness whereof we the undersigned their Ministers Plenipotentiary have in their Name and in Virtue of our Full Powers signed with our Hands the present Definitive Treaty, and caused the Seals of our Arms to be affix'd thereto.

Done at Paris, this third Day of September, In the Year of our Lord one thousand seven hundred & Eighty three. —

D Hartley   John Adams..   B Franklin   John Jay ——

The Treaty of Paris, last page

The Treaty, which provided the formal recognition by Great Britain of the Independence of the United States, was the result of highly successful diplomacy by the American plenipotentiaries. With the surrender of Lord Cornwallis at Yorktown in October 1781, virtually all hostilities ceased. But the British still occupied Charleston, Savannah, New York and many frontier posts. The continental Army was almost incapable of further effort.

The British were acutely aware of the futility of any further offensive military action; they were also acquainted with the high cost of maintaining troops in America. Consequently they were in the mood for peace and were ready to enter upon negotiations in the spring of 1782.

The victorious allies were divided by conflicting interests. The United States was allied with France and France was bound in an alliance with Spain. France's position was influenced by her commitments to Spain. The American commissioners in Paris had been instructed by Congress to do nothing without the advice and consent of the French. The American diplomats, notably John Jay, became persuaded that the interests of France were not the best interests of the United States and began separate negotiations with the British. After many tortuous and extended parleys they agreed upon tentative terms which were then, for the first time, communicated to the French minister, who could then do little more than sputter a protest.

The preliminary and conditional articles of peace with Great Britain were signed on November 30, 1782. This had the effect of an armistice which would prevail until England, France and Spain might conclude their own treaties. America could not conclude the final treaty until France and England had come to terms; and France delayed her action in order to give Spain adequate time in which to negotiate. After many months all was arranged and the Definitive Treaty of Peace between Great Britain and the United States was signed on September 3, 1783.

The present document is lent to the Freedom Train exhibit by the National Archives.

22. Roger Williams Speaks Out for Complete Religious Freedom

A DISTINGUISHED American historian describes Roger Williams as "colonial thinker, religious liberal, and earliest of the fathers of American democracy." In his own day, however, he was known quite differently.

Williams, a young, well-educated English minister, had come to Boston in 1631 to begin a career in an atmosphere of new freedom. He left his native England because life was being made increasingly uncomfortable for any who dared express opposition to the attempts of the government to impose uniformity of religious practice. For all dissenters, and especially the Puritans, the future seemed cloudy and bleak.

In Boston, Williams quickly discovered that the freedom of the new world was a curious thing. The Puritans crossed the Atlantic because they dissented from the authorities in England, but once they themselves were ensconced in the seats of authority they wanted no more dissent. With them freedom was a one-way philosophy: they claimed it for themselves, but would not grant it to others. It should be added that Williams was uncompromising in his convictions and did nothing to ingratiate himself with the Massachusetts authorities. Not only did he differ with them on the subject of religious freedom, but he nettled them in perhaps an even more sensitive spot: their purse. He was eloquent in his defense of the Indians and was caustic in voicing his objections to the defrauding and exploitation of the natives by the Puritans and by the English government. His denunciations of the imperialistic expropriation of American soil and his views on religious liberty combined to make him a figure which Massachusetts would be happy not to have in the community. He had been chosen, over the opposition of the magistrates, as teacher of the Salem Church in 1634. Finally, the following year, the General Court of Massachusetts Bay Colony found him guilty of disseminating "new and dangerous opinions against the authorities of magistrates" and ordered him banished from the colony.

The authorities attempted to seize him, but he had been warned in advance and escaped in the dead of winter. After many privations and suffering the young minister assembled enough hardy followers to found the earliest Rhode Island settlement, Providence, in 1636. By 1643 four settlements had been established in the Narragansett area. In Rhode Island, Williams granted full and general religious liberty as a matter of law and of principle, for he held to his belief that no government should attempt or be permitted to force any form of religion on anybody and that every person should be free to worship God in his own way. This broad tolerance was unique in the American colonies. Williams also established a system of land ownership far more democratic than that which existed in Massachusetts. His political system was likewise marked by its liberality.

Even from a distance the Massachusetts authorities were made fearful by the existence of such "ungodly and subversive notions." If they could not suffer Williams to remain in their midst neither could they allow him and his followers to grow happy and prosperous on their southern border, for contagion—and especially the contagion of ideas—knows no borders. An armed band from Massachusetts invaded Rhode Island and seized a few of the inhabitants. Then Massachusetts tried a more subtle

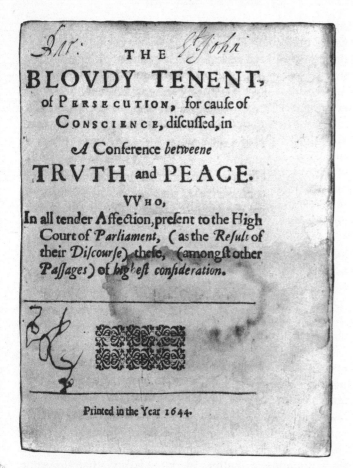

Roger Williams's Famous Statement on Religious Freedom Appeared in This Book, Printed in 1644 (See No. 22)

23. Thomas Jefferson Writes the Virginia Bill for Establishing Religious Freedom

Thomas Jefferson thought that his Bill of Establishing Religious Freedom ranked with his authorship of the Declaration of Independence—and that each was more important than his presidency of the United States.

Following the Declaration of Independence, the Virginia House of Delegates had repealed all Acts of Parliament concerning religion, yet there was still considerable support for those who favored some form of government subsidy of religion. Various proposals were made to declare Christianity the religion of the state and to maintain ministers of all denominations by levying taxes on the general populace. Jefferson, who believed firmly in the "natural rights of mankind," was opposed to all such measures and so drafted a bill designed to protect all citizens, regardless of race or creed, in their freedom of conscience.

Jefferson's Bill for Establishing Religious Freedom was first introduced in the Virginia House of Delegates in June 1779. It stunned the majority of the House and immediately became the subject of such stormy debate that no action was taken at that time. By 1784 conservative tidewater members of the Virginia House, who opposed the bill, almost succeeded in putting through a law levying a tax for the public support of religion. Leading the fight against this proposal was another Virginian destined for greatness, James Madison, whose timely motion for postponement prevented its passage. Jefferson and Madison then brought the issue of religious freedom before the voters in an intensive campaign of speeches and publications. In 1785 Jefferson went to Europe, where he succeeded Benjamin Franklin as United States Minister to France. In Jefferson's absence Madison carried on the fight and finally, on January 16, 1786, the bill was passed.

The preamble of the bill, a ringing declaration of free faith, was modified slightly by the Virginia legislature. Then follows the short, almost staccato resolution which paved the way for a new era of religious freedom and toleration in American history.

Jefferson concluded his bill with an admonition to posterity that to repeal or restrict it in the future would be "an infringement of natural right."

The aim of this great contribution to humanity, as explained by Jefferson himself, was "to comprehend, within the mantle of its protection, the Jew and the Gentile, the Christian and the Mohametan, the Hindoo and infidel of every denomination."

This particular copy of Jefferson's Bill for Establishing Religious Freedom was printed in 1784 along with a number of other bills designed to revise the laws of

approach to the problem. They attempted to secure for themselves a patent for the Narragansett region; this would enable them to snuff out the independent existence of the unwelcome neighbors to the south.

To forestall this action Williams went to England to request a charter for his Colony. He was successful and the charter for the Providence Plantations in the Narragansett Bay region was issued on March 14, 1644.

It was while in England that Williams took up the pen in the liberal cause as a pamphleteer, opposing the Puritan attempt to establish a national church and compulsory uniformity. In his best known work, *The Bloudy Tenent of Persecution* (1644), he proclaimed his celebrated statement for religious freedom. He expanded his grounds for believing that "God requireth not an uniformity of Religion," and contended that all individuals and religious bodies—pagans, Jews, and Catholics as well as Protestants—were entitled to religious liberty as a natural right. His statement on religious freedom stands out like a beacon light in an age when religious intolerance darkened the minds of men.

The first edition (1644) of *The Bloudy Tenent of Persecution* is lent to the Freedom Train exhibit by the Library of Congress.

Virginia. A committee of five, including Jefferson, had been appointed by the Virginia legislature in November 1776 to draw up this revision of the laws. The Bill for Establishing Religious Freedom, however, was entirely Jefferson's work. It gives him high rank among those who have championed man's intellectual and spiritual liberty.

Sections I and II of the Bill are reprinted from the Library of Congress copy lent to the Freedom Train.

SECTION I. Well aware that the opinions and belief of men depend not on their own will, but follow involuntarily the evidence proposed to their minds; that Almighty God hath created the mind free, and manifested his supreme will that free it shall remain by making it altogether insusceptible of restraint; that all attempts to influence it by temporal punishments, or burthens, or by civil incapacitations, tend only to beget habits of hypocrisy and meanness, and are a departure from the plan of the holy author of our religion, who being lord both of body and mind, yet chose not to propagate it by coercions on either, as was in his Almighty power to do, but to extend it by its influence on reason alone; that the impious presumption of legislators and ruler, civil as well as ecclesiastical, who, being themselves but fallible and uninspired men, have assumed dominion over the faith of others, setting up their own opinions and modes of thinking as the only true and infallible, and as such endeavoring to impose them on others, hath established and maintained false religions over the greatest part of the world and through all time: That to compel a man to furnish contributions of money for the propagation of opinions which he disbelieves and abhors, is sinful and tyrannical; that even the forcing him to support this or that teacher of his own religious persuasion, is depriving him of the comfortable liberty of giving his contributions to the particular pastor whose morals he would make his pattern, and whose powers he feels most persuasive to righteousness; and is withdrawing from the ministry those temporary rewards, which proceeding from an approbation of their personal conduct, are an additional incitement to earnest and unremitting labours for the instruction of mankind; that our civil rights have no dependence on our religious opinions, any more than our opinions in physics or geometry; that therefore the proscribing any citizen as unworthy the public confidence by laying upon him an incapacity of being called to offices of trust and emolument, unless he profess or renounce this or that religious opinion, is depriving him injuriously of those privileges and advantages to which, in common with his fellow citizens, he has a natural right; that it tends also to corrupt the principles of that very religion it is meant to encourage, by bribing, with a monopoly of worldly honours and emoluments, those who will externally profess and conform to it; that though indeed these are criminal who do not withstand such temptation, yet neither are those innocent who lay the bait in their way; that the opinions of men are not the object of civil government, nor under its jurisdiction; that to suffer the civil magistrate to intrude his powers into the field of opinion and to restrain the profession or propagation of principles on supposition of their ill tendency is a dangerous falacy, which at once destroys all religious liberty, because he being of course judge of that tendency will make his opinions the rule of judgment, and approve or condemn the sentiments of others only as they shall square with or differ from his own; that it is time enough for the rightful purposes of civil government for its officers to interfere when principles break out into overt acts against peace and good order; and finally, that truth is great and will prevail if left to herself; that she is the proper and sufficient antagonist to error, and has nothing to fear from the conflict unless by human interposition disarmed of her natural weapons, free argument and debate; errors ceasing to be dangerous when it is permitted freely to contradict them.

SECTION II. We, the General Assembly of Virginia do enact that no man shall be compelled to frequent or support any religious worship, place or ministry whatsoever, nor shall be enforced, restrained, molested or burthened in his body or goods, nor shall otherwise suffer, on account of his religious opinions or belief; but that all men shall be free to profess, and by argument to maintain, their opinions in matters of religion, and that the same shall in no wise diminish, enlarge or affect their civil capacities.

24. Stephen Daye Prints the First Book in the North American Colonies (1640)

ONE of the most interesting and valuable of all the exhibits on the Freedom Train is one of the few surviving copies of the first edition of *The Whole Booke of Psalmes Faithfully Translated into English Metre*, popularly known as the Bay Psalm Book.

For comment on this unusual item one cannot do better than quote the eminent bibliographer, George Parker Winship, from his recent book on *The Cambridge Press, 1638–1692:*

"The third output from the Press was 'the Psalms newly turned into metre.' It is the first thing printed in English America that can be called a book and the first that can still be seen. It has long ranked among the world's most famous books. This is due largely to the enormous influence that printed matter has had upon the expansion of the United States, economically and culturally, and in part to the persistent vogue of book collecting which has kept pace with the prosperity that followed the expansion. Its fame is also an inheritance of considerable antiquity, going back to the time when this was a new book. Many of the earliest settlers of Massachusetts were acutely conscious of the significance of what they had done when they separated themselves from their homeland. Their leaders were historically minded, fully aware of the importance of preserving the record of their proceedings. They understood the symbolic significance of a printing press as evidence of a cultural foundation, when this was added to the equipment of the colony, alongside of the college. These leaders and their associates who remained in England realized equally the practical advantages of press and college as encouragements to possible settlers who were hesitating to separate themselves from the refinements of life to which they had been accustomed in the Mother Country. These considerations, consciously or subconsciously, go far to explain the noteworthy fact that eleven copies of this Bay Psalm Book of 1640 are still in existence in public or private libraries. Eight of these never left New England where five of them were collected by Thomas Prince before the middle of the eighteenth century.

"The Bay Psalm Book is famous for reasons with which the work itself has nothing to do. It is also an extremely important book, for reasons that have nothing whatever to do with its fame, and which have not yet been convincingly explained. These reasons have to do with the religious development of the English people, and when they come to be clearly comprehended the spiritual foundation of the English character will be easier to understand."

Known to survive, in varying degrees of completeness and in various bindings, are eleven copies of the Bay Psalm Book. Normally, scholars are but little interested in the monetary value of such esteemed items, but the Bay Psalm Book deviates somewhat from the usual. On January 28, 1947, a perfect copy of the first edition of this little book was sold at public auction in New York City. It was bought, on behalf of Yale University, for the sum of $151,000. This is the highest price ever paid for a book at a public auction.

The copy of the Bay Psalm Book displayed on the Freedom Train exhibit lacks a few pages, but it retains the calf binding in which it was first bound. It is lent to the Freedom Train by Dr. A. S. W. Rosenbach.

25. President Washington Declares That America Has Given to Mankind a Policy of Freedom Worthy of Emulation (1790)

DURING President Washington's tour of various New England states in 1790, he arrived in Newport, Rhode Island, on August 17. Included in the presidential party were Secretary of State Thomas Jefferson, Gov-

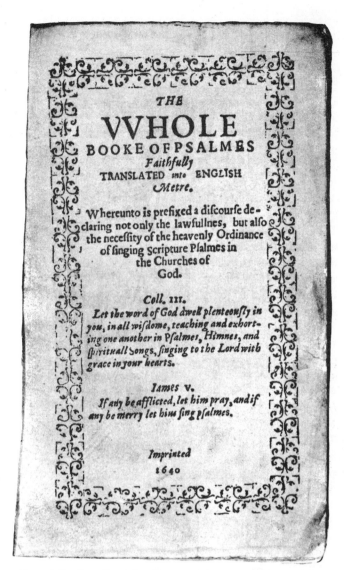

One of the Few Surviving Copies of the First Book Printed in the North American Colonies (See No. 24)

ernor George Clinton of New York, Judge John Blair, Senator Theodore Foster of Rhode Island, and others. Upon his arrival he was met by a committee representing the city. Among the representatives of the clergy was Moses Seixas, who was the Warden of the Hebrew Congregation and a member of King David's Lodge. When, on the following day various deputations appeared at Washington's quarters to present the distinguished visitor with formal addresses of welcome, Warden Seixas spoke for the Hebrew Congregation.

After expressing "the most cordial affection and esteem for your person and merits" the address continued:

"With pleasure we reflect on those days, those days of difficulty and danger, when the God of Israel, who delivered David from the peril of the sword—shielded your head in the day of battle—and we rejoice to think that the same spirit who rested in the bosom of the greatly beloved Daniel, enabling him to preside over the provinces of the Babylonish Empire, rests, and ever will rest upon you, enabling you to discharge the arduous duties of Chief Magistrate in these states.

"Deprived as we heretofore have been of the invaluable rights of free citizens, we now (with a deep sense of gratitude to the Almighty Dispenser of all Events) behold a Government erected by the majesty of the people, a Government which gives to bigotry no sanction, to persecution no assistance, but generously affording to all liberty of conscience and immunities of citizenship, deeming everyone, of whatever nation, tongue, or language equal parts of the great Government machine. This so ample and extensive Federal Union whose basis is philanthropy, mutual confidence and public virtue, we cannot but acknowledge to be the work of the Great God who ruleth in the armies of Heaven and among the inhabitants of the earth, doing whatever seemeth Him good. . . ."

To this address, dated August 17, 1790, Washington sent the following acknowledgment. In his reply the president uses some phrases taken from the original address, but he adds his own eloquent sentiment on the subject of freedom and toleration. This original two-page manuscript, lent to the Freedom Train exhibit by Mr. Howard L. Milkman, is in the handwriting of a secretary. The signature is, of course, that of Washington. To the second page of the manuscript has been added a later postscript in an unidentified hand which quaintly declares that the letter is "Original & Valuable."

To the Hebrew Congregation in Newport
Rhode Island

Gentlemen

While I receive with much satisfaction, your address replete with expressions of affection and esteem; I rejoice in the opportunity of assuring you, that I shall always retain a grateful remembrance of the cordial welcome I experienced in my visit to Newport, from all classes of Citizens.

The reflection on the days of difficulty and danger which are past is rendered the more sweet, from a consciousness that they are succeeded by days of uncommon prosperity and security. If we have wisdom to make the best use of the advantages with which we are now favored, we cannot fail, under the just administration of a good Government, to become a great and a happy people.

The Citizens of the United States of America have a right to applaud themselves for having given to mankind examples of an enlarged and liberal policy: a policy worthy of imitation. All possess alike liberty of conscience and immunities of citizenship. It is now no more that toleration is spoken of, as if it was by the indulgence of one class of people, that another enjoyed the exercise of their inherent natural rights. For happily the Govern-

ment of the United States, which gives to bigotry no sanction, to persecution no assistance, requires only that they who live under its protection, should demean themselves as good citizens, in giving it on all occasions their effectual support.

It would be inconsistent with the frankness of my character not to avow that I am pleased with your favorable opinion of my administration, and fervent wishes for my felicity. May the Children of the Stock of Abraham, who dwell in this land, continue to merit and enjoy the good will of the other Inhabitants; while everyone shall sit in safety under his own vine and fig tree, and there shall be none to make him afraid. May the father of all mercies scatter light and not darkness in our paths, and make us all in our several vocations useful here, and in his own due time and way everlastingly happy.

Go. Washington

26. "The Federalist" Explains and Defends the Constitution (1788)

THE Constitution formulated by the convention in Philadelphia was to encounter serious opposition in the pivotal states of Massachusetts, Virginia and New York, but in the last the fight was more bitter, for the greater part of the state was distinctly anti-Federal. Here the popular governor, George Clinton, supported by Yates, Lansing, Melancton Smith, Lamb and others of more local reputation, organized the opposition. The Clintonians, smugly confident, unconcerned about the problems of their neighbors, convinced of the high destiny of their state, were unwilling to turn over the profitable impost revenues to a federal government. Many great landholders, jealous and conservative, joined paper-money men and numerous office-holders, who feared the loss of the impost would curtail their salaries. Federalist opinion prevailed only in New York City and the immediate neighborhood.

At this critical period Hamilton and Jay performed an effective, disinterested act of patriotic statesmanship. Both had been influential in making the Philadelphia convention possible, yet neither was wholly satisfied with the Constitution which it drafted.

In frequent discussions before the convention met they had found their ideas to be essentially similar—so similar indeed that Hamilton borrowed many of Jay's phrases in expounding them. Both favored an aristocratic rather than a democratic republic; both held that the state governments ought to be abolished as sovereign entities. They demanded a vigorous executive invested with wide powers. But while Hamilton openly avowed his preference for monarchy, Jay detested it and insisted that the ultimate source of all political authority resided in the people.

To the Hebrew Congregation in Newport
Rhode Island.

Gentlemen.

While I receive, with much satisfaction, your Address replete with expressions of affection and esteem; I rejoice in the opportunity of assuring you, that I shall always retain a grateful remembrance of the cordial welcome I experienced in my visit to Newport, from all classes of Citizens.

The reflection on the days of difficulty and danger which are past is rendered the more sweet, from a consciousness that they are succeeded by days of uncommon prosperity and security. If we have wisdom to make the best use of the advantages with which we are now favored, we cannot fail, under the just administration of a good Government, to become a great and a happy people.

The Citizens of the United States of America have a right to applaud themselves for having given to mankind examples of an enlarged and liberal policy: a policy worthy of imitation. All possess alike liberty of conscience and immunities of citizenship. It is now no more that toleration is spoken of, as if it was by the indulgence of one class of people, that another enjoyed the exercise of their inherent natural rights. For happily
the

Washington's "To Bigotry No Sanction" Letter on Religious Freedom (See No. 25) the Government of the United States, which gives to bigotry no sanction, to persecution no assistance, requires only that they who live under its protection, should demean themselves as good citizens, in giving it on all occasions their effectual support.

It would be inconsistent with the frankness of my character not to avow that I am pleased with your favorable opinion of my administration, and fervent wishes for my felicity. May the children of the Stock of Abraham, who dwell in this land, continue to merit and enjoy the good will of the other Inhabitants; while every one shall sit in safety under his own vine and figtree, and there shall be none to make him afraid. May the father of all mercies scatter light and not darkness in our paths, and make us all in our several vocations useful here, and in his own due time and way everlastingly happy.

G Washington

1790. August
Reply of Genl. Washington
to Address of the Hebrews
of Newport Rhode Island
With Autograph Signature
of G.º Washington
Original & Valuable

George Washington's Letter, second page

Hamilton's plan was quickly rejected in the convention, yet he never lost faith in it. Nor did he ever gain complete confidence in the Constitution. Several years before he died he complained bitterly of his support of a plan of government in which he had never had faith "from the beginning" and which he described as "a frail and worthless fabric." This support of a plan which was highly distasteful to him he explained in his last utterance to the convention: "No man's ideas are more remote from the plan than my own are known to be; but is it possible to deliberate between anarchy and convulsion on one side and the chance of good to be expected from the plan on the other?"

Jay was more mild in his remarks on the Constitution. After careful study of the document he wrote to John Adams: "For my part I think it much better than the one we have, and therefore that we shall be gainers by the Exchange; especially as there is Reason to hope that Experience and the good Sense of the People, will correct what may prove to be unexpedient in it. A Compact like this, which is the Result of Accomodation & Compromise, cannot be supposed to be perfectly consonant to the Wishes and opinions of any of the Parties. It corresponds a good Deal with your favorite & I think just Principles of Government, whereas the present Confederation seems to have been formed without the least attention to them."

Before the convention had adjourned Hamilton was already hurling newspaper polemics against the enemy. Attacking Clinton in an anonymous letter in the *Daily Advertiser* of July 21, he declared that the Governor's attempts to prejudice the people against the Constitution before they had even seen it were unjust and amply demonstrated that the Governor preferred his "own power" to the "public good." Clintonian quills scratched away and tongues wagged with the rumor that Hamilton had "palmed himself off" on Washington and that he had been "dismissed" from Washington's family. A hasty refutation came from Mount Vernon. Thus the battle was begun. By late September arguments flooded the newspapers. The authors of many of the letters were well known, but they signed their letters: "Plain Truth," "Brutus," "Caesar," "An Old Whig," "Sidney," "Detector," "Cato," "Rough Hewer," "Baptist," and a variety of others. Clinton, as "Cato," launched his pedantic arguments against the Constitution; Hamilton, as "Caesar," replied with personal abuse of the Governor. Other quills contributed sardonic humor and burlesque: a welcome relief from the drowsy lucubrations which dragged through column after column. "Roderick Razor" defended the Constitution in the *Daily Advertiser* by liberal quotations from "Squire Sour Crout" and "Squire Clip Purse Van Clink de Gelt." A Clintonian wit, "one of the Nobility," pretended to urge the adoption of the Constitution "without the least hesitation, examination, alteration or amendment," describing the mass of the people

as "mere orang outangs—blockheads, numskulls, asses, monkeys, sheep, owls, and lobsters,—and only created to be subservient to the pleasures and interest of their superiors." Continuing, he declared that "all the offices of the government are, by the laws of nature, appropriated to men of family, fortune and genius."

It was in the midst of the newspaper hurly-burly of October that two of the Federalist leaders realized that invective would only confirm their opponents in their views. They determined to publish a long and partisan, but scholarly, exposition of the Constitution, together with a rebuttal of the Clintonian arguments. Thus was conceived the *Federalist*, described as one of the great American contributions to political theory and one marking an epoch in the development of free constitutional government. Hampton L. Carson, an eminent legal historian, declared that this monumental work "for comprehensiveness of design, strength, clearness and simplicity . . . has no parallel among the writings of men, not even excepting or overlooking those of Montesquieu and Aristotle," and Wendell in his *Literary History of America* describes it as "so wisely thoughtful that one may almost declare it the permanent basis of sound thinking concerning American constitutional law."

Through the vicissitudes of fortune Jay was never able to discharge his scheduled responsibilities. Hence *The Federalist* became chiefly the work of Hamilton and Madison.

It is not clear whether the suggestion first came from Hamilton or from Jay, nor is there any certainty when the design was first formed. It is probable that it arose from one of the many conferences of Jay and Hamilton, possibly early in October 1787. The first number, hastily written by Hamilton while returning on a Hudson sloop from legal duties in Albany, was published in the New York *Independent Journal* for Saturday, October 27, under the signature of "Publius." Eighty-five numbers were published in various newspapers during the course of the next seven months. When the plan was once formed Jay and Hamilton enlisted the aid of James Madison and divided the preparation of the essays.

The Federalist papers, hastily written but following the conception of a grand design, were published in various newspapers from October 1787 until May 1788. Of the 85 lengthy essays all but eight of them appeared in the New York press. In the late spring of 1788 they were published in book form.

The two-volume copy of the original publication, lent to the Freedom Train by Mr. Henry Bradley Martin, has several special association values. This is the copy that Alexander Hamilton had specially bound for presentation to General Washington. When Washington received it he placed his signature on each of the title pages and added them to his library. Later, James Madison added his manuscript annotations regarding the authorship of each of the essays. In this he was incorrect in attributing the first essay to John Jay.

27. John Jay Revises the Manuscript of "Federalist" Essay Number 5

THERE has been much dispute concerning the authorship of some numbers of *The Federalist* (see item No. 26), but it is clear that John Jay wrote only five of them. Four essays (numbers 2 through 5) by Jay, treating the dangers from foreign force and influence, were published in the early weeks of November 1787. Then, for almost sixty numbers, he contributed nothing. The explanation given by William Jay and George Pellew is that this interruption was caused by an injury Jay received in the celebrated "Doctor's Riot" in New York City. This is hardly an explanation, as the riot did not occur until April 1788 and by that time at least 77 of the 85 numbers had been published. Jay's failure to contribute his share was caused by a breakdown in his health in the winter of 1787. During that summer, Dr. Charlton, the family physician, had forced him to take a rest of five or six weeks at Rye and Bedford. His health was partly regained, but in November he suffered an attack of what was first diagnosed as tuberculosis and later rheumatism. He had not recovered by February, when he still complained of an excruciating pain in his left side. When he was able to work again he wrote a defense of the powers of the Senate, especially the power of making treaties, which was published on March 7 as essay number 64.

The present four-page manuscript, lent to the Freedom Train by Mr. William Jay Iselin, is Jay's original draft of essay number 5 and concludes his discussion of the "Dangers from Foreign Force and Influence" which he began to treat in number 2. This is one of the only three manuscripts that have survived of the original 85. It is entirely in the handwriting of Jay and contains many corrections and revisions. The first page alone contains changes involving 70 words.

28. Edmund Randolph Presents to the Convention the Virginia Plan for the Constitution

FOLLOWING the adoption of the Articles of Confederation as a frame of government in 1781, it had become increasingly clear that the weak federation of independent states which it established was most unsatisfactory.

By 1787 the need for improvement was so clearly recognized that the Congress of the Confederation invited the states to send delegates to a convention at Philadelphia "for the sole and express purpose of revising the Articles of Confederation."

When the convention was organized on May 25, 1787, many of the delegates had already come to the conclusion that far more than a revision of the Articles of Confederation was required to meet the need for an effective national government. Members of the delegation from Virginia had privately prepared a plan for a new government and this plan they quickly brought forward. This Virginia Plan, of which James Madison was the chief author, was presented in the form of a series of resolutions introduced on the floor of the convention by Edmund Randolph on May 29. It struck directly at the root of the difficulties under which the country had been laboring since the Declaration of Independence.

In a brilliant speech of presentation, Randolph summed up the situation confronting the country. He described the problems with which the Confederation, made "in the infancy of the science of constitutions," was powerless to cope. The great need, he said, was for a government that could defend the country against invasions, that could settle differences between the states, that could deal with sedition within the states, that could defend itself against encroachments by the states, and that would be superior to the state constitutions.

That a government with the power necessary to do these things was successfully advocated in 1787, while only six years earlier the thirteen states had, with utmost difficulty, established a loose and feeble confederation, is explained by the events of the intervening years. With no control over taxation or trade, no executive or judiciary, and no authority to enforce its laws on the states, the Congress under the Articles of Confederation was completely unable to discharge the elementary functions of a national government worthy of the name. In the expanding West there was a strong demand for free trade through New Orleans, then in Spanish hands. The increasingly important western fur trade was falling to the British. American ships had been excluded from trade with Canada and the West Indies, and foreign commerce was being further strangled by British imperial policy. Commerce among the states was blocked and restricted by local regulations and tariffs. Internal prosperity was stifled by lack of a national currency, and the states added to the confusion of business by issuing their own currency.

But foremost in the minds of many responsible people was the example of the rebellion of debtors in Massachusetts led by Daniel Shays. Washington wrote that "There are combustibles in every State which a spark might set fire to." In presenting the Virginia Plan, Randolph pointed with alarm to the "Prospect of anarchy" which was so widely evident. The remedy, he said, lay in the resolutions he was offering which would set up a government with effective power.

The Virginia Plan proposed a national legislature of two houses, modeled on the various state legislatures. The members of the lower house were to be chosen directly by the people and those of the upper house were to be elected by the lower house from nominees of the state legislatures. Representatives in the national legislature were to vote individually and not by states, but representatives were to be apportioned among the states on the basis of wealth and population. The power to levy taxes and other specified powers were to be granted to the national legislature. For enforcement of the laws a national executive and a judiciary were to be established.

The Virginia Plan sought to establish a national government operating directly on individuals instead of on the states as did the government of the Articles of Confederation. In this respect Randolph's resolutions were as revolutionary as the Declaration of Independence. In considering the plan in long debate during which the differences between the small and the larger states became so heated that the convention nearly broke up, the delegates to the convention recognized the merits of its basic approach. With changes and refinements, the Virginia Plan was woven into the basic fabric of the Constitution.

The original manuscript, from James Madison's Notes of Debates, is lent to the Freedom Train exhibit by the Library of Congress. It is in the handwriting of Edmund Randolph who gave it to Madison, as a footnote in the hand of the latter explains.

"He expressed his regret that it should fall to him, rather than those who were of longer standing in life and political experience, to offer the great subject of this mission. But as the convention had originated from Virginia, and his colleagues supposed that some proposition was expected from them, they had imposed this task on him.

"He then commented on the difficulty of the crisis, and the necessity of preventing the fulfilment of the prophicies of the American downfal.

"He observed that in revising the federal system we ought to inquire 1. into the properties which such a government ought to possess 2. the defects of the confederation, 3. the danger of our situation etc. A. the remedy

"1. The Character of such a government ought to secure 1. against foreign invasion. 2. against dissentions between members of the union, or seditions in particular states. 3. to secure to the several states various blessings, of which an isolated situation was incapable. 4. to be able to defend itself against incroachment. & 5. to be paramount to the state constitutions.

"2. In speaking of the defects of the confederation he professed a high respect for its authors, and considered them as having done all that patriots could do, in the then infancy of the science, of constitution of confederacies,—when the inefficiency of requisitions was unknown—no commercial discord had arisen among any states—no rebellion had appeared as in Massts.—foreign debts had not become urgent—the   of paper money had not been seen—treaties had not been violated—and perhaps nothing better could be obtained from the jealousy of the states with regard to their sovereignty.

"He then proceeded to enumerate the defects: 1. that the confederation produced no security against foreign invasion; congress not being permitted to prevent a war nor to support it by its own authority—of this he cited many examples; most of which tended to show that they could not cause infractions of treaties or of the law of nations to be punished; that particular states might by their conduct provoke war without controul; and that neither militia nor draughts being fit for defense on such occasions, inlistment only could be successful, and these could not be executed with money.

"2. That the federal government could not check the quarrels between states, nor a rebellion in any, not having constitutional power nor means to interpose according to the exigency.

"3. That there were many advantages, which the U. S. might acquire, which were not attainable under the confederation—such as a productive impost—counteraction of the commercial regulations of other nations—pushing of commerce ad libitum— etc. etc.

"4. that the federal government could not defend itself against the incroachments from the states.

"5. that it was not even paramount to the State constitutions, ratified as it was in many of the states.

"3. He next reviewed the danger of our situation, appealed to the sense of the best friends of the U. S.— the prospect of anarchy from the laxity of government every where; and to other considerations.

"4. He then proceeded to the remedy; the basis of which he said, must be the republican principle.

"He then proposed as conformable to his ideas the following resolutions, which he explained one by one.

(Here insert ye Resolutions annexed)

He concluded with an exhortation, not to suffer the present opportunity of establishing general peace, harmony, happiness, and liberty in the U. S. to pass away unimproved.°

[Then, in the handwriting of James Madison:]

"° This abstract of the speech was furnished to J. M. by E. Randolph and is in his handwriting, as a report of it from him had been relied on, it was omitted by J. M."

29. President Washington Annotates His Copy of the Proposed Constitution (1787)

Among the notations and corrections appearing on this printed copy of the Constitution are several that are clearly in the handwriting of General Washington. But these few scattered annotations provide no adequate clue to Washington's real influence on the work of the Constitutional Convention.

Tired, troubled with rheumatism, and with his estates in desperate need of careful management, Washington agreed with great reluctance to become a member of the delegation from Virginia to the Constitutional Convention which met in Philadelphia in May 1787. He was under no illusions concerning the significance and the extreme difficulty of the task, for it became clear early in the Convention that far more than the mere revision of the Articles of Confederation was necessary. He was convinced that the "political concerns of this country are suspended by a thread" and, with characteristic vigor, plunged into the work. When the convention opened Washington was elected its President and the unanimous vote of the delegates amply attested their full confidence in his character and ability. During the four summer months in which the Convention labored and struggled to formulate a workable and yet acceptable plan of government, Washington presided almost constantly. He felt it his duty as chairman to take no part in the debates; his vote is recorded only five times and these when the delegation from Virginia was evenly divided. But he followed the discussions most carefully. By his conciliatory attitude, his willingness to modify his own views to accomplish a larger purpose, and by the sheer weight of his character, he exercised profound influence in the meetings.

One of his thoughtful contemporaries concluded that Washington's service to his country in connection with the Constitution should rank second only to his military service. In reflecting some years later on those uncertain times, another delegate to the Convention wrote of Washington's influence: "Had not the Constitution come out under his name, it would never have been ratified." Concerning the results of the Convention, the Constitution itself, Washington recognized that it had many imperfections but "considering the heterogeneous mass of which the Convention was composed and the diversity of interest . . . to be attended to," it had as few basic defects as could be expected. Because of the availability of the amending process to rectify errors and to permit adaptation to changing needs, Washington wrote in October 1789, "I think it would be wise for the people to accept what is offered them. . . ."

This printed draft of the Constitution as it was reported to the Committee on Detail in August 1787 was Washington's personal copy. It is lent to the Freedom Train exhibit by the National Archives. At this stage in the drafting of the Constitution the separate sovereignties of the various states had not, in the thinking of the delegates, been merged into the *United* States, as is indicated by the opening sentence: "We the People of the States of New Hampshire, Massachusetts . . . etc."

30. Charles Pinckney Suggests the "Habeas Corpus" Clause for Inclusion in the Constitution (1787)

"The writ of *habeas corpus,*" writes E. S. Corwin, "is the most important single safeguard of personal liberty known to Anglo-American law." It was somewhat after the determination of the trial-by-jury provision (see No. 31) that the *habeas corpus* clause was inserted, on Monday, August 20, 1787. Exhibited on the Freedom Train, the official Journal of the Convention, kept by the secretary, William Jackson, in his large and legible but inflexible handwriting, records that on this day certain propositions were introduced and referred to a select committee. Jackson's Journal has always been too meagre a source for any detailed knowledge of the Convention. The present is a case in point, for he does not identify the person who introduced these propositions, one of which includes *habeas corpus*. But we learn from James Madison's Notes that all were moved by Charles Pinckney of South Carolina.

Pinckney, "the bright young man" of the Convention (his thirtieth birthday fell in the month after its adjournment) came to Philadelphia with a ready-made plan for a constitution for the United States. While the Convention, somewhat understandably, preferred to work out its own, it did adopt a surprising number of ideas from Pinckney's draft. Some thirty years later Pinckney rather spoiled this record by claiming that almost the whole of the final Constitution came from his original draft—in which case the Convention certainly wasted a great deal of breath. However, he must receive the credit for the *habeas corpus* clause, along with a number of other useful provisions, but it was Gouverneur Morris who on August 28 altered Pinckney's vague "most urgent and pressing occasions" to the far more precise "in cases of rebellion or invasion."

The manuscript of Pinckney's original plan, submitted to the Convention on May 29, cannot be found. Although historians have been partially able to reconstruct it from other documents, it remains impossible to say whether or not this or a similar *habeas corpus* provision was ever included in it. The Journal of the Constitutional Convention is from the manuscript collections of the Library of Congress.

It was moved and seconded to insert the words "and support" between the word "raise" and the word "armies" in the 14 clause, 1 sect, 7 article.

which passed in the affirmative. It was moved and seconded to strike out the words "build and equip" and to insert the words "provide and maintain" in the 15 clause, 1 sect. 7 article

which passed in the affirmative. It was moved and seconded to insert the following as a 10th clause, in the 1 sect. of the 7. article "To make rules for the government and regulation of the land and naval forces"

which passed in the affirmative. It was moved and seconded to annex the following proviso to the last clause "provided that in time of peace the army shall not consist of more than   thousand men"

which passed in the negative. It was moved and seconded to insert the following as a clause in the 1 sect. of the 7 article "to make laws for regulating and disciplining the militia of the several States, reserving to the "several States the appointment of their militia Officers." It was moved and seconded to postpone the last clause in order to take up the following

"To establish an uniformity of exercise and arms for the militia—and rules for their government when called into service under the authority of the United States: and to establish and regulate a militia in any State where it's legislature shall neglect to do it."

It was moved and seconded to refer the two last motions to a Committee

which passed in the affirmative and they were referred to the Committee of eleven.

And then the House adjourned till Monday next at 10 o'clock A. M.

Monday August 20th, 1787

It was moved and seconded to refer the following propositions to the Committee of five

which passed in the affirmative. Each House shall be the Judge of it's own privileges, and shall have authority to punish by imprisonment every person violating the same: or who, in the place where the Legislature may be sitting and during the time of it's session, shall threaten any of it's members for any thing said or done in the House: or who shall assault any of them therefor —or who shall assault, or arrest any witness or other person ordered to attend either of the Houses in his way going or returning; or who shall rescue any person arrested by their order.

Each Branch of the Legislature, as well as the Supreme Executive shall have authority to require the opinions of the Supreme Judicial Court upon important questions of law, and upon solemn occasions.

The privileges and benefit of the writ of habeas corpus shall be enjoyed in this government in the most expeditious and ample manner: and shall not be suspended by the Legislature except upon the most urgent and pressing occasions, and for a limited time not exceeding   months.

31. The Right to Trial by Jury Is, for the First Time, Added to the Constitution

ALTHOUGH the original Constitution contained no formal Bill of Rights, a lack which aroused much criticism and was shortly remedied, it would be a great mistake to assume that the members of the Philadelphia Convention had any hostility to civil liberties or that they failed to make any provision for them. When Alexander Hamilton, in the 84th number of *The Federalist*, sought to answer the arguments of critics on this score, he was able to point to eight "provisions in favor of particular privileges and rights" in the text of the Constitution itself. He and the other Federalist proponents of the Constitution argued that a Bill of Rights against a government of delegates and limited powers was unnecessary or worse. The people granted the government certain specific powers; the rest they retained. Bills of Rights, he said, "would even be dangerous. They would contain various exceptions to powers not granted; and, on this very account, would afford a colorable pretext to claim more than were granted. For why declare that things shall not be done which there is no power to do?"

Among the provisions cited by Hamilton is that limiting judgment in cases of impeachment to removal from office and disqualification for further office holding. Suspension of the writ of *habeas corpus* is warranted only in cases of rebellion or invasion or when the public safety requires it. Bills of attainder or *ex post facto* laws are prohibited. The trial for all crimes, except in cases of impeachment, is to be by jury. The testimony of two witnesses to the same overt act or confession in open court is required for conviction for treason. "Corruption of blood, or forfeiture" for treason may apply only to the person convicted. These are certainly important limitations upon the newly created Federal executive, legislative, and judicial branches, against foreseen possibilities of oppression and in favor of the individual citizen.

The provision in the Constitution for trial by jury was merely expanded by the Sixth Amendment which added details which the Convention had not felt necessary to mention.

In the surviving manuscript records of the Convention it is possible to perceive in several instances the exact point at which these Rights provisions were added to the growing document. On July 26 the Convention adjourned and did not reconvene until August 6, while its Committee of Detail, consisting of John Rutledge of South Carolina, Edmund Randolph of Virginia, Nathaniel Gorham of Massachusetts, Oliver Ellsworth of Connecticut, and James Wilson of Pennsylvania, took the resolutions already adopted by the Convention, declarations of principle agreed upon, and from them hammered out an actual draft Constitution. A few surviving papers show us the Committee of Detail actually at work. One of the most remarkable and fascinating of these is a long paper originally penned by Randolph, but including numerous corrections and interlineations in the hand of Rutledge; for some unexplained reason this passed into the keeping of George Mason and is now in the small but important group of his papers in the Library of Congress. The Randolph-Rutledge manuscript is midway in the process of turning general principles into concrete provisions, and in it we can see the addition whereby John Rutledge added trial by jury to the document: "That Trials for Crim[ina]l offenses be in the State where the off[ens]e was com[mitte]d—by Jury—And a right to make all Laws necessary to carry the foregoing Powers into Exe[cutio]n—" There is, in the printed report of the Committee of Detail which the Convention received and began to consider on August 6, the following provision as Article XI, Section 4: "The trial of all criminal offences (except in cases of impeachments) shall be in the state where they shall be committed; and shall be by Jury"—obviously a revision of Rutledge's original wording. The final draft of the Constitution merely transposes the two clauses and adds a third to provide for cases when the offense was not committed in any state.

This original document is from the manuscript collections of the Library of Congress.

32. Pennsylvania Becomes the Second State to Ratify the Federal Constitution (1787)

"INDIVIDUALS entering into society, must give up a share of liberty to preserve the rest. The magnitude of the sacrifice must depend as well on situation and circumstance, as on the object to be obtained. It is at all times difficult to draw with precision the line between those rights which must be surrendered, and those which may be reserved . . . that it [the Constitution] will meet the full and entire approbation of every State is not perhaps to be expected. . . . That it may promote the lasting welfare of that country so dear to us all, and secure her freedom and happiness, is our most ardent wish." Thus wrote George Washington, President of the Federal Convention that drafted the Constitution of the United States. It remained for the states to accept the Constitution through ratification.

Through the summer months of 1787 delegates from the thirteen states met in Philadelphia to debate and devise necessary modifications in the plan of government as it feebly operated under the Articles of Confederation. They ended by formulating a new plan. They found that one of the sharpest cleavages to be resolved in their work was between the group desiring a strong Federal government and the anti-Federalists, such as George Mason and Edmund Randolph of Virginia, and Elbridge Gerry of Massachusetts, who upheld the autonomy of the states. Benjamin Franklin, Philadelphia's foremost citizen, put forth the final efforts of his long career by creating a spirit of compromise. Submission of the Constitution by the Federal Convention to the Congress of the Confederation had to be followed by ratification from nine states before it would be adopted.

On November 6, Pennsylvania held elections for members of its State Convention, and on November 21 this body assembled. Its discussions were prolonged, with many delegates urging the necessity of including a bill of rights in the Constitution. News of the Constitution's ratification by the state of Delaware on December 7 spurred the Pennsylvania delegates to agreement, and on December 12 Pennsylvania by vote of 46 to 23 became the second state to ratify the Constitution. On the following day at Philadelphia, officials marched in solemn procession from the State House to the Court House in order to hear the formal proclamation of Pennsylvania's approval of the Constitution. A few days later, on December 18, New Jersey also ratified the new frame of government, but not until June 21, 1788, did the ninth ratification occur through action by the New Hampshire State Convention. Thereafter, the Constitution became effective for those states which had previously ratified it.

Pennsylvania's ratification, inscribed on parchment, was sent to the central government, and is now in the official custody of the National Archives. This is the original document in the Freedom Train exhibit. In this instrument, the entire Constitution is written out, beginning with the unifying phrase, "We the people of the United States," in bold black letters resembling those of the original Constitution. The three-line ratification of it that follows includes the signatures of 45 members of the State Convention. Preceding the others is the signature of Frederick Augustus Muhlenberg, President of the Convention and Pennsylvania's representative at the Continental Congress. Two years later his name appeared on an even more significant document when, as Speaker of the House of Representatives, he placed his signature on the Bill of Rights.

Among the patriotic men of Pennsylvania who signed

the State's ratification were Timothy Pickering, Anthony Wayne, Benjamin Rush, and James Wilson. Rush and Wilson had been signers of the Declaration of Independence and Wilson had been eloquent throughout the meetings of the Federal Convention in advocating a strong Federal constitution. Rush, Treasurer of the U.S. Mint from 1799–1813, is noted for his discoveries in medicine and his philanthropy as much as for his numerous patriotic services. Timothy Pickering had served in the Continental Army as Adjutant General and Quartermaster General and later (in the Federal government) was successively Postmaster General, Secretary of War, and Secretary of State. He concluded his career as Senator from Massachusetts. "Mad Anthony" Wayne won renown through his military exploits in the Revolution and his later success in subduing the Indians in Ohio.

33. Congress Approves the Bill of Rights for the Constitution (1789)

JUST a little over a hundred years intervened between the English Bill of Rights granted by William and Mary in 1689 and the American Bill of Rights. Both arose from the insistence of the people upon a recognition by the government of what they termed their natural rights. This idea of a compact or contract between those governing and those governed, stems from the time of John Locke and Montesquieu. These political theorists held that individuals possessed certain natural rights above and beyond the law of the state. Some of these rights were alienable and could be transferred to the government, but others were "inalienable" and could not be surrendered. There should be, therefore, a "frame" of government in which the alienable rights were entrusted to the state in return for just and efficient government, and there should be a "bill of rights" setting forth the inalienable rights of the people upon which the state was especially forbidden to infringe.

Freedom of speech, freedom of the press, freedom of religion—these are but three of the precious liberties inscribed on the piece of yellowing parchment known as the Bill of Rights. Where the peoples of other nations had struggled for centuries to gain these same "inalienable rights," the American people wrote them into the basic law of the land only a few short years after independence. They had forged "the great American charter of personal liberty and human dignity."

The Constitution itself, before amendment, was primarily a blueprint for a national government. Except for guaranteeing such rights as that of trial by jury, the privilege of the writ of *habeas corpus,* and protection against bills of attainder or *ex post facto* laws, the Constitution did not specifically mention individual rights, but

was concerned with establishing a workable frame of government. Significantly, however, Article V provided the machinery by which it could be amended. The previous frame of government established by the thirteen colonies in the Articles of Confederation provided for the possibility of amending the Articles, but only on condition that every one of the thirteen states would ratify the change. This principle of unanimity was one of the defects which made it desirable to revise the Articles of Confederation in the achievement of a more flexible government. Article V of the Constitution established the principle that majorities of two-thirds or three-fourths would replace the old unanimity in adopting any proposed amendment.

The Constitution was submitted to the various state legislatures for ratification in September 1787. It immediately encountered strong opposition. Objections were raised to certain organizational features of the government outlined by the Constitution, but more strenuous objections were directed against the omission of specific guarantees of personal rights and liberties. Supporters of the Constitution relied upon the arguments that a bill of rights in a government of delegated and limited powers was unnecessary. Essay number 84 of *The Federalist* expounded this view. Opponents of the Constitution, however, with the memory of colonial grievances under British imperial rule still fresh in their minds, held out for a written bill of rights. Further, most states, beginning with Virginia in June 1776, had adopted declarations setting forth the inviolate rights of the people. Other states to formulate distinct Bills of Rights were Maryland, North Carolina, Vermont, Massachusetts, and New Hampshire.

Ratification of the Constitution was carried through by a narrow margin in many states, such as Pennsylvania and Virginia, with the assurance that amendments would be made on the basis of proposals by the various state conventions. With the ratification of New Hampshire on June 21, 1788, the necessary ninth state, the Constitution became effective. Congress, which was to meet on March 4, 1789, encountered difficulties in organization and did not convene until early April. Toward the close of his inaugural address to the first Congress on April 30, President Washington reminded Congress of its responsibility in promoting "the characteristic rights of freemen." Within a week after Washington's address, James Madison of Virginia, who had been elected to Congress under pledge to use his influence to bring about adoption of a bill of rights, announced to the House of Representatives his intention of proposing a number of amendments to the Constitution (see item No. 40). On June 8, Madison offered to the House a selected list of amendments based upon numerous proposals advocated by various states when they had ratified the Constitution. He declared: "We ought not disregard their inclination, but on principle of amity, and moderation, conform to their wishes, and expressly declare the great rights of mankind secured under this Constitution." A select committee of the House reported out 17 amendments, which were reduced to 12 by the Senate. These were agreed to by a joint resolution of the Senate and House on September 25, 1789. It is the original of this document, on which are inscribed the 12 amendments proposed by Congress, that we call the Bill of Rights. The signatures of Frederick Augustus Muhlenberg and John Adams appear on the document as the Speaker of the House and the President of the Senate respectively.

Congress ordered copies of the resolution made and submitted to the various states for ratification on September 26, 1789. Ten of the proposed 12 amendments were ratified by the necessary three-fourths of the states, and became a part of the law of the land on December 15, 1791, with the ratification of Virginia, the eleventh state to take this action. (It is interesting to note that Connecticut, Georgia, and Massachusetts "ratified" the Bill of Rights by formal action of their legislatures in 1939, the 150th anniversary of the passage of the joint resolution by Congress.)

Contained in these 10 amendments are the basic "Constitutional rights" of the American people. These amendments guarantee certain fundamental personal and property rights that cannot be abridged by Congress or the other branches of the national government; among them are freedom of religion, freedom of speech, freedom of the press, freedom of assembly, the right to petition the government for redress of grievances, freedom from unreasonable search and seizure, the right to a trial by jury, and just compensation for property taken for public use.

The American Bill of Rights had great influence on the political thought of leaders of the French Revolution and upon it they patterned their "Declaration of the Rights of Man and of the Citizen" issued in 1789. From France, the wave of liberty spread over Europe and many other countries adopted the principles enunciated in the American Bill of Rights.

The original official Joint Resolution of September 25, 1787, known as the Bill of Rights, is displayed on the Freedom Train. The ink and writing on the large sheet of parchment (28 x 29 inches) has faded through the years, but the principles they enunciate have never lost their freshness or their vigor. The document was kept in the custody of the Department of State until transferred to the National Archives where it is preserved as a part of the general records of the United States government.

Congress of the United States
begun and held at the City of New-York, on
Wednesday the fourth of March, one thousand seven hundred and eighty nine

THE Conventions of a number of the States, having at the time of their adopting the Constitution, expressed a desire in order to prevent misconstruction or abuse of its powers, that further declaratory and restrictive clauses should be added: And as extending the ground of public confidence in the Government, will best insure the benificent ends of its institutions.

RESOLVED by the Senate and House of Representatives of the United States of America in Congress assembled, two thirds of both Houses concurring, that the following Articles be proposed to the Legislatures of the several States as amendments to the Constitution of the United States, all or any of which Articles, when ratified by three fourths of the said Legislatures, to be valid to all intents and purposes, as part of the said Constitution, viz.

ARTICLES in addition to, and amendment of the Constitution of the United States of America, proposed by Congress, and ratified by the Legislatures of the several States, pursuant to the fifth Article of the original Constitution.

Article the first . . . After the first enumeration required by the first Article of the Constitution, there shall be one Representative for every thirty thousand until the number shall amount to one hundred after which the proportion shall be so regulated by Congress, that there shall be not less than one hundred Representatives for every forty thousand persons, until the number of Representatives shall amount to two hundred, after which the proportion shall be so regulated by Congress, that there shall not be less than two hundred Representatives, nor more than one Representative for every fifty thousand persons.

Article the second . . . No law, varying the compensation for the services of the Senators and Representatives, shall take effect, until an election of Representatives shall have intervened.

Article the third . . . Congress shall make no law respecting an establishment of religion, or prohibiting the free exercise thereof, or abridging the freedom of speech, or of the press; or the right of the people peaceably to assemble, and to petition the Government for a redress of grievances.

Article the fourth . . . A well-regulated Militia, being necessary to the security of a free State, the right of the people to keep and bear Arms, shall not be infringed.

Article the fifth . . . No soldier shall, in time of peace be quartered in any house, without the consent of the Owner, nor in time of war, but in a manner to be prescribed by law.

Article the sixth . . . The right of the people to be secure in their persons, houses, papers, and effects, against unreasonable searches and seizures, shall not be violated, and no Warrants shall issue, but upon probable cause, supported by Oath or affirmation, and particularly describing the place to be searched, and the persons or things to be seized.

Article the seventh . . . No person shall be held to

Congress OF THE United States,

begun and held at the City of New York, on

Wednesday, the fourth of March, one thousand seven hundred and eighty nine.

THE Conventions of a number of the States having, at the time of their adopting the Constitution, expressed a desire, in order to prevent misconstruction or abuse of its powers, that further declaratory and restrictive clauses should be added: And as extending the ground of public confidence in the Government, will best ensure the beneficent ends of its institution.

RESOLVED, by the Senate and House of Representatives of the United States of America in Congress assembled, two thirds of both Houses concurring, that the following Articles be proposed to the Legislatures of the several States, as Amendments to the Constitution of the United States; all, or any of which articles, when ratified by three fourths of the said Legislatures, to be valid to all intents and purposes, as part of the said Constitution, vizt.

ARTICLES in addition to, and amendment of the Constitution of the United States of America, proposed by Congress, and ratified by the Legislatures of the several States, pursuant to the fifth Article of the original Constitution.

Article the first... After the first enumeration required by the first article of the Constitution, there shall be one Representative for every thirty thousand, until the number shall amount to one hundred, after which, the proportion shall be so regulated by Congress, that there shall be not less than one hundred Representatives, nor less than one Representative for every forty thousand persons, until the number of Representatives shall amount to two hundred, after which the proportion shall be so regulated by Congress, that there shall not be less than two hundred Representatives, nor more than one Representative for every fifty thousand persons.

Article the second... No law, varying the compensation for the services of the Senators and Representatives, shall take effect, until an election of Representatives shall have intervened.

Article the third... Congress shall make no law respecting an establishment of religion, or prohibiting the free exercise thereof; or abridging the freedom of speech, or of the press; or the right of the people peaceably to assemble, and to petition the Government for a redress of grievances.

Article the fourth... A well regulated Militia, being necessary to the security of a free State, the right of the people to keep and bear arms, shall not be infringed.

Article the fifth... No soldier shall, in time of peace, be quartered in any house, without the consent of the owner, nor in time of war, but in a manner to be prescribed by law.

Article the sixth... The right of the people to be secure in their persons, houses, papers, and effects, against unreasonable searches and seizures, shall not be violated, and no warrants shall issue, but upon probable cause, supported by oath or affirmation, and particularly describing the place to be searched, and the persons or things to be seized.

Article the seventh... No person shall be held to answer for a capital, or otherwise infamous crime, unless on a presentment or indictment of a grand jury, except in cases arising in the land or naval forces, or in the Militia, when in actual service in time of War or public danger; nor shall any person be subject for the same offence to be twice put in jeopardy of life or limb; nor shall be compelled in any criminal case, to be a witness against himself, nor be deprived of life, liberty, or property, without due process of law; nor shall private property be taken for public use, without just compensation.

Article the eighth... In all criminal prosecutions, the accused shall enjoy the right to a speedy and public trial, by an impartial jury of the State and district wherein the crime shall have been committed, which district shall have been previously ascertained by law, and to be informed of the nature and cause of the accusation; to be confronted with the witnesses against him; to have compulsory process for obtaining witnesses in his favor, and to have the assistance of counsel for his defence.

Article the ninth... In suits at common law, where the value in controversy shall exceed twenty dollars, the right of trial by jury shall be preserved, and no fact, tried by a jury, shall be otherwise re-examined in any Court of the United States, than according to the rules of the common law.

Article the tenth... Excessive bail shall not be required, nor excessive fines imposed, nor cruel and unusual punishments inflicted.

Article the eleventh... The enumeration in the Constitution, of certain rights, shall not be construed to deny or disparage others retained by the people.

Article the twelfth... The powers not delegated to the United States by the Constitution, nor prohibited by it to the States, are reserved to the States respectively, or to the people.

Frederick Augustus Muhlenberg, Speaker of the House of Representatives.

John Adams, Vice-President of the United States, and President of the Senate.

ATTEST,

John Beckley, Clerk of the House of Representatives.

Sam. A. Otis Secretary of the Senate.

The Bill of Rights (See No. 33)

answer for a capital, or otherwise infamous crime, unless on a presentment or indictment of a Grand Jury, except in cases arising in the land or naval forces, or in the Militia, when in actual service in time of War or public danger; nor shall any person be subject for the same offence to be twice put in jeopardy of life or limb; nor shall be compelled in any Criminal Case to be witness against himself, nor be deprived of life, liberty, or property, without due process of law; nor shall private property be taken for public use, without just compensation.

Article the eighth . . . In all criminal prosecutions, the accused shall enjoy the right to a speedy and public trial, by an impartial jury of the State and district wherein the crime shall have been committed, which district shall have been previously ascertained by law, and to be informed of the nature and cause of the accusation; to be confronted with the witnesses against him; to have compulsory process for obtaining Witnesses in his favor, and to have the Assistance of Counsel for his defence.

Article the ninth . . . In suits at common law, where the value in controversy shall exceed twenty dollars, the right of trial by jury shall be preserved, and no fact tried by a jury shall be otherwise re-examined in any Court of the United States, than according to the rules of the common law.

Article the tenth . . . Excessive bail shall not be required, nor excessive fines imposed, nor cruel and unusual punishments inflicted.

Article the eleventh . . . The enumeration in the Constitution, of certain rights, shall not be construed to deny or disparage others retained by the people.

Article the twelfth . . . The powers not delegated to the United States by the Constitution nor prohibited by it to the States, are reserved to the States respectively, or to the people.

34. George Mason Drafts a Proposed Declaration of Rights for the Constitution (1788)

GEORGE MASON, master of Gunston Hall and of a 5,000-acre plantation on the Potomac not far from Alexandria, Virginia, was an aristocrat to his fingertips. But, far more important to history: he was an uncompromising republican, a bitter enemy of slavery and one of America's greatest exponents of civil liberties. Neither an orator nor a practical politician, he still had great influence among the leaders of his day because of his clear intellect and literary gifts. It was Mason who drafted the Bill of Rights, adopted by the Virginia Convention on June 12, 1776. This was the basis of all the later state bills of rights. It was the first such document to be in-

corporated in, and even made preliminary to, a written constitution.

After independence had been won on the battlefield and at the conference table, George Mason was among those who had become increasingly convinced that America must have a stronger central government than the Articles of Confederation could ever provide. In 1787 he was a member of the Virginia delegation to the Constitutional Convention. A week or two before the end, however, he became dissatisfied with certain of the provisions of the draft Constitution. He wrote out sixteen concrete "Objections to this Constitution of Government," and on September 15, 1787, the next-to-last meeting of the convention, he viewed with alarm, as Madison tells us: "the dangerous power and structure of the Government, concluding that it would end either in monarchy, or a tyrannical aristocracy; which, he [Mason] was in doubt, but one or other, he was sure. This constitution had been formed without the knowledge or idea of the people. A second Convention will know more of the sence of the people, and be able to provide a system consonant to it. It was improper to say to the people, take this or nothing. As the Constitution now stands, he could neither give it his support or vote in Virginia; and he could not sign here what he could not support there. With the expedient of another Convention, as proposed he could sign."

No second convention was authorized, and Mason was one of the three members who refused to sign the engrossed Constitution.

Mason therefore found himself associated with Patrick Henry, Richard Henry Lee, and James Monroe as one of the Anti-Federalist leaders in the struggle over ratification in the pivotal state of Virginia. In the Virginia Convention, whch sat from June 2 to 27, 1788, the question at issue finally narrowed down to whether amendments to the proposed Constitution, including a bill of rights, should be made a condition of Virginia's ratification, or whether the state should first ratify and then urge the passage of amendments upon the new government. The Anti-Federalists' resolution that prior to ratification the desired amendments ought to be referred to the other states was defeated. However, the convention promptly resolved that necessary amendments should be "recommended to the consideration of the Congress which shall first assemble under the said Constitution." A committee of twenty, including Mason, was appointed to draft them, and two days later they brought in twenty proposed amendments and a bill of rights in twenty articles. The latter was clearly based on the exhibited draft, which Mason probably prepared somewhat earlier for the Anti-Federalist opposition in the Virginia convention. It was an expansion of the Virginia Bill of Rights which Mason had originally drafted twelve years earlier.

The new clauses by Mason are of great importance to the national Bill of Rights, the first ten amendments to the Constitution. Madison, in drawing up proposed amendments to the Constitution which he brought in to the House of Representatives on June 8, 1789, manifestly drew heavily upon the bill of rights proposed by his own state convention the year before. In the national bill, Amendment III, prohibiting the quartering of soldiers, is Article 18 of the Virginia proposals with minor verbal changes. Amendment IV of the national Bill of Rights, on unreasonable searches and seizures, is a condensation of Article 14, and the provision of Amendment II, "the right of the people to keep and bear arms shall not be infringed," came from Article 17 of the Virginia suggestions, which begins "That the people have a right to keep and bear arms."

George Mason's original draft of the Declaration of Rights, lent to the Freedom Train by the Library of Congress, thus assumes added importance. (The order of paragraphs follows the original text.)

Amendments proposed to the new Constitution of Government

That there be a Declaration or Bill of Rights, asserting and securing from Encroachment the essential and unalienable Rights of the People, in some such Manner as the following:

1. That all Freemen have certain essential inherent Rights, of which they cannot, by any Compact, deprive or divest their posterity; among which are the Enjoyment of Life and Liberty, with the Means of acquiring, possessing, and protecting property, and pursuing and obtaining Happiness and Safety.—

2. That all power is naturally vested in, and consequently derived from the People; that Magistrates therefore are their Trustees and Agents, and at all Times amenable to them.

3. That Government ought to be instituted for the common Benefit, Protection and Security of the People; and that whenever any Government shall be found inadequate or contrary to these purposes, a Majority of the Community hath an indubitable, unalienable, and indefeasible right to reform, alter, and establish another, or abolish it, in such Manner as shall be judged most conducive to the Public Weal; and that the Doctrine of non-resist[ance] against arbitrary power & oppression is absurd, slavish & destructive of the good and Happiness of Mankind.

4. That no Man, or set of Men, are entitled to exclusive or separate public Emoluments or privileges from the Community, but in Consideration of public Services; which not being descendible, neither ought the Offices of Magistrate Legislator, or Judge, or any other public Office to be hereditary.

5. That the Legislative, executive, and judiciary powers of Government should be separate and distinct, and that the Members of the two first may be restrained from oppression, by feeling and participating in the public Burthens, they should, at fixed periods, be reduced to private Station, return in to the Mass of the people, and the Vacancys be supplied by certain & regular Elections; in which all or any part of the former Members to be eligible, or ineligible, as the Rules of the Constitution of Government, and the Laws shall direct.—

6. That the right of the people to participate in the Legislature is the best Security of Liberty, and the Foundation of all free Government; for this purpose Elections ought to be free & frequent; and all men having sufficient Evidence of permanent common Interest with, and Attachment to the Community, ought to have the Right of Suffrage and no aid, charge, Tax or fee can be set, rated or levyed upon the People, without their own Consent, or that of their Representatives so elected, nor can they be bound by any Law to which they have not, in like manner, assented, for the public Good.—

7. That all power of suspending Laws, or the Execution of Laws, by any Authority, without Consent of the representatives of the people in the Legislature, is injurious to their rights, and ought not to be exercised.

8. That in all capital or criminal prosecutions, a man hath a right to demand the Cause and Nature of his Accusation, to be confronted with the Accusers and Witnesses, to call for Evidence, be admitted Counsel in his Favour, and to a fair and speedy Trial by an impartial Jury of his Vicinage; without whose unanimous Consent he can not be found guilty, (except in the Government of the Land and naval Forces in time of actual War, Invasion or Rebellion) nor can he be compelled to give Evidence against himself.

9. That no freeman ought to be taken, imprisoned, or disseized of his Freehold, Liberties, privileges, or Franchises, or outlawed, or exiled, or in any Manner destroyed, or deprived of his Life, Liberty, or Property but by the Law of the Land.—

10. That every freeman restrained of his Liberty, is entitled to a Remedy, to enquire into the Lawfulness thereof, and to remove the same is unlawful, and that such Remedy ought not to be denied, or delayed.—

13. That excessive Bail ought not to be required, nor excessive Fines imposed, nor cruel and unusual punishments inflicted.—

14. That every free man has a right to be secure from all unreasonable Searches and Seizures of his Person, his papers, and his property all Warrants therefore to search suspected places, or to seize any freeman, his papers, or property, without Information upon Oath (or Affirmation of a person religiously scrupulous of taking an Oath) of legal and sufficient Cause, are grievous and oppressive; and all general Warrants to search suspected places, or to apprehend any suspected person, without specially naming or describing the place or person, are dangerous, and ought not to be granted.—

11. That in Controversies respecting property, and in Suits between Man and Man, the ancient Trial by Jury of Facts, where they arise, is one of the greatest Securities to the Rights of a free people, and ought to remain sacred and inviolable.—

16. That the people have a right to Freedom of Speech, and of Writing and publishing their Sentiments; that the Freedom of the Press is one of the great Bulwarks of Liberty, and ought not to be violated.—

15. That the people have a right peaceably to assemble together to consult for their common Good or to instruct their Representatives, and that every freeman has a right to petition, or apply to the Legislature for Redress of Grievances.—

12. That every Freeman ought to find a certain Remedy, by Recourse to the Laws, for all Injurys or Wrongs he may receive in his person, property, or character. He ought to obtain Right and Justice freely, without Fale, compleatly and without Denial, promptly and without Delay; and that all Establishments or Regulations contravening these Rights are oppressive and unjust.—

17. That the people have a Right to mass & to bear arms; that a well regulated militia, composed of the Body of the people, trained to Arms, is the proper natural and safe Defense of a free State; That standing Armys in time of peace are dangerous to Liberty, and therefore ought to be avoided, as far as the Circumstances and Protection of the Community will admit; and that in all Cases, the Military should be under strict subordination to and governed by the Civil Power.

13. That no Soldier in time of peace ought to be quartered in any House without the Consent of the owner; and in time of War, only by the Civil Magistrate in such Manner as the Laws direct.—

19. That any person religiously scrupulous of bearing Arms ought to be exempted, upon payment of an Equivalent, to employ another to bear Arms in his Stead.

20. That Religion, or the Duty which we owe to our Creator, and the Manner of discharging it, can be directed only by Reason and Conviction, not by Force or Violence, and therefore all men have an equal natural and unalienable right to the free Exercise of Religion, according to the Dictates of Conscience, and that no particular religious Sect or Society of Christians ought to be favoured or established by Law, in preference to others.—

35. Virginia Proposes Amendments Protecting Civil Liberties as She Ratifies the Constitution

FOREMOST in every event leading to formulation of the constitutional framework for the United States was Virginia, the "Old Dominion." Her sons bestirred themselves with untiring zeal to build a frame of government that would be workable and compatible with the ideas for which they believed the Revolution had been fought. As the inherent weaknesses of government under the Articles of Confederation became apparent, Virginia was quick to approve and appoint a delegation to the Federal Convention at Philadelphia in 1787. Members of this delegation, however, were not unanimous in their approval of the instrument finally adopted as a Constitution and later submitted to the states for ratification. George Mason and Edmund Randolph refused to give their signature of approval to the Constitution, even though they had contributed greatly to its construction and their fellow-Virginian, George Washington, was serving as President of the Convention.

When the 168 members of the Virginia State Convention met at Richmond in June 1788, disagreement continued between the Federalist and Anti-Federalist factions. Debates grew more lengthy and lively. Patrick Henry spoke against ratification. George Washington at Mount Vernon and many others throughout the Confederation followed the proceedings at Richmond with interest. While the requisite number of nine States (Delaware, Pennsylvania, New Jersey, Georgia, Maryland, Massachusetts, New Hampshire, South Carolina, Connecticut) had ratified the Constitution by this time, Virginia and New York had yet to take action. By virtue of their large populations and tremendous areas, the decisions of these two states might determine the success or failure of the new government under the Constitution.

In Richmond, James Madison exerted all his diplomatic energies and patriotic fervor for ratification. Edmund Randolph was eventually converted. Others favoring the Constitution were Henry (Light Horse Harry) Lee, John Marshall, and George Wythe. Madison's assurance that a bill of rights would be incorporated in the Constitution by exercising the amending powers granted in Article V finally silenced the arguments of many of the opposition. On June 25, 1788, Virginia ratified the Constitution by a vote of 89 to 79. On the following day, June 26, however, the Convention drew up a series of 40 amendments and guarantees of individual liberties that it recommended for adoption by the Congress as amendments to the Constitution.

Under the influence of Jean-Jacques Rousseau's philosophy of the natural rights of man and John Locke's theories of political compacts, the first sentence of these amendments declared "That there are certain natural rights of which men, when they form a social compact cannot deprive or divest their posterity, among which are the enjoyment of life and liberty, with the means of acquiring, possessing and protecting property, and pursuing and obtaining happiness and safety." The original of these amendments inscribed on parchment, which is displayed on the Freedom Train, is a part of the general records of the United States Government now in the custody of the National Archives. There is a notable similarity in the language of the Virginia amendments with that employed in the Declaration of Independence and in Virginia's own Bill of Rights. With George Mason on the committee of 20 which drafted the document, it was natural that this similarity should appear, as he was the author of the Declaration of Rights adopted by Virginia in 1776.

When the first Congress of the United States assembled under the new Constitution in April 1789, James Madison was a member of the House of Representatives. He redeemed his pledge to the Virginia Convention by introducing a series of amendments to the Constitution on June 8, 1789. A select committee of the House reported out seventeen amendments which the Senate reduced to twelve, and of which all but two were finally ratified by the states. These form the constitutional cornerstone of our civil liberties. Ratification of the Bill of Rights was completed on December 15, 1791, when the necessary two-thirds majority was assured by the approval of Virginia.

36. Congress Works on the Drafts of the First Amendments to the Constitution (1789)

THE House of Representatives of the First Congress, under the leadership of James Madison, proposed a series of amendments to the Constitution in the nature of a bill of rights. It submitted seventeen articles or amendments to the Senate for consideration. A printed copy of this proposal, dated August 24, 1789, and with notations written by an unidentified hand, is exhibited on the Freedom Train. The names of John Beckley and Samuel A. Otis appear as Clerk of the House and Secretary of the Senate respectively.

The Senate reduced the number of articles in the first amendments as proposed by the House from 17 to 12. In the draft on exhibit, the preamble appeared as used in the final version: "The Conventions of a Number of the States having, at the time of their adopting the Constitution, expressed a Desire, in order to prevent misconstruction or abuse of its Powers, that further declaratory and restrictive Clauses should be added: And as extending the Ground of public Confidence in the Government, will best insure the benificent ends of its Institution." Nine articles are, aside from capitalization and punctuation, the same as those finally submitted to the States for ratification: the remaining three articles, which have been crossed out in this draft (Articles 1, 3, and 8), were modified somewhat in the final draft sent to the States. There are no signatures or names appended to this Senate draft. These two documents are from the records of the United States Senate now in the custody of the National Archives.

37. Congress Requests the President to Submit the Bill of Rights to the States for Ratification

THE movement for amendments to the Constitution guaranteeing fundamental civil rights culminated in the approval by Congress, on September 25, 1789, of twelve amendments. It was next necessary to secure the ratification of each amendment by at least three-fourths of the states. By the resolution of which the original signed manuscript is on exhibit, passed by the House on September 24 and concurred in by the Senate on September 26, 1789, the President was requested to transmit copies of the amendments to the executives of Rhode Island and North Carolina. These two states had not as yet ratified the Constitution and therefore could take no formal action on the amendments at that time. Before approval of the amendments by the required three-fourths of the states was obtained, however, three more states joined the Union by ratifying the Constitution. This addition of North Carolina, Rhode Island, and Vermont raised to eleven the number of states whose approval was necessary to give effect to the proposed amendments. On December 15, 1791, the necessary eleventh state, Virginia, ratified all of the amendments submitted by Congress. Although two of the twelve amendments submitted to the states failed to secure the necessary three-fourths vote, Virginia's action gave effect to the ten amendments known as the Bill of Rights. This document is from the National Archives.

CONGRESS OF THE UNITED STATES
In the House of Representatives,

Thursday the 24th of September, 1789

RESOLVED by the Senate and House of Representatives of the United States of America, in Congress assembled, that the President of the United States be requested to transmit to the Executives of the several States which have ratified the Constitution, Copies of the Amendments proposed by Congress to be added thereto, and like Copies to the Executives of the States of Rhode Island, and North Carolina.

Attest   John Beckley, Clerk

UNITED STATES OF AMERICA

In Senate September the 26th, 1789

RESOLVED, that the Senate do concur in this Resolution. Attest   Sam. A. Otis

[59]

38. Virginia's Ratification of the Bill of Rights Makes the First Ten Amendments a Part of the Constitution

THIS is the original document lent by the National Archives to the Freedom Train, whereby the Commonwealth of Virginia notified the Congress of the United States that Virginia, as of December 15, 1791, had ratified all of the amendments to the Constitution proposed by Congress. Virginia's action was most important, for by its approval the necessary ratification by three-fourths of the States of the ten amendments known as the Bill of Rights had been obtained.

It was fitting that Virginia, which had played so prominent a role in America's struggle for national independence and later for a Bill of Rights, now by its action gave effect to the amendments which guaranteed the independence and freedom of the individual.

39. Thomas Jefferson Deplores the Lack of a Bill of Rights in the Constitution (1787)

THOMAS JEFFERSON was in Europe during the greater part of the Critical Period under the Articles of Confederation and during all the anxious months when the Constitution was being formulated and ratified. From 1784 to 1789 he represented the United States at the court of Louis XVI. He took time from diplomacy, however, to keep in touch with events in America through an extensive correspondence. He wrote to no one more confidentially or on more important subjects than to James Madison, the Virginia scholar-statesman eight years his junior. Their political association was the result of a harmony in opinions and objectives, and may best be regarded as that of a senior and a junior partner in a common enterprise, rather than that of master and pupil.

It was therefore natural that when reports of the result of the Constitutional Convention's labors reached Jefferson in Paris, he should give his impressions of it to his friend Madison. He did so in this original letter of December 20, 1787, exhibited on the Freedom Train— probably not realizing the eminent role Madison had himself played in the framing of the Constitution. Jefferson found many things which commanded his approval, but he deplored the absence of two items. The second, less important, was the lack of any provision for rotation in office. The first was the absence of a specific Bill of Rights.

The fact that a large number of Jefferson's countrymen at home were also dissatisfied at this lack of a Bill of Rights accounted for much of the opposition to the Con-

stitution in the ratifying conventions which met in the states. In order to obtain certain of their narrow majorities, the Federalists were obliged to promise the subsequent passage of a Bill of Rights, and it was James Madison who took upon himself the redemption of these pledges after the new Congress was in session. About a year and a half after Jefferson wrote his letter of December 1787, Madison was able to report that he had a set of such amendments on their way through the legislative machinery.

Dear Sir,

My last to you was of October the 8th, by the Count de Moustier. Yours of July the 18th, September the 6th and October the 24th, were successively received, yesterday, the day before, and three or four days before that. I have only had time to read the letters; the printed papers communicated with them, however interesting, being obliged to lie over till I finish my despatches for the packet, which despatches must go from hence the day after to-morrow. I have much to thank you for; first and most for the cyphered paragraph respecting myself. These little informations are very material towards forming my own decisions. I would be glad even to know, when any individual member thinks I have gone wrong in any instance. If I know myself, it would not excite ill blood in me, while it would assist to guide my conduct, perhaps to justify it, and to keep me to my duty, alert. I must thank you, too, for the information in Thomas Burke's case; though you will have found by a subsequent letter, that I have asked of you a further investigation of that matter. It is to gratify the lady who is at the head of the convent wherein my daughters are, and who, by her attachment and attention to them, lays me under great obligations. I shall hope, therefore, still to receive from you the result of all the further inquiries my second letter had asked. The parcel of rice which you informed me had miscarried, accompanied my letter to the Delegates of South Carolina. Mr. Bourgoin was to be the bearer of both, and both were delivered together into the hands of his relation here, who introduced him to me, and who, at a subsequent moment, undertook to convey them to Mr. Bourgoin. This person was an engraver, particularly recommended to Dr. Franklin and Mr. Hopkinson. Perhaps he may have mislaid the little parcel of rice among his baggage. I am much pleased that the sale of western lands is so successful. I hope they will absorb all the certificates of our domestic debt speedily, in the first place, and that then, offered for cash, they will do the same by our foreign ones.

The season admitting only of operations in the cabinet, and these being in a great measure secret, I have little to fill a letter. I will, therefore, make up the deficiency, by adding a few words on the Constitution proposed by our convention.

I like much the general idea of framing a government, which should go on of itself, peaceably, without needing continual recurrence to the State legislatures. I like the organization of the government into legislative, judiciary and executive. I like the power given the legislature to levy taxes, and for that reason solely, I approve of the greater House being chosen by the people directly. For though I think a House so chosen, will be very far inferior to the present Congress, will be very illy qualified to legislate for the Union, for foreign nations, etc., yet this evil does not weigh against the good, of preserving inviolate the fundamental principle, that the people are not to be taxed but by representatives chosen immediately by themselves. I am captivated by the compromise of the opposite claims of the great and little States, of the latter to equal, and the former to proportional influence. I am much pleased, too, with the substitution of the method of voting by person, instead of that of voting by States; and I like the negative given to the Executive, conjointly with a third of either House; though I should have liked it better, had the judiciary been associated for that purpose, or invested separately with a similar power. There are other good things of less moment. I will now tell you what I do not like. First, the omission of a bill of rights, providing clearly, and without the aid of sophism, for freedom of religion, freedom of the press, protection against standing armies, restriction of monopolies, the eternal and unremitting force of the habeas corpus laws, and trials by jury in all matters of fact triable by the laws of the land, and not by the laws of nations. To say, as Mr. Wilson does, that a bill of rights was not necessary, because all is reserved in the case of the general government which is not given, while in the particular ones, all is given which is not reserved, might do for the audience to which it was addressed; but it is surely a *gratis dictum*, the reverse of which might just as well be said; and it is opposed by strong inferences from the body of the instrument, as well as from the omission of the cause of our present Confederation, which had made the reservation in express terms. It was hard to conclude, because there has been a want of uniformity among the States as to the cases triable by jury, because some have been so incautious as to dispense with this mode of trial in certain cases, therefore, the more prudent States shall be reduced to the same level of calamity. It would have been much more just and wise to have concluded the other way, that as most of the States had preserved with jealousy this sacred palladium of liberty, those who had wandered, should be brought back to it; and to have established general right rather than general wrong. For I consider all the ill as established, which may be established. I have a right to nothing, which another has a right to take away; and Congress will have a right to take away trials by jury in all civil cases. Let me add, that a bill of rights is what the people are en-titled to against every government on earth, general or particular; and what no just government should refuse, or rest on inference.

The second feature I dislike, and strongly dislike, is the abandonment, in every instance, of the principle of rotation in office, and most particularly in the case of the President. Reason and experience tell us, that the first magistrate will always be re-elected if he may be re-elected. He is then an officer for life. This once observed, it becomes of so much consequence to certain nations, to have a friend or a foe at the head of our affairs, that they will interfere with money and with arms. A Galloman, or an Angloman, will be supported by the nation he befriends. If once elected, and at a second or third election outvoted by one or two votes, he will pretend false votes, foul play, hold possession of the reins of government, be supported by the States voting for him, especially if they be the central ones, lying in a compact body themselves, and separating their opponents; and they will be aided by one nation in Europe, while the majority are aided by another. The election of a President of America, some years hence, will be much more interesting to certain nations of Europe, than ever the election of a King of Poland was. Reflect on all the instances of history, ancient and modern, of elective monarchies, and say if they do not give foundation for my fears; the Roman Emperors, the Popes while they were of any importance, the German Emperors till they became hereditary in practice, the Kings of Poland, the Deys of the Ottoman dependencies. It may be said, that if elections are to be attended with these disorders, the less frequently they are repeated the better. But experience says, that to free them from disorder, they must be rendered less interesting by a necessity of change. No foreign power, nor domestic party, will waste their blood and money to elect a person, who must go out at the end of a short period. The power of removing every fourth year by the vote of the people, is a power which they will not exercise, and if they were disposed to exercise it, they would not be permitted. The King of Poland is removable every day by the diet. But they never remove him. Nor would Russia, the Emperor, etc., permit them to do it. Smaller objections are, the appeals on matters of fact as well as laws; and the binding all persons, legislative, executive, and judiciary by oath, to maintain that constitution. I do not pretend to decide, what would be the best method of procuring the establishment of the manifold good things in this constitution, and of getting rid of the bad. Whether by adopting it, in hopes of future amendment; or after it shall have been duly weighed and canvassed by the people, after seeing the parts they generally dislike, and those they generally approve, to say to them, "We see now what you wish. You are willing to give to your federal government such and such powers; but you wish, at the same time, to have such and such fundamental rights secured to you, and certain sources of convulsion taken away. Be it so. Send together deputies again. Let them establish your fundamental rights by a sacrosanct declaration, and let them pass the parts of the Constitution you have approved. These will give powers to your federal government sufficient for your happiness."

This is what might be said, and would probably produce a speedy, more perfect and more permanent form of government. At all events, I hope you will not be discouraged from making other trials, if the present one should fail. We are never permitted to despair of the commonwealth. I have thus told you freely what I like, and what I dislike, merely as a matter of curiosity; for I know it is not in my power to offer matter of information to your judgment, which has been formed after hearing and weighing everything which the wisdom of man could offer on these subjects. I own, I am not a friend to a very energetic government. It is always oppressive. It places the governors indeed more at their ease, at the expense of the people. The late rebellion in Massachusetts has given more alarm, than I think it should have done. Calculate that one rebellion in thirteen States in the course of eleven years, is but one for each State in a century and a half. No country should be so long without one. Nor will any degree of power in the hands of government, prevent insurrections. In England, where the hand of power is heavier than with us, there are seldom half a dozen years without an insurrection. In France, where it is still heavier, but less despotic, as Montesquieu supposes, than in some other countries, and where there are always two or three hundred thousand men ready to crush insurrections, there have been three in the course of the three years I have been here, in every one of which greater numbers were engaged than in Massachusetts, and a great deal more blood was spilt. In Turkey, where the sole nod of the despot is death, insurrections are the events of every day. Compare again the depredations of their insurgents, with the order, the moderation and the almost self-extinguishment of ours. And say, finally, whether peace is best preserved by giving energy to the government, or information to the people. This last is the most certain, and the most legitimate engine of government. Educate and inform the whole mass of the people. Enable them to see that it is their interest to preserve peace and order, and they will preserve them. And it requires no very high degree of education to convince them of this. They are the only sure reliance for the preservation of our liberty. After all, it is my principle that the will of the majority should prevail. If they approve the proposed constitution in all its parts, I shall concur in it cheerfully, in hopes they will amend it, whenever they shall find it works wrong. This reliance cannot deceive us, as long as we remain virtuous; and I think we shall be so, as long as agriculture is our prin-

cipal object, which will be the case, while there remains vacant lands in any part of America. When we get piled upon one another in large cities, as in Europe, we shall become corrupt as in Europe, and go to eating one another as they do there. I have tired you by this time with disquisitions which you have already heard repeated by others a thousand and a thousand times; and therefore, shall only add assurances of the esteem and attachment with which I have the honor to be, dear Sir, your affectionate friend and servant.

P. S. The instability of our laws is really an immense evil. I think it would be well to provide in our constitutions, that there shall always be a twelvemonth between the engrossing a bill and passing it; that it should then be offered to its passage without changing a word; and that if circumstances should be thought to require a speedier passage, it should take two-thirds of both Houses, instead of a bare majority.

40. James Madison Informs Jefferson of His Introduction of Resolutions Providing for a Bill of Rights (1789)

ABOUT a year and a half after Thomas Jefferson wrote his letter of December 20, 1787 (see item No. 39), James Madison was able to report that he had a set of such amendments on their way through the legislative machinery. In the original letter exhibited on the Freedom Train, dated June 13, 1789, Madison wrote:

"The newspapers enclosed will show you the form and extent of the amendments which I thought it advisable to introduce to the House of Representatives, as most likely to pass through two-thirds of that House and of the Senate, and three-fourths of the States. If I am not mistaken, they will, if passed, be satisfactory to a majority of those who have opposed the Constitution."

The Bill of Rights as passed by Congress and ratified by the necessary number of states conformed generally to Jefferson's suggestions. Amendment I provided for freedom of religion and of the press, and Amendment VI strengthened the provision of Article III, Section 2, of the Constitution in favor of trial by jury. There was no express provision for Habeas Corpus—Jefferson had perhaps missed the emphatic wording of the Constitution on that point (Article I, Section 9) but Amendments IV and V contained additional provisions against unreasonable seizures of persons and the deprivations of liberty without due process of law. "Restriction against monopoly," by which Jefferson probably meant monopolies granted by the Government, remained unprovided for, but evidently this was regarded as unnecessary since such monopolies were so contrary to the spirit of the Constitution.

In view of the above, it was quite fitting that Thomas

Jefferson, who returned from France to become our first Secretary of State, should have been the one to officially certify to the several States on March 1, 1792, that the Bill of Rights had been properly ratified and was thenceforth a part of the Constitution of the United States.

N. York. June 13th 1789.

Dear Sir

The letter herewith enclosed from Col. H. Lee with the papers accompanying it fully explain themselves. Inclosed also is a letter from Mr. P. Carr, who has been here several weeks. One of his inducements to visit N. York during the present vacation, was a hope of falling in with you on your visit to America. I regret much both your disappointments. It is not yet in my power to say when the cause of yours will be removed. Every step taken under the new System is marked with tardiness; the effect of that want of precidents which give a mechanical motion to business under old establishments.

To the above inclosures is added a chart of the Great falls copied from a draught sent me by Col: Lee. I should have observed that all the papers from him, except this are duplicates, the originals having been consigned by a conveyance from Alexanda to the care of Mr. Mason who resides at Bordeaux, to be forwarded to Paris.

This will go by a Gentleman, Mr. Joy, who is returning to London, and will be forwarded by such opportunity as he may judge sufficiently certain. Considering it is likely to be long on the way, and having written pretty lately to you, I shall suspend further communications, till a more direct & convenient channel presents itself. The newspaper inclosed will shew you the form and extent of the amendments which I thought it adviseable to introduce to the H. of Representatives (as most likely to pass thro' 2/3 of that He. & of the Senate & 3/4 of ye States). If I am not mistaken they will if passed, be satisfactory to majority of those who have opposed the Constitution. I am persuaded they will be so to a majority of that Description in Virginia. I wish you all happiness & am Dear Sir yrs most affectly
Js. Madison Jr

note—Let the amendments follow—
Mr. Jefferson

which explained the provisions contained in the proposed Constitution and which influenced its final ratification.

I. A republic a word used in various senses—has been applied to aristocracies and monarchies
  1. to Rome under the Kings
  2. to Sparta though a senate for life
  3. to Carthage though the same
  4. to United Netherland, though Stadholder, Hereditary order
  5. to Poland though Aristocracy and monarchy
  6. to G Britain though Monarchy etc.
II. Again great confusion about the words democracy Aristocracy Monarchy
  I. Democracy defined by some Rousseau etc. a government exercised by the collective body of the People
    2. Delegation of their power has been made the Criterion of Aristocracy
  II. Aristocracy has been used to designate governments
    1. Where an *independent* few possessed sovereignty
    2. Where the representatives of the people possessed it
  III. Monarchy—where Sovereignty in the hands of a single man
    General idea—Independent in his Situation in any other sense would apply to State of New York etc.
III. Democracy in my sense where the whole power of the government is in the people
  1. whether exercised by themselves or
  2. by their representatives chosen by them either mediately or immediately and legally accountable to them - - - - -
IV. Aristocracy where whole sovereignty is permanently in the hands of a few for life or hereditary -
V. Monarchy where the whole sovereignty is in the hands of one man for life or hereditary - - -
VI. Mixed government where these three principles unite

41. Alexander Hamilton Prepares an Outline for Parts of "The Federalist"

HAMILTON was the principal author of *The Federalist* (see items Nos. 26 and 27). He planned and wrote, or collaborated in writing, more than half of all the essays.

The present manuscript, lent to the Freedom Train exhibit by the Library of Congress, is Hamilton's original manuscript outline of subjects of part of the essays

42. Secretary of the Treasury Hamilton Outlines His "Report on the Public Credit"

IN THE formation of the new national government President Washington wished to appoint Robert Morris, the financier of the War of Independence, as Secretary of the Treasury. Washington then turned to his old friend Alexander Hamilton. Hamilton had previously

I A republic a word used in various senses —

      has been applied to aristocracies and monarchies

        1 to Rome under the Kings
        2 to Sparta though a senate for life
        3 to Carthage though the same
        4 to United Netherland, though Stadholder Hereditary noble
        5 to Poland though Aristocracy and monarchy
        6 to G Britain though Monarchy &c

II Again great confusion about the words democracy Aristocracy
    Monarchy.

      1 Democracy defined by some Rousseau &c a government
        exercised by the collective body of the People
      2 Delegation of their power has been made the Criterion
        of Aristocracy.

    II Aristocracy has been used to designate governments
      1 where an independent few possessed sovereignty
      2 Where the representatives of the people possessed it

    III Monarchy. where sovereignty in the hands of a
      single man.
        General idea — Independent in his situation
        in any other sense would apply to State of N York
        &c

III Democracy in my sense where the whole power of the government
    is in the people
      1 whether exercised by themselves or
      2 by their representatives chosen by them either
        mediately or immediately and legally
        accountable to them — — — — — —

IV Aristocracy where whole sovereignty is permanently
    in the hands of a few for life or hereditary —

V Monarchy where the whole sovereignty is in the hands
    of one man for life or hereditary — —

VI Mixed government where these three principles unite

Alexander Hamilton's Outline of Subjects for "The Federalist," 1788 (See No. 41).

made a number of striking suggestions aimed at the re-organization of the finances of the new nation, but he was without any practical experience in the management of finances on a large scale.

He accepted the post and at once plunged into the difficulties of a field at once complex and novel. He did it with characteristic vigor and imagination. The results demonstrate a bold courage and a firm grasp of the details of a complicated subject. As Secretary of the Treasury Hamilton reached the climax of his career in public service.

His "Report on the Public Credit" is clearly one of the greatest of his state papers. Within a few days of his secretaryship Congress called upon him for a comprehensive plan for the establishment and the administration of the finances of the nation. With astonishing speed he produced such a plan. He made certain fundamental assumptions: that the new government should and would punctually and completely meet its financial engagements, both foreign and domestic. He wished to present his report personally to Congress, but those who feared that his presence and eloquence would overwhelm the otherwise calm judgment of many members, blocked the suggestion. He was forced to submit it in writing.

After much acrimonious debate, all of his basic recommendations were adopted. As a result, in the words of Allan Nevins, "he created as from the void a firm public credit." And at that time a firm public credit was the paramount item of which the new nation had need.

The following type text reproduces the exact contents of the page of the original manuscript outline of Hamilton's "Report on the Public Credit" that is exhibited on the Freedom Train. It is from the collections of the Library of Congress.

"an undue share of the public burthen.

"Among other substantial reasons, which recommend, as a provision for the public debt, duties upon articles of consumption, in preference to taxes on houses and lands, is this . . . It is very desirable, if practicable to reserve the latter fund for objects and occasions, which will more immediately interest the sensibility of the whole community, and more directly affect the public safety. It will be a consolatory reflection, that so capital a resource remains untouched by that provision; which, while it will have a very sensible influence on favour of public Credit, will be materially conducive to the tranquillity of the Public mind, in respect to external danger, and will really operate as a powerful guarantee of peace. In proportion as the estimation of our resources is exalted in the eyes of foreign Nations, the respect for us must increase; and this must beget a proportionable caution neither to insult nor injure us with levity. While on the contrary the appearance of exhausted resources, (which would perhaps be a consequence of mortgaging the rev-

enue to be derived from land for the interest of the public debt) might tend to invite both insult and injury, by inspiring an opinion, that our efforts to resent or repel them were little to be dreaded.

"It may not be unworthy of a reflection, that while the idea of residuary resources in so striking a particular cannot fail to have many beneficial consequences; the suspension of taxes on real estate"

43. Alexander Hamilton Prepares a Draft of the Farewell Address for Submission to President Washington (1796)

PRESIDENT WASHINGTON had reluctantly accepted Hamilton's resignation as Secretary of the Treasury, but his retirement from public office on January 31, 1795, did not disrupt the intimate collaboration which had long existed between them.

Washington had wished to retire from the presidency in 1793 and had asked James Madison, in May 1792, to formulate notes to be used in the preparation of a farewell address. Madison did a draft, but this was pigeonholed when Washington gave up his plan for retirement. But now Washington was not to be dissuaded. He took Madison's notes and wove them into the structure of the new address he was preparing. The resulting document (see document No. 47) became Washington's first draft of the Farewell Address. Washington then showed this manuscript to Hamilton in Philadelphia and asked him to "redress" it. Hamilton then made a syllabus of points before he began to work on his "major draft."

Hamilton's original manuscript, called an "abstract of points to form an address," bears no date, but it was probably written prior to July 5, 1796. Washington then took Hamilton's "major draft" and incorporated many of Hamilton's ideas, and especially his phrases, in his own final version of the Farewell Address which he sent to David C. Claypoole, proprietor and editor of the *American Daily Advertiser*, for publication in the issue of Monday, September 19, 1796.

Hamilton's original manuscript is lent to the Freedom Train by the Library of Congress.

I. The period of a new Election approaches it is his duty to announce his intention to decline—

II. He had hoped that long ere this it would have been in his power and particularly had nearly come to a final resolution in the year 1792 to do it but the peculiar situation of affairs & advice of confidential friends dissuaded
    political cowardice

III. In acquiescing in a further election he still hoped a year or two longer would have enabled him to withdraw but a continuance of causes has delayed till now—when the position of our Country abroad and at home justify him in pursuing his inclination

IV. In doing it has not been unmindful of his relation as a dutiful citizen to his Country nor is now influenced by the some allege diminution of zeal for its interest or gratitude for its past kindness but by a belief that the step is compatible with both.

V. The impressions under which he first accepted were explained on the proper occasion—

VI. In the execution of it has contributed the best exertions of a very fallible judgment acknowledged his insufficiency—experienced his disqualifications for the difficult trust & every day a stronger sentiment from that cause to yield the plan—advance into the decline of life, every day more sensible of weight of years of the necessity of repose the duty to seek retirement & Add

VII. It will be among the purest enjoyments which can sweeten the remnant of his days to partake in a private station in the midst of his fellow Citizens the laws of a free Govern. the ultimate object of his care and wishes—

W. as to Rotation

44. The American Flag is Unfurled to Battle for the First Time

ON June 14, 1777, the Continental Congress had resolved that the flag of the thirteen United States was to consist of thirteen alternate red and white stripes, with thirteen white stars in a field of blue. The garrison at Fort Schuyler (formerly Fort Stanwix, the site of which is now included in the city of Rome, New York) succeeded in improvising a flag that conformed to the pattern established by Congress. Shirts were cut up to form the white stripes, bits of scarlet cloth were joined for the red, and the blue ground for the stars came from a cloak belonging to Captain Abraham Swartwout.

The document exhibited on the Freedom Train is the only authoritative account known of the first military raising of the American flag. It occurs in the manuscript "Journal of the most Material Occurrences proceeding the Siege of Fort Schuyler (formerly Fort Stanwix) with an Account of that Siege &c. . . .", the original of which was lent by Dr. A. S. W. Rosenbach.

The relevant passages of this manuscript journal by William Colbreath follow:

"Augt. 3d. Early this Morning a Continental Flagg made by the Officers of Col. Gansevoorts Regiment was hoisted and a Cannon Levelled at the Enemies Camp was fired on the Occasion, A Small Party was sent out to the Landing to see if the Enemy had Destroy'd any of our Batteaus last Night, This Party found the Batteau Man that was missing wounded thro the Brain Stabb'd in the Right Breast and Scalped he was alive when found, and brought to the Garrison But Died Shortly after the Beautteax Lay at the Landing no ways Damaged about three o Clock this Afternoon the Enemy Shewed themselves to the Garrison on all Sides Carry'd off some Hay from a Field near the Garrison at which a Flag brought up Capt Tice came into the Fort with a Proffer of Protection if the Garrison wou'd Surrender, which was Rejected with disdain."

45. Francis Scott Key Writes "The Star Spangled Banner"

THE "STAR SPANGLED BANNER" is one of the great national anthems composed under the immediate stress of a momentous event. It was inspired by an incident that proved to be a turning point in the War of 1812. During the summer of 1814, the British had captured the city of Washington and set fire to the Capitol. The next objective was the subjugation of the city of Baltimore. The citizens, untrained as they were, were hastily mobilized for defense. In September 1814, more than forty British ships proceeded up Chesapeake Bay, put ashore troops at North Point for a land attack, and then stood off Fort McHenry, at the entrance to Baltimore Harbor, for a naval bombardment that lasted for nearly twenty-five hours, on September 13 and 14.

While the British ships were preparing for the bombardment, a lawyer from Georgetown, D. C., Francis Scott Key, reached the Admiral's ship under a flag of truce, in an effort to secure the release of a prominent citizen, Dr. William Beanes, who was being held as a hostage aboard the British flagship. The request was granted, but both Key and Beanes were detained on shipboard because of the impending bombardment.

It was thus that Key, guarded on the cartel ship, *Minden*, anxiously witnessed the entire siege of Fort McHenry. When the shelling finally ceased during the night, he was in ignorance of the outcome of the battle. Dawn showed that the Stars and Stripes still floated over the desperately defended fort, and that the British attack had been futile.

In his exultation, Key, still waiting on the ship, jotted down some lines on the back of an old letter. As the British fleet withdrew, Key was put ashore. He found Baltimore jubilant over the victory that had spared it the fate of Washington. Immediately upon reaching his hotel, Key wrote out his notes in the form of a song with the meter of a popular tune of the day called "Anacreon in Heaven". He showed it next morning to his brother-in-law, Judge Joseph Nicholson, who at once took it to a

O say can you see, ~~through~~ by the dawn's early light,
What so proudly we hail'd at the twilight's last gleaming,
Whose broad stripes & bright stars through the perilous fight
O'er the ramparts we watch'd, were so gallantly streaming?
And the rocket's red glare, the bomb bursting in air,
Gave proof through the night that our flag was still there,
O say does that star spangled banner yet wave
O'er the land of the free & the home of the brave?

On the shore dimly seen through the mists of the deep,
Where the foe's haughty host in dread silence reposes,
What is that which the breeze, o'er the towering steep,
As it fitfully blows, half conceals, half discloses?
Now it catches the gleam of the morning's first beam,
In full glory reflected now shines in the stream,
'Tis the star-spangled banner — O long may it wave
O'er the land of the free & the home of the brave!

And where is that band who so vauntingly swore,
That the havoc of war & the battle's confusion
A home & a Country should leave us no more?
— ~~Their blood~~
Their blood has wash'd out their foul footstep's pollution.
No refuge could save the hireling & slave
From the terror of flight or the gloom of the grave,
And the star-spangled banner in triumph doth wave
O'er the land of the free & the home of the brave.

O thus be it ever when freemen shall stand
Between their lov'd home & the war's desolation!
Blest with vict'ry & peace may the heav'n rescued land
Praise the power that hath made & preserv'd us a nation!
Then conquer we must, when our cause it is just,
And this be our motto — "In God is our trust,"
And the Star-spangled banner in triumph shall wave
O'er the land of the free & the home of the brave. —

The Original of "The Star Spangled Banner" in Francis Scott Key's Own Hand (See No. 45)

Washington's Accounting of His Expenses as Commander-in-Chief (See No. 46)

local printer who struck it off in the form of handbills. These circulated rapidly and soon the song echoed throughout the city, was reprinted in newspapers and so carried to other towns. From its first publication, the "Star Spangled Banner" enjoyed general popularity. It was commonly regarded as the National Anthem long before Congress passed a bill giving it this official designation in 1931.

The original manuscript belonging to the Walters Art Gallery, which is that exhibited on the Freedom Train, is the document that Key wrote out on the night of September 14, 1814, when he reached Baltimore after the battle. It is the one used by the printer as copy for the handbills that first made the song known to the public. The paper descended in Judge Nicholson's family until it was acquired by Henry Walters in 1907. Four other copies of the poem are known to have been made by Key, one of which is now in the Library of Congress.

These all were made for friends long afterward, about 1840, when the song was already an established national favorite. What became of the first notes Key made on shipboard is unknown, but presumably he destroyed them after writing the present neat manuscript.

46. General Washington Submits the Account of his Expenses during the Revolutionary War

When George Washington was chosen by the Continental Congress to be Commander-in-Chief of the American armies, he stated in his acceptance that he would accept no payment for his services but that he would keep an exact account of his expenses, for he did not doubt that Congress would one day reimburse him.

At the close of the war he laboriously made out two copies of his expense accounts, one of which has been preserved in the National Archives and is now displayed in the Freedom Train exhibit.

His account book covers the period from June 1776 to 1783. As rendered by Washington it was compiled from various expense books and memoranda kept by aides, stewards, housekeepers, and others, and is necessarily, therefore, a summary. It contains, however, many items of special interest. Among these is a series of entries of payments for espionage service. Although Washington kept secret the names of his agents, some have been identified from other sources. He testifies in a note to the obligations due them from the public.

The double columns on most pages are explained by the necessity of reducing the amounts to a common basis. Because the different colonies each had its own currency, the rate of exchange between the local currency and "Lawful" or coin currency varied throughout the war and with each locality.

So accurately had Washington's accounts been kept that when they were finally settled the skilled accountants of the Treasury found that in the sums which totalled more than 160,000 dollars there was a discrepancy of only "89/90 of one dollar" more due to Washington than his accounts show.

Washington's account book has been lent to the exhibit from the records of the Treasury Department now in the custody of the National Archives.

47. President Washington Makes a Political Legacy to the Nation in a Farewell Address (1796)

SOME of the background of this famous utterance which has been termed "one of the world's most remarkable documents" has already been given (see item No. 43). The main facts can be briefly summarized.

Washington had thought of retiring from the presidency at the end of his first term and, in anticipation of this, had asked James Madison to prepare the draft of a farewell message. This Madison did, but the manuscript was pigeon-holed when the pressure of events and the entreaties of friends persuaded the President to postpone his retirement. But in 1796 he was adamant. He was now in his middle sixties. He had led a strenuous life—mostly in the service of his country. He had now grown weary of the strife and turmoil of politics. He wished to make a statement which would definitely eliminate him from the possibility of a third term. He wished also to take this opportunity to offer for the "solemn contemplation" of his fellow-citizens certain ad-

vice on the conduct of national affairs which would present both his hopes and his reflections which arose from long experience in public life.

Upon the basis of Madison's notes Washington prepared his first draft of the Farewell Address. It is this original manuscript, entirely in Washington's handwriting, which is lent to the Freedom Train exhibit by the New York State Library. This manuscript Washington later showed to Alexander Hamilton with the request that he "redress" it. After numerous conferences with John Jay, Hamilton prepared his own major draft of an address. Using his own draft and the combined suggestions of Hamilton and Jay, Washington then prepared the version which was sent to the editor of the *American Daily Advertiser* through whose columns it was released to the American people.

Keenly aware of the many disturbing forces at work in the infant republic, Washington stressed the necessity of firm union and a strong central government. "The name AMERICAN, which belongs to you in your national capacity, must always exalt the just pride of Patriotism, more than any appellation derived from local discrimination." He warned against sectional jealousies, which he recognized were stimulated by parties who seek to gain local power by misrepresenting the opinions and aims of other districts. To Washington the constitutional separation of powers and the system of checks and balances made party politics unnecessary. It had seemed to him that political opposition was factionalism, antagonistic not only to the orderly functioning of the Administration but the ultimate success of the new government. He cautioned against the "Baneful effects of the Spirit of Party," which stemmed from "the strongest passions of the human mind." In the management of government he urged the preservation of public credit. He did not, however, advocate foolish economies, for he noted that "timely disbursements to prepare for danger frequently prevent much greater disbursements to repel it."

He was far-sighted and penetrating in his observations on domestic matters, but it was in the field of foreign affairs that his views have had such significant influence on the future conduct of American international relations. It was clear to Washington that because the United States was small and weak it was absolutely essential for the country to gain time "to settle and mature its yet recent institutions, and to progress without interruption to that degree of strength and consistency . . . necessary to give it . . . the command of its own fortunes." To this end he urged that good faith and justice be observed toward all nations, and especially that friendliness and fairness should not be permitted to yield to "inveterate antipathies" or "passionate attachments" for particular countries. Washington observed that: "The Nation which indulges toward another an habitual hatred or an habitual fondness is in some degree a slave."

In addition to his admonitions for the general conduct of foreign affairs, there is found in the Farewell Address what many have interpreted as the basic statement of isolationism—once such a valid guide for American foreign policy. Washington was reflecting the colonial experience of over a hundred years of embroilment in the conflict of Europe and the increasing difficulties of maintaining neutrality during the current war between France and England. In his judgment America's best interests lay in remaining aloof from European struggles:

"Europe has a set of primary interests, which to us have none or a very remote relation.—Hence she must be engaged in frequent controversies, the causes of which are essentially foreign to our concerns. Hence therefore it must be unwise in us to implicate ourselves, by artificial ties in the ordinary vicissitudes of her politics, or the ordinary combinations and collisions of her friendships or enmities. Our detached and distant situation invites us to pursue a different course. . . . 'Tis our true policy to steer clear of permanent alliances, with any portion of the foreign world. . . . Taking care always to keep ourselves, by suitable establishments, on a respectable defensive posture, we may safely trust to temporary alliances for extraordinary emergencies."

48. President Lincoln Proposes a Plan for the Abolition of Slavery (1862)

THE Emancipation Proclamation has received wide and honored praise. But it did not represent Lincoln's only solution to the problem of slavery. In this original document, lent to the Freedom Train exhibit by Dr. A. S. W. Rosenbach, we are sharply reminded of a neglected phase of Lincoln's broad statesmanship. It merits the attention of the American public. No better clarification can be found than in the words of Professor J. G. Randall, an eminent authority on Lincoln and his times:

"Where Lincoln gave thought to large-scale national planning in the matter of liberating the slaves, such thought was not embraced within the bounds of the emancipation proclamation. Speaking relatively and with a view to the President's main concept for solving the problem, it is correct to regard the proclamation as of minor importance. The famous edict was to Lincoln a war measure of limited scope, of doubtful legality, and of inadequate effect. In his reaching out for an adequate solution the President developed an elaborate blueprint for freedom in terms of gradual emancipation by voluntary action of the slave states with Federal cooperation in two matters: foreign colonization of emancipated Negroes and compensation to slaveowners.

"This blueprint was envisaged not merely with refer-ence to the war, though its integration with a broad war policy was a vital factor; beyond the war the President's solution was projected into a peaceminded future with a view to the ultimate, statesmanlike elimination of an institution in which, as Lincoln felt, North and South had a common responsibility and a community of interest. Though the plan failed, a familiarity with it becomes necessary to an understanding of wartime currents and especially of Lincoln's manner of tackling a large problem. As one studies the President's pathetically earnest efforts to promote this 'proposition,' one is impressed with his conservatism, his sense of fair dealing, his lack of vindictiveness, his attention to legal adjustments, his respect for self-determination in government, his early vision of state-and-federal cooperation, and his coordination of a domestic reform with the nation's paramount purpose to restore the Union and then to preserve it. The proposition is also significant as perhaps the major instance in which Lincoln tried manfully to enlist the support of Congress. On no other matter did he so far extend his presidential leadership in attempted legislation. The only other project of the period that compares with it is that of reconstruction, but in that case Lincoln did not rely upon congressional enactment of a presidentially sponsored measure.

"Announced in a special message to Congress on March 6, 1862, and fully elaborated in his message of December 1 of that year, Lincoln's plan was unfolded as part of a grand concept of a large and growing people, a nation of untouched resources whose future, he hoped, would not be frustrated 'by any political folly or mistake.' A long-term policy was envisaged, to be completed 'at any time or times' before 1900."

Fellow-citizens of the Senate and House of Representatives: Herewith is a draft of a bill to compensate any State which may abolish slavery within its limits, the passage of which, substantially as presented, I respectfully and earnestly recommend.

July 14, 1862.   Abraham Lincoln

Be it enacted by the Senate and House of Representatives of the United States of America, in Congress assembled, That whenever the President of the United States shall be satisfied that any State shall have lawfully abolished slavery within and throughout such State, either immediately or gradually, it shall be the duty of the President, assisted by the Secretary of the Treasury, to prepare and deliver to such State an amount of six per cent. interest-bearing bonds of the United States equal to the aggregate value, at ———— dollars per head, of all the slaves within such State as reported by the census of the year one thousand eight hundred and sixty; the whole amount for any one State to be delivered at once if the abolishment be immediate, or in equal annual instalments if it be grad-

Friends and Fellow Citizens

The quotation ~~which you will~~
find in this ~~following~~ address, was composed
and intended to have been published, in the
year 1792; in time to have announced to
the Electors of the Presiden[t] & Vice President of the United
States, the determination of the former ~~which has~~ previ-
ous to the sd Election ~~therein expressed~~ before the Election ~~could then be~~
~~actually made~~: but the solicitude my confidential ~~of a warm~~ friend,
~~who was apprised of my intention, and~~
~~in whose judgment I did very much rely~~
~~(particularly in one who was privy to the~~
~~draught *) that I would suspend my deter-~~
~~mination~~, added to the peculiar situation
of our foreign affairs, at that epoch, in du-
ced

* ~~Mr Madison~~

been blessed amidst the tumults which have
harrassed other countries... Please you with
undefiled hands — an uncorrupted heart —
and with ardent vows to heaven for the welfare & happiness of that country in which I
and my forefathers to the third or fourth
Ancestry drew our first breath. —

G: Washington

Washington's Farewell Address, last page

ual, interest to begin running on each bond at the time of its delivery, and not before.

And be it further enacted, That if any State, having so received any such bonds, shall at any time afterward by law reintroduce or tolerate slavery within its limits, contrary to the act of abolishment upon which such bonds shall have been received, said bonds so received by said State shall at once be null and void, in whosesoever hands they may be, and such State shall refund to the United States all interest which may have been paid on such bonds.

49. President Lincoln Signs the Emancipation Proclamation (1863)

Although Abraham Lincoln was a lifelong opponent of the slave system, he reached his great decision to attack the "peculiar institution" of the South only because he felt the success of the Union cause required it. As 1862 and the second year of war progressed, the failure of the North to achieve any decisive military success concentrated greater attention than ever on the issue of emancipation.

The abolitionists had increased the vigor of their propaganda and, in response to a changing public opinion, Congress was whittling away at slavery. In July a law was passed emancipating many slaves of disloyal owners. In a message to Congress in March 1862, Lincoln urged recognition of the principle of compensation to the states that would abolish slavery. A resolution to that effect was passed, but no slaveholding state could be persuaded to free its slaves on such a basis. In April, slavery was abolished by Congress in the District of Columbia, with compensation to slaveowners; and in June slavery was prohibited in the territories.

Urged by many to strike a blow at the heart of the Confederacy by emancipating the slaves, Lincoln did not abandon his paramount belief that the great purpose of the war was to preserve the Union. He was fearful of driving from the Union the loyal, slaveholding border states, and he knew that many in the Union armies were not anti-slavery men. In his famous letter of August 22, 1862, he wrote to Horace Greeley, editor of the *New York Tribune*:

"My paramount object in this struggle is to save the Union, and it is not either to save or destroy slavery. If I could save the Union without freeing any slave, I would do it; and if I could save it by freeing all the slaves, I would do it; and if I could save it by freeing some and leaving others alone, I would also do that."

Lincoln determined upon his course of action by midsummer of 1862. On July 22, he presented to his cabinet a draft of a preliminary proclamation. Although his mind was made up on the issue, he accepted the advice of Secretary of State Seward that it ought not to be given out in a time of disaster lest it be considered a "shriek on the retreat" of the government. He waited for a more propitious occasion. In September the Army of the Potomac turned back the forces under Lee at the costly battle of Antietam. A doubtful victory, if one at all, it was seized upon as the most likely opportunity to present itself.

It was on September 22, 1862, that President Lincoln issued his preliminary Proclamation of Emancipation. By virtue of his authority as Commander-in-Chief of the Army and Navy, he declared that on January 1, 1863, all slaves within any state or district then declared to be in rebellion against the United States "shall be then, thenceforth, and forever free."

On the appointed day, duly informed that the states in arms against the government had ignored his appeal, Lincoln issued the document shown here, fulfilling to the letter his preliminary proclamation by defining the areas to which emancipation applied. Although undertaken strictly as a war measure, the Proclamation of Emancipation was the climax of the growing detestation on the part of the American people for the institution of human slavery.

By The President of The United States of America:
A Proclamation

Whereas, on the twenty-second day of September, in the year of our Lord one thousand eight hundred and sixty-two, a proclamation was issued by the President of the United States, containing, among other things, the following, to wit:

"That on the first day of January, in the year of our Lord one thousand eight hundred and sixty-three, all persons held as slaves within any State, or designated part of a State, the people whereof shall then be in rebellion against the United States, shall be then, thenceforward, and forever free; and the Executive Government of the United States, including the military and naval authority thereof, will recognize and maintain the freedom of such persons, and will do no act or acts to repress such persons, or any of them, in any efforts they may make for their actual freedom.

"That the Executive will, on the first day of January aforesaid, by proclamation, designate the States and parts of States, if any, in which the people thereof respectively shall then be in rebellion against the United States; and the fact that any State, or the people thereof, shall on that day be in good faith represented in the Congress of the United States by members chosen thereto at elections wherein a majority of the qualified voters of such State shall have participated, shall in the absence of strong countervailing testimony be deemed conclusive evidence that such State and the people thereof are not then in rebellion against the United States."

Now, therefore, I, Abraham Lincoln, President of the United States, by virtue of the power in me vested as commander-in-chief of the army and navy of the United States, in time of actual armed rebellion against the authority and government of the United States, and as a fit and necessary war measure for suppressing said rebellion, do, on this first day of January, in the year of our Lord one thousand eight hundred and sixty-three, and in accordance with my purpose so to do, publicly proclaimed for the full period of 100 days from the day first above mentioned, order and designate as the States and parts of States wherein the people thereof, respectively, are this day in rebellion against the United States, the following, to wit:

Arkansas, Texas, Louisiana (except the parishes of St. Bernard, Plaquemines, Jefferson, St. John, St. Charles, St. James, Ascension, Assumption, Terre Bonne, Lafourche. St. Mary, St. Martin, and Orleans, including the city of New Orleans), Mississippi, Alabama, Florida, Georgia, South Carolina, North Carolina, and Virginia (except the forty-eight counties designated as West Virginia, and also the counties of Berkeley, Accomac, Northampton, Elizabeth City, York, Princess Ann, and Norfolk, including the cities of Norfolk and Portsmouth), and which excepted parts are for the present left precisely as if this proclamation were not issued.

And by virtue of the power and for the purpose aforesaid, I do order and declare that all persons held as slaves within said designated States and parts of States are, and henceforward shall be, free; and that the Executive Government of the United States, including the military and naval authorities thereof, will recognize and maintain the freedom of said persons.

And I hereby enjoin upon the people so declared to be free to abstain from all violence, unless in necessary selfdefense; and I recommend to them that, in all cases when allowed, they labor faithfully for reasonable wages.

And I further declare and make known that such persons of suitable condition will be received into the armed service of the United States to garrison forts, positions, stations, and other places, and to man vessels of all sorts in said service. And upon this act, sincerely believed to be an act of justice, warranted by the Constitution upon military necessity, I invoke the considerate judgment of mankind and the gracious favor of Almighty God.

In witness whereof, I have hereunto set my hand, and caused the seal of the United States to be affixed.

Done at the city of Washington, this first day of

January, in the year of our Lord one thousand eight hundred and sixty-three, and of the Independence of the United States of America the eighty-seventh.

(L. S.)

Abraham Lincoln

By the President: William H. Seward, Secretary of State.

50. A Joint Resolution of Congress Proposes the Thirteenth Amendment to the Constitution

WITH the advance of the Union armies as the Civil War drew to a close, the effective area to which Lincoln's Emancipation Proclamation of January 1, 1863, applied was increased until slavery was in fact abolished in all the states which were in arms against the government on that date. But slavery still existed in those slaveholding border states which had not seceded and in those parts of the South under Union control on the date of the Proclamation.

In order to place above question the step he had taken with doubtful constitutional authority and to remove slavery from the whole country, Lincoln urged upon Congress the adoption of a resolution proposing a Constitutional amendment prohibiting slavery in all parts of the nation. Exhibited on the Freedom Train is the original proposal, dated January 11, 1864, by which the Senate proposed a joint resolution to amend the Constitution.

After a long and bitter fight in Congress, this project was sent to the states for ratification in January 1865. Extraordinary measures were recognized as necessary to win the approval of the required three-fourths of the states. With Lee's surrender and the collapse of the Confederacy soon thereafter, it became possible for the Federal military authorities to force ratification by a sufficient number of Southern states so that the Thirteenth Amendment was declared effective December 18, 1865.

This document is from the collections of the National Archives.

51. President Lincoln Delivers a Brief Address at Gettysburg (1863)

LINCOLN's Gettysburg Address is not only a lofty page in American literature; it has become a part of the universal language of liberty and human dignity. Of the nobility of sentiment and the beauty little can be said that has not already been well said. It has long since been securely enshrined in the pages of history. It will live on to inspirit the heart of man as long as men of good will cherish freedom.

But of the circumstances under which it was written and delivered some relevant things need be said, for the facts themselves are often more interesting than the legends.

It was the plan of the committee in charge of the preparation of the cemetery at Gettysburg to have a distinguished orator and a great poet do the principal honors at the dedication ceremonies. The idea of an impressive program of ceremonies was almost an afterthought. It was a simple problem of sanitation that gave birth to the proposal for a cemetery at Gettysburg, for the former battlefield was littered with the rotting cadavers of horses and men. It was a cooperative effort of eighteen states in which Pennsylvania took the lead. As the work progressed the potential stature of the project slowly dawned upon the committee which was headed by David Wills of Gettysburg. Elaborate dedicatory ceremonies then seemed in order. It was not difficult to find the orator, for Edward Everett was the foremost speaker of his day. He regarded the occasion as so solemn and important that he requested additional time for the preparation of his address and the ceremonies were postponed from the original date of October 23 to November 19. But no "great poet" could be found, for the poetic muse had been one of the unsung casualties of the war.

Hundreds of printed invitations to attend the ceremonies were sent out in the proper perfunctory manner by the committee. One of these routinely went to President Lincoln. Lincoln replied and accepted the invitation.

Lincoln's acceptance produced a turmoil in the committee. It is probable that they thought he would be too busy to attend, for they had received many such refusals from far lesser figures than the President of the United States. Now that the President had indicated that he would attend, a dilemma confronted the committee. Should he be asked to speak or could he possibly be left to sit in silence. Some felt that Lincoln would be unable to muster enough dignity for the solemnity of the event and that the interjection of some of his broad humor might wreck the ceremonies. The politeness of protocol at last prevailed and Wills, on November 2, sent the President a letter asking him to speak. The letter reflected the thinking of the committee and its phrasing might well have been considered a gratuitous insult; the President was requested to make "a few appropriate remarks" in formally setting apart the grounds "to their sacred use."

Official duties kept the President extremely busy in the early days of November, but he did find time to think of the necessary "few appropriate remarks." Before Lincoln and his official party took the special train to Gettysburg on Wednesday, November 18, he had certainly written the first page and possibly even the second and final page of the first draft of the Address. There is

By the President of the United States of America:

A Proclamation.

Whereas, on the twenty-second day of September, in the year of our Lord one thousand eight hundred and sixty-two, a proclamation was issued by the President of the United States, containing, among other things, the following, to wit:

"That on the first day of January, in the "year of our Lord one thousand eight hundred "and sixty-three, all persons held as slaves within "any State or designated part of a State, the people "whereof shall then be in rebellion against the "United States, shall be then, thenceforward, and "forever free; and the Executive Government of the "United States, including the military and naval "authority thereof, will recognize and maintain "the freedom of such persons, and will do no act "or acts to repress such persons, or any of them, "in any efforts they may make for their actual "freedom.

"That the Executive will, on the first day

The Emancipation Proclamation (See No. 49)

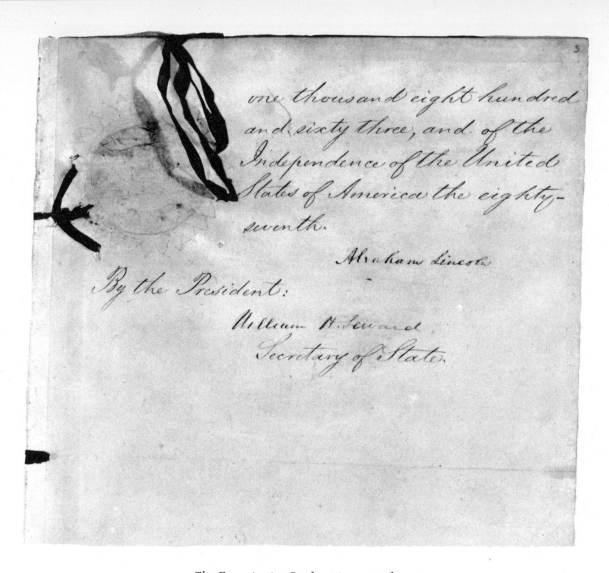

The Emancipation Proclamation, second page

no evidence whatever that Lincoln did any writing of the speech while on the train from Washington. Alas for the legend of the back of an old torn envelope! A double alas to the legend that it was written on the train with a pencil borrowed from Andrew Carnegie! It is perfectly clear what happened on the train during its slow journey. Lincoln conversed with his companions; he read a copy of the *New York Herald* to catch up with current news; and at various stops en route he received proffered gifts of flowers and kissed a number of babies. It is true that toward the end of the journey he excused himself from his companions with a remark to the effect that he had a brief speech to make on the morrow and perhaps he ought to give it a little thought. It is probable that he was merely tired and used this pretext to get a little rest from the bustling conversation of the official party.

Upon reaching Gettysburg that evening he was escorted to the home of his host, David Wills, the chairman of the committee on ceremonies. The evening was so busy that he could have had little, if any, time to work on his brief manuscript. It was on the morning of the day of dedication that Lincoln probably revised his first draft. Certainly it was during this morning in the Wills house that the President wrote his second draft and it is this second draft which Lincoln held in his hand while making the Address. This "reading copy," the manuscript exhibited on the Freedom Train, is lent by the Library of Congress, to which the three children of John Hay, his secretary, presented it in 1916.

As Lincoln delivered his speech he did not read exactly what he had written into the manuscript. From the stenographic reports it would seem that he omitted the word "poor" in the phrase "our poor power to detract" and, on the inspiration of the moment, he added the

Four score and seven years ago our fathers
brought forth, upon this continent, a new nation, conceived in Liberty, and dedicated to the proposition
that all men are created equal.

Now we are engaged in a great civil war, test-
ing whether that nation, or any nation, so conceived,
and so dedicated, can long endure. We are met
here on a great battle-field of that war. We have
come to dedicate a portion of it as a final rest-
ing place for those who here gave their lives that
that nation might live. It is altogether fitting
and proper that we should do this.

But in a larger sense we can not dedicate—
we can not consecrate— we can not hallow this
ground. The brave men, living and dead, who struggled here, have consecrated it far above our poor power
to add or detract. The world will little note,
nor long remember, what we say here, but
can never forget what they did here. It is
for us, the living, rather to be dedicated
here to the unfinished work which they have,
thus far, so nobly carried on. It is rather

Lincoln's Own Manuscript of the Gettysburg Address, second page

solemn phrase "under God" to make the final words read "that this nation, under God, shall have a new birth of freedom—and that government of the people, by the people, for the people, shall not perish from the earth."

52. Henry Laurens of South Carolina Denounces the Institution of Slavery (1776)

HENRY LAURENS was one of the great merchants and planters of South Carolina. After leading many early colonial protests against British tyranny he became one of the conspicuous statesmen of the American Revolution. He succeeded John Hancock as the president of the Continental Congress. His career might have ended in a great blaze of glory had he himself not ended up in the Tower of London as a prisoner of war. It was shortly after he had embarked upon an important mission to secure financial aid from Holland that the British intercepted his ship and seized him. While a prisoner in London he was denied all diplomatic privileges and was otherwise roughly treated. He was finally released in exchange for Lord Cornwallis (see document No. 20).

This original letter was written to his son John only a few weeks after the adoption of the Declaration of Independence. It breathes the defiant spirit of liberty and it especially attacks the institution of slavery as an abhorrent denial of freedom. Laurens laments the destruction of current crops—"no small sacrifice at the shrine of liberty, and yet very small compared with that I am willing to make; not only crops, but land, life and all must follow in preference to sacrificing liberty to mammon." Then he discusses the institution of human slavery: "You know, my dear son, I abhor slavery. I was born in a country where slavery had been established by British kings and parliaments as well as by the laws of that country ages before my existence . . . I nevertheless disliked it." He declares that he is "not one of those who dare trust in Providence for defense and security of their own liberty while they enslave and wish to continue in slavery thousands who are as well entitled to freedom as themselves . . . the day I hope is approaching when, from principles of gratitude as well as justice, every man

[78]

will strive to be foremost in showing his readiness to comply with the golden rule." He describes his plan to manumit his own slaves, who represent a property value of £20,000 sterling. He is conscious of the fact that he "shall appear to many as a promoter not only of strange, but of dangerous doctrines," yet "I will do as much as I can in my time, and leave the rest to a better hand."

The original manuscript letter displayed in the Freedom Train exhibit is from the collections of Mr. Frederic R. Kirkland. It was once purchased by a political club in Boston for presentation to President Lincoln. While it was being especially bound, Lincoln was assassinated and the presentation was never made.

53. General Robert E. Lee Accepts the Presidency of Washington College (1865)

MANY American personages from out of the past require a note of identification and a splash of background to gain even a small measure of recognition from the modern reader. Robert E. Lee needs none. His fame is established and secure against the corrosion of ignorance, and apathy and of time itself. General Lee's words, like his actions, have a distinctive and a particular eloquence which needs neither annotation nor interpretation.

The present original manuscript letter, lent to the Freedom Train exhibit by Washington and Lee University, is the one in which the General accepts the presidency of Washington College (it was not until after his death in 1870 that the name was changed to Washington and Lee).

At the close of the war the tiny college found itself in a state of physical dilapidation and financial distress. This gave it no unique position, for many sections of the South lay in the ruins of war. There was an urgent need for courageous rebuilding . . . a need for leadership in taking up the new and heavy tasks of peace. But many in the South were full weary, and impoverished and embittered.

Lee himself was in financial trouble when he received the offer from the committee of the college. He had turned down several tempting business offers which would have given him financial independence, for they did not seem to present the opportunity he was seeking.

In accepting the college presidency Lee the warrior became Lee the conciliator. For this he was pre-eminently qualified, for no American has ever enjoyed greater moral prestige south of the Mason-Dixon line than Robert E. Lee. And during the remaining few years of his life Lee labored to spread his message: "All should unite in honest efforts to obliterate the effects of war, and to restore the blessings of peace." He had accepted the presidency of Washington College because, as he explained to the members of the committee in the letter now exhibited, "I think it the duty of every citizen in the present condition of the country, to do all in his power to aid in the restoration of peace and harmony."

54. President Lincoln Declares that America Much Needs "A Good Definition of the Word Liberty" (1864)

LINCOLN's speech, popularly known as "The Baltimore Address," was made at the Sanitary Fair held in Baltimore on April 18, 1864. These fairs raised funds for the support of the work of the United States Sanitary Commission, a war relief organization which had first been organized in June 1861. The work of the Commission had been so eminently successful that the President, no matter what the pressure of his war duties, could not decline the invitation to speak. But, between the time of his acceptance and the delivery of his address, the entire North had been profoundly shocked by an event at Fort Pillow, Tennessee. As the war had drawn out its weary course, Negro soldiers had been incorporated in the Union Army. Some of these Negro troops had been a part of the garrison at Fort Pillow when it was overrun by Confederate forces under the command of General Forrest. For some weeks preceding the capture of the fort General Forrest had delivered himself of much loose and inflammatory talk of what would happen when his forces seized any Negroes in the uniform of the Union Army. He declared bluntly that they would not be treated as prisoners of war, but as simple property. When the small garrison at Fort Pillow was overwhelmed by superior forces Forrest's men, as well as many of his officers, proceeded to murder the prisoners in cold blood. It was a simple mass murder arising out of race hatred. With the news of the "Fort Pillow Massacre" Northern tempers flared and demanded retaliation. The more hotheaded demanded the execution of Southern prisoners and the extirpation of the ruling classes of the South as a measure of revenge. When Lincoln spoke at Baltimore the facts had not yet been completely ascertained. He advised caution and moderation. Several weeks later Lincoln asked the members of his Cabinet their opinions on the proper course of action, for the facts demonstrated that the rumors had been unusually correct. Before any action was taken, however, the roaring crescendo of Northern military operations dimmed the memory and the significance of the tragic affair at Fort Pillow.

In the portion of his speech evidently written before receipt of the first news from Fort Pillow Lincoln discusses the difficulty of defining the word "liberty." It is

Powhatan Co: 24 Aug '65

Gentlemen

I have delayed for some days, reply-
ing to your letter of the 5 Inst: informing me of my
election by the Board of Trustees, to the Presidency of
Washington College, from a desire to give the subject
due consideration. Fully impressed with the
responsibilities of the office, I have feared that I
should be unable to discharge its duties, to the satisfaction of the Trustees, or to the benefit of the Country.
The proper education of youth requires not only
great ability, but I fear more strength than I now
possess, for I do not feel able to undergo the labour
of conducting classes in regular courses of instruction.
I could not therefore undertake more than the
general administration & supervision of the Institution. There is another subject which has caused
me serious reflection, & is I think worthy of the consideration of the Board. Being excluded from
the terms of amnesty in the proclamation of the
President of the U.S. of the 29th May last, & an object
of censure to a portion of the Country, I have thought
it probable that my occupation of the position of
President, might draw upon the College a feeling
of hostility; & I should therefore cause injury to an
Institution, which it would be my highest desire
to advance. I think it the duty of every citizen

Robert E. Lee's Acceptance of the Presidency of Washington College (See No. 53) in the present condition of the Country, to do all in his power to aid in the restoration of peace & harmony, & in no way to oppose the policy of the State or Genl Governments, directed to that object. It is particularly incumbent on those charged with the instruction of the young, to set them an example of submission to authority, & I could not consent to be the cause of animadversion upon the College—

Should you however take a different view, & think that my services in the position tendered me by the Board will be advantageous to the College & Country, I will yield to your judgment & accept it. Otherwise I must most respectfully decline the office.

Begging you to express to the trustees of the College my heartfelt gratitude for the honor conferred upon me, & requesting you to accept my cordial thanks for the kind manner in which you have communicated its decision,

I am Gentn with great respect
your most Obt Sevt
R E Lee

Messrs John W. Brockenbrough Rector
S McD Reid, Alfred Leyburn
Horatio Thompson D.D. Bolivar Christian   } Committee
J. J. Kirkpatrick

a problem that remains with us. If Lincoln's sentiments were tomorrow repeated in the Assembly of the United Nations they would lose none of their poignant relevance.

The original manuscript of the Baltimore Address, entirely in Lincoln's handwriting, is lent to the Freedom Train exhibit by Dr. A. S. W. Rosenbach.

Ladies and Gentlemen—Calling to mind that we are in Baltimore, we can not fail to note that the world moves. Looking upon these many people, assembled here, to serve, as they best may, the soldiers of the Union, it occurs at once that three years ago, the same soldiers could not so much as pass through Baltimore. The change from then till now, is both great and gratifying. Blessings on the brave men who have wrought the change and the fair women who strive to reward them.

But Baltimore suggests more than could happen within Baltimore. The change within Baltimore is part only of a far wider change. When the war began, three years ago, neither party, nor any man, expected it would last till now. Each looked for the end, in some way, long ere to-day. Neither did any anticipate that domestic slavery would be much affected by the war. But here we are; the war has not ended, and slavery has been much affected—how much needs not now to be recounted. So true is it that man proposes, and God disposes.

But we can see the past, though we may not claim to have directed it; and seeing it, in this case, we feel more hopeful and confident for the future.

The world has never had a good definition of the word liberty, and the American people, just now, are much in want of one. We all declare for liberty, but in using the same *word* we do not all mean the same *thing*. With some the word liberty may mean for each man to do as he pleases with himself, and the product of his labor; while with others the same word may mean for some men to do as they please with other men, and the product of other men's labor. Here are two, not only different, but incompatable things, called by the same name— liberty. And it follows that each of the things is, by the respective parties, called by two different and incompatable names—liberty and tyranny.

The shepherd drives the wolf from the sheep's throat, for which the sheep thanks the shepherd as a *liberator,* while the wolf denounces him for the same act as the destroyer of liberty, especially as the sheep was a black one. Plainly the sheep and the wolf are not agreed upon a definition of the word liberty, and precisely the same difference prevails to-day among us human creatures, even in the North, and all professing to love liberty. Hence we behold the processes by which thousands are daily passing from under the yoke of bondage, hailed by some as the advance of liberty, and bewailed by others as the destruction of all liberty. Recently, as it seems, the people of Maryland have been doing something to define liberty; and thanks to them that, in what they have done, the wolf's dictionary has been repudiated.

It is not very becoming for one in my position to make speeches at great length; but there is another subject upon which I feel that I ought to say a word. A painful rumor, true I fear, has reached us of the massacre, by the rebel forces, at Fort Pillow, in the West end of Tennessee, on the Mississippi River, of some three hundred colored soldiers and white officers, who had just been overpowered by their assailants. There seems to be some anxiety in the public mind whether the government is doing its duty to the colored soldier, and to the service, at this point. At the beginning of the war, and for some time, the use of colored troops was not contemplated; and how the change of purpose was wrought, I will not now take time to explain. Upon a clear conviction of duty I resolved to turn that element of strength to account; and I am responsible for it to the American people, to the Christian world, to history, and on my final account to God. Having determined to use the negro as a soldier, there is no way but to give him all the protection given to any other soldier. The difficulty is not in stating the principle, but in practically applying it. It is a mistake to suppose the government is indifferent to this matter, or is not doing the best it can in regard to it. We do not to-day *know* that a colored soldier or white officer commanding colored soldiers, has been massacred by the rebels when made a prisoner. We fear it, believe it, I may say, but we do not *know* it. To take the life of one of their prisoners, on the assumption that they murder ours, when it is short of certainty that they do murder ours, might be too serious, too cruel a mistake. We are having the Fort Pillow affair thoroughly investigated; and such investigations will probably show conclusively how the truth is—If, after all that has been said, it shall turn out that there has been no massacre at Fort Pillow, it will be almost safe to say there has been none, and will be none elsewhere. If there has been the massacre of three hundred there, or even the tenth part of three hundred, it will be conclusively proved; and being so proved, the retribution shall as surely come. It will be matter of grave consideration in what exact course to apply the retribution, but in the supposed case, it must come.

55. Susan B. Anthony and Elizabeth Cady Stanton Petition Congress for Women's Right to Vote

THE Nineteenth Amendment to the Constitution for the enfranchisement of women was the result of the unceasing efforts of many American women over a period of more than seven decades. Two of the outstanding and earliest leaders in this struggle for woman suffrage, neither of whom lived to see the Nineteenth Amendment enacted, were Elizabeth Cady Stanton and Susan B. Anthony.

The first real beginning of the movement for woman suffrage occurred in 1848 at the first convention for woman's rights held at Seneca Falls, New York. It was upon the insistence of Elizabeth Cady Stanton, wife of a noted anti-slavery leader, that the convention adopted a resolution calling for woman suffrage.

In 1851 she met Susan B. Anthony and from that time on the two women worked together in the crusade for woman's rights for more than 50 years. Miss Anthony, a school teacher who had given up her profession in order to fight social injustice, had become convinced that only through equal rights could women become effective workers for social betterment.

The two women were instrumental in organizing the National Woman Suffrage Association in 1869, whose objective was declared by resolution to be the securing of the vote for women by a 16th Amendment to the Constitution. Mrs. Stanton was made president and Miss Anthony chairman of the executive committee. The petition here exhibited was sent by this organization in 1873 to the Forty-Second Congress asking them respectfully "to enact appropriate legislation to protect women citizens in the several States of the Union in their right to vote." On the back of this petition, which was written on the stationery of the Association, is printed the Association's constitution and a list of the officers, including 40 vice-presidents.

In 1890 the two leading woman suffrage societies were merged to form the National American Woman Suffrage Association. Mrs. Stanton was elected its first president and served until 1892 when Miss Anthony succeeded her as president for the next eight years. Mrs. Stanton and Miss Anthony remained active in the movement until their deaths shortly after the turn of the century.

The exhibited original document is from the collections of the National Archives. The text:

To the Honorable Senate and House of Representatives in Congress assembled.

We the undersigned citizens of the United States, but deprived of some of the privileges and immunities of citizens, among which is the right to vote, beg leave to submit the following Resolution:—

Resolved: That we, the officers and members of the National Woman Suffrage Association, in Convention assembled; Respectfully ask Congress to enact appropriate legislation during its present session to protect women citizens in the several States of this Union, in their right to vote.

> Susan B. Anthony Pres.
> Matilda Joslyn Gage Ch. Ex. Com.
> Elizabeth Cady Stanton

56. Matilda Hindman Petitions Congress against Depriving the Women of Utah of the Right to Vote (1874)

LITTLE progress had been made in the advancement of the cause for woman suffrage in the United States from the beginning of the movement in the middle of the nineteenth century until 1869 when Wyoming, organized as a territory, gave women the right to vote. In 1870 the territorial legislature of Utah also granted suffrage to women.

In December 1873, Senator Frederick Frelinghuysen of New Jersey introduced a bill in the Senate which related to the laws of the territory of Utah. One provision of this bill would have disfranchised the women voters of Utah.

Perturbed by the proposed measure, Matilda Hindman, a suffragette from Pennsylvania, sent a petition to Congress pleading that the bill be rejected because "if it becomes law it will do great injury to a large number of the citizens of that Territory."

Utah was admitted to the Union on January 4, 1896, with a provision for woman suffrage in its constitution, the third state to take such a step.

This original signed petition is lent to the Freedom Train by the National Archives.

To the Senate and House of
Representatives in Congress
Assembled

Senator Frelinghuysen on the 3d of December 1873 presented to the Senate of the United States,

A Bill to aid in the execution of the laws of the Territory of Utah, and for other purposes; which was read twice and order to be printed and,

Whereas; there are certain sections in that Bill which if it becomes a law will do great injury to a large number of the citizens of that Territory.

First; In that it will disfranchise the women who are now voters,

Second; It will prevent women from serving on either petit or grand juries,

Third; It will subject them to fine and imprisonment if they attempt to vote,

Fourth; It will prohibit the Legislature of the Territory from ever passing a law to
restore these rights.

See Sections 5, 6, 7, 19, 22 and 24 of said Bill; and,

Whereas, Senator Logan on the 4th day of December 1873 also presented to the Senate of the United States A Bill with the above named provisions, and containing another section which reads as follows: Sec. 23. That the common law of England, as it existed in the colonies at the date of the Declaration of Independence, is, hereby extended over and declared to be in force in the Territory of Utah, so far as the same is practicable and

Whereas, These Sections seem unjust and oppressive, your petitioner in behalf of women, and by authority of the Woman Suffrage Association of the State of Pennsylvania, would respectfully pray your Honorable bodies not to pass a law containing the above named section, nor any law whatever, by which the women of Utah will be disfranchised, or in any way deprived of their civil and political rights. We pray you, for the following reasons, to grant our petition.

First. Because the disfranchising of these women will render them wholly subject to the power of the men who are voters in that Territory, as they will be compelled to obey laws which they had no voice in making and which they will have no power of repealing, however unjust, cruel or oppressive they may be, and thus will many of these women become more hopelessly subject to the corrupt influences existing in that Territory.

Second. A law that disfranchises any class of citizens, except for high crimes and misdemeanors, is cruel and tyrannical in its nature; and no such law can be enacted by a truly Democratic government.

Third. Such a law would force one half of the people of Utah to be governed without their consent; would compel them to pay tax without representation; and deprive them of a trial by a jury of their peers; all of which are direct violations of the fundamental principles of our government.

Fourth. As the United States Government has never disfranchised any of its citizens except great criminals, such a law as this would place these women, who are charged with no crime, in the category of felons and traitors.

Fifth. If the common law of England is extended over, and declared to be in force in the Territory of Utah, married women will be entirely subject to the will of their husbands, and the *legitimate* mother rendered powerless; as the common law declares, "the very being and existence of the wife is suspended during marriage;" "And the mother as such has no power."

It gives the husband complete control over the wife.

Gives him a right to the custody of her person, to her strict obedience, to her time, property, services and children.

This law subjects woman to the most cruel proscriptions; as "it regards marriage as a relation between servant and master, a relation of servitude on the part of the wife and supremacy on the part of the husband."

Matilda Hindman
Agent of the Pennsylvania Woman
Suffrage Association

57. The Nineteenth Amendment Enfranchises the Women of the United States

"The right of citizens of the United States to vote shall not be denied or abridged by the United States or by any State on account of sex."

BY the Nineteenth Amendment to the Constitution, American women were granted the right to vote and thus was brought to a successful conclusion a struggle of more than seventy years to achieve woman suffrage.

Although a few courageous American women had earlier raised their voices in favor of woman suffrage, it was not until 1848 that it attracted any wide public attention and support. In that year at the first convention for women's rights, held at Seneca Falls, New York, a resolution was adopted declaring that "it is the duty of the women of this country to secure to themselves the sacred right to the elective franchise." This was done at the vigorous insistence of Elizabeth Cady Stanton.

Recognizing the need of forming well-integrated organizations if they were to make any progress, the leading women suffragists in 1869 formed two groups to carry on the campaign: the National Woman Suffrage Association headed by Elizabeth Cady Stanton and Susan B. Anthony and the American Woman Suffrage Association led by Lucy Stone. In 1890 both united to form the National American Suffrage Association.

The leaders of the movement were soon convinced that they could not expect any action by Congress until the experiment of woman suffrage had been made by some of the States and pressure upon Congress could be exerted. They directed their efforts, therefore, along the lines of national and state action. By the time Congress had approved the Nineteenth Amendment in 1919, full woman suffrage had already been granted in fifteen states. Twenty other states had granted a limited suffrage to women.

In 1878, a proposed amendment for woman suffrage, written by Susan B. Anthony, was introduced in the Senate, but was reported unfavorably in committee. This same amendment was proposed without success in every Congress from 1878 until 1919, when it was finally approved and sent to the States for ratification.

Many objections were raised to the woman suffrage amendment in Congressional debate. Some Congressmen claimed that the amendment would violate states' rights while others feared that such suffrage would interfere with the traditional duties of women in the home.

President Woodrow Wilson, who had formerly favored state action on the matter, in 1918 sent a message to Congress urging the adoption of the amendment. The House promptly agreed but the Senate failed to act before adjournment. In May 1919 the House again acted favorably and on June 5, 1919, the Senate also approved it. The wording of the adopted amendment was exactly the same as that written by Susan B. Anthony in 1878.

With this prospect of ultimate success women suffragists now concentrated their efforts on obtaining speedy ratification. The National American Woman Suffrage Association, under the leadership of Mrs. Carrie Chapman Catt and Miss Alice Paul, put into action a well-organized plan for securing approval by the States. Wisconsin ratified it on June 10, 1919. By May 22, 1920, thirty-five states had ratified—one short of the number necessary to make the amendment effective. Finally, on August 18, 1920, Tennessee became the thirty-sixth state to ratify and on August 26, 1920, the Secretary of State proclaimed the Nineteenth Amendment a part of the Constitution.

The Nineteenth Amendment is represented in the exhibit by the original engrossed joint resolution of Congress proposing the amendment from the collections of the National Archives. This resolution is bound in a volume containing several other engrossed copies of laws passed by Congress.

58. Congress Establishes a New Landmark of Freedom in the Northwest Ordinance (1787)

ONE of the pressing problems facing the new government established under the Articles of Confederation in March 1781 was the development of a policy for the administration and settlement of the extensive lands northwest of the Ohio River. Numerous settlements had already been made there. Deep in the interior lay the French villages that George Rogers Clark had conquered during the Revolution. Together with Detroit and other fur-trading centers acquired by the Treaty of Paris in 1783, there was a scattered population of several thousands.

Massachusetts, Connecticut, Virginia, and New York held claims to lands in the northwest under their ancient charters from the English Crown. When the Articles of Confederation were drawn up in 1777, Maryland refused to agree to them unless these other states ceded their various territorial claims to the Congress. Since the Articles of Confederation required approval by each of the thirteen states before it became operative, Maryland possessed considerable bargaining power.

To break the impasse that threatened the Confederation, New York consented to cede her claims; and Congress offered to reimburse any state for expenses incurred in defending the northwest. Connecticut also offered to give over all her claim with the exception of some territory around Lake Erie, which became known as the "Western Reserve." Maryland, satisfied that her terms would be complied with, signed the Articles of Confederation on March 1, 1781. New York, Virginia, Massachusetts, and Connecticut ceded to the Congress of the Confederation their respective rights and that body then began to concern itself with the administration of the vast territory.

A few days after Virginia's cession of her claims was received by Congress, in 1784, Thomas Jefferson drafted an ordinance for the government of the territory. He set forth the momentous principle that the territories to be organized from the western lands should ultimately be admitted into the Union as states enjoying all the rights and privileges of the older ones and that slavery should be prohibited in the territories after 1800. Jefferson's proposal had not received the approval of Congress before he left for his post as Minister to France.

Large-scale colonization of the northwest first required the establishment of law and order. A group of New Englanders, many of them Revolutionary War veterans, organized the Ohio Company of Associates in Boston in 1786 to buy and settle large tracts of land in the northwest. Spokesmen for the company, led by the Reverend Manasseh Cutler, put pressure on Congress for a cession of land and the creation of an efficient territorial government.

On July 11, 1787, a committee including Edward Carrington, Nathan Dane, and R. H. Lee reported "An Ordinance for the government of the Territory of the United States northwest of the river Ohio." The third reading of the ordinance occurred on July 13, 1787, and passed with but one dissenting vote. (The distinction between an ordinance and a statute or act was not very clearly drawn. Both had the force of law but certain acts of the Congress of the Confederation were called ordinances.) One of the first actions of the Congress assembled under the new Constitution was to re-enact the Ordinance of 1787, so that it would continue to be operative under the new constitutional organization. This was approved by President Washington on August 7, 1789.

The Ordinance of 1787 provided for a temporary government by a governor, a secretary, and judges with full authority to make laws and enforce them. Looking to the future, the ordinance provided that when there were 5,000 free males in the territory a representative legislature was to be established, and upon the attainment of 60,000 population the territory would be admitted to the Union on an equal footing with the original states "in all respects whatever." It declared that this compact between the people in the original states and the people in the territory was "unalterable, unless by common consent."

This compact, outlined in six articles, included the rights of religious freedom, of habeas corpus, of trial by jury, and of proportional representation in the legislature, and it abolished slavery or involuntary servitude.

On the subject of education, the ordinance states: "Religion, morality, and knowledge being necessary to good government and the happiness of mankind, schools and the means of education shall forever be encouraged." This was written before the Bill of Rights was even enacted and it shows the continuing vigilance of the legislators for the principles of liberty for a free and enlightened people.

The first legal American settlement was established at Marietta, on April 7, 1788, by the Ohio Company. On March 1, 1803, the State of Ohio was received into the Union, "Provided the same shall be republican, and not repugnant to the Ordinance of 1787." President Jefferson, who had written the first draft of the Ordinance of 1784, signed the act by which Ohio was admitted. Other states formed in whole or in part from the Northwest Territory and admitted later into the Union were: Indiana (1816), Illinois (1818), Michigan (1837), and Wisconsin (1848). When they entered the Union, the ordinance was no longer binding upon them; however, in acts authorizing their admission, a proviso similar to Ohio's was included, or the State Constitution used phraseology similar to that of the ordinance.

The Northwest Ordinance of 1787 as the first organic act prepared by the new government of the United States for any of its territories ranks with the Constitution and the Bill of Rights as an expression of the political philosophy of the new nation. Daniel Webster doubted whether "one single law of any lawgiver, ancient or modern, has produced effects of more distinct, marked, and lasting character than the Ordinance of 1787." It established the pattern for America's administration of public lands and, as the United States pushed its frontiers to the Pacific, it provided the frame of reference and precedent for future action regarding continental territories.

The printed official copy of the Northwest Ordinance of 1787 displayed on the Freedom Train is from records of the Northwest Territory among general records of the Department of State now in the custody of the National Archives. The signature at the conclusion of the two printed pages is that of Charles Thomson, who was secretary of the Continental Congress during its entire history from 1774 to 1789.

59. President McKinley Insists That the Filipinos be Given the Basic Civil Liberties of American Citizens (1900)

WITH the end of the War with Spain in 1898, the American possession of the Philippine Islands by right of conquest was reinforced by the payment of $20,000,000 to Spain. The task of governing the islands, beginning with the military occupation of Manila in August of that year, has been marked by American efforts to resolve the basic conflict between the democratic spirit of the American Constitution and the responsibilities of a world power burdened with insular possessions.

The question has been aptly phrased: "Does the Constitution follow the flag?"

While the course of American policy toward the Philippines has not been uniformly smooth and beyond criticism, it has generally been based on the conviction that American principles of government and individual freedom could and should be extended to the Islands. Even before the final ratification of the treaty of peace with Spain, President McKinley appointed a temporary commission to investigate conditions in the Philippines. This commission concluded that, because of the Filipinos' lack of education and political experience and their racial and linguistic diversities, they were not yet prepared to discharge the responsibilities of self-government. Consequently, the President decided to appoint a new commission with a definite authority that would become a permanent part of the Philippine administration.

The exhibit on the Freedom Train represents two pages of the original signed instructions of President McKinley to William H. Taft, whom he had appointed President of the Philippine Commission. Prepared by Secretary of State Elihu Root for the President's signature, the instructions outline the basic procedure the Commission was to follow in setting up the beginnings of self-government. The instructions clearly point out the democratic philosophy by which the Commission should guide itself.

The Commission was to devote its attention first "to the establishment of municipal governments, in which the natives of the islands . . . shall be afforded the opportunity to manage their own local affairs to the fullest extent to which they are capable." And when competent natives could be found for administration duties, they were "to receive the offices in preference to any others."

The Commission was directed to "bear in mind that the government they are establishing is designed, not for our satisfaction or for the expression of our theoretical views, but for the happiness, peace, and prosperity of the people of the Philippine Island. . . ."

Expanded and applied as fully as circumstances have permitted, the philosophy of McKinley's early instructions to the Philippine Commission has ultimately made possible the full realization of the goal of self-government within a democratic framework.

The independence of the Philippines was proclaimed by President Harry S. Truman on July 4, 1946 (see item number 60).

The Secretary of War,   April 7, 1900.
    Washington, D. C.

Sir:

In the message transmitted to the Congress on the 5th of December, 1899, I said, speaking of the Philippine Islands: "As long as the insurrection continues the military arm must necessarily be supreme. But there is no reason why steps should not be taken from time to time to inaugurate governments essentially popular in their form as fast as territory is held and controlled by our troops. To this end I am considering the advisability of the return of the Commission, or such of the members thereof as can be secured, to aid the existing authorities and facilitate this work throughout the islands."

To give effect to the intention thus expressed, I have appointed Hon. William H. Taft, of Ohio, Professor Dean C. Worcester, of Michigan, Hon. Luke I. Wright, of Tennessee, Hon. Henry C. Ide, of Vermont, and Professor Bernard Moses, of California, Commissioners to the Philippine Islands to continue and perfect the work of organizing and establishing civil government already commenced by the military authorities, subject in all respects to any laws which Congress may hereafter enact. The Commissioners named will meet and act as a board, and the Hon. William H. Taft is designated as President of the board. It is probable that the transfer of authority from military commanders to civil officers will be gradual, and will occupy a considerable period. Its successful accomplishment, and the maintenance of peace and order in the meantime, will require the most perfect cooperation between the civil and military authorities in the island, and both should be directed, during the transition period, by the same executive department. The Commission will therefore report to the Secretary of War, and all their action will be subject to your approval and control.

You will instruct the Commission to proceed to the city of Manila, where they will make their principal office, and to communicate with the Military Governor of the Philippine Islands, whom you will at the same time direct to render to them every assistance within his power in the performance of their duties. Without hampering them by too specific instructions, they should in general be enjoined, after making themselves familiar with the conditions and needs of the country, to devote their attention in the first instance to the establishment of municipal governments in which the natives of the islands, both in the cities and in the rural communities, shall be afforded the opportunity to manage their own local affairs to the fullest extent of which they are capable, and subject to the least degree of supervision and control which a careful study of their capacities and observation of the workings of native control show to be consistent with the maintenance of law, order and loyalty. The next subject in order of importance should be the organization of government in the larger administrative divisions corresponding to counties, departments or provinces, in which the common interests of many or several municipalities falling within the same tribal lines, or the same natural geographical limits, may best be subserved by a common administration. Whenever the Commission is of the opinion that the condition of affairs in the islands is such that the central administration may safely be transferred from military to civil control, they will report that conclusion to you, with their recommendations as to the form of central government to be established for the purpose of taking over the control.

Beginning with the 1st day of September, 1900, the authority to exercise, subject to my approval, through the Secretary of War, that part of the power of government in the Philippine Islands, which is of a legislative nature, is to be transferred from the Military Governor of the islands to this Commission, to be thereafter exercised by them in the place and stead of the Military Governor, under such rules and regulations as you shall prescribe, until the establishment of the civil central government for the islands contemplated in the last foregoing paragraph, or until Congress shall otherwise provide. Exercise of this legislative authority will include the making of rules and orders, having the effect of law, for the raising of revenue by taxes, customs duties and imposts; the appropriation and expenditure of public funds of the islands; the establishment of an educational system throughout the islands; the establishment of a system to secure an efficient civil service; the organization and establishment of courts; the organization and establishment of municipal and departmental governments, and all other matters of a civil nature for which the Military Governor is now competent to provide by rules or orders of a legislative character.

The Commission will also have power, during the same period, to appoint to office such officers under the judicial, educational and civil service systems, and in the municipal and departmental governments, as shall be provided for. Until the complete transfer of control the Military Governor will remain the chief executive head of the government of the islands, and will exercise the executive authority now possessed by him and not herein expressly assigned to the Commission, subject, however, to the rules and orders enacted by the Commission in the exercise of the legislative powers conferred upon them. In the meantime, the municipal and departmental governments will continue to report to the Military Governor, and be subject to his administrative supervision and control, under your direction; but that supervision and control will be confined within the narrowest limits consistent with the requirement, that the powers of government in the municipalities and departments shall be honestly and effectively exercised, and that law and order and individual freedom shall be maintained.

All legislative rules and orders, establishments of government and appointments to office by the Commission will take effect immediately, or at such times as they shall designate, subject to your approval and action upon the coming-in of the Commission's reports, which are to be made from time to time as their action is taken. Wherever civil governments are constituted under the direction of the Commission, such military posts, garrisons and forces will be continued for the suppression of insurrection and brigandage, and the maintenance of law and order, as the Military Commander shall deem requisite, and the military forces shall be at all times subject under his orders to the call of the civil authorities for the maintenance of law and order and the enforcement of their authority. In the establishment of municipal governments the commission will take as the basis of their work the governments established by the Military Governor under his order of August 8, 1899, and under the report of the board constituted by the Military Governor by his order of January 29, 1900, to formulate and report a plan of municipal government, of which His Honor, Cayetano Arellano, President of the Audiencia, was Chairman, and they will give to the conclusions of that board the weight and consideration which the high character and distinguished abilities of its members justify. In the constitution of departmental or provincial governments, they will give especial attention to the existing government of the Island of Negros, constituted, with the approval of the people of that island, under the order of the Military Governor of July 22, 1899, and after verifying, so far as may be practicable, the reports of the successful working of that government, they will be guided by the experience thus acquired, so far as it may be applicable to the conditions existing in other portions of the Philippines. They will avail themselves, to the fullest degree practicable, of the conclusions reached by the previous Commission to the Philippines.

In the distribution of powers among the governments organized by the Commission, the presumption is always to be in favor of the smaller sub-division, so that all the powers which can properly be exercised by the municipal government shall be vested in that government, and all the powers of a more general character which can be exercised by the departmental government shall be vested in that government, and so that in the governmental system, which is the result of the process, the central government of the islands, following the example of the distribution of the powers between the States and the National Government of the United States, shall have no direct administration except of matters of purely general concern, and shall have only such supervision and control over local governments as may be necessary to secure and enforce faithful and efficient administration by local officers.

The many different degrees of civilization and varieties of custom and capacity among the people of the different islands preclude very definite instruction as to the part which the people shall take in the selection of their own officers; but these general rules are to be observed: That in all cases the municipal officers, who administer the local affairs of the people, are to be selected by the people, and that wherever officers of more extended jurisdiction are to be selected in any way, natives of the islands are to be preferred, and if they can be found competent and willing to perform the duties, they are to receive the offices in preference to any others. It will be necessary to fill some offices for the present with Americans, which after a time may well be filled by natives of the islands. As soon as practicable, a system for ascertaining the merit and fitness of candidates for civil office should be put in force. An indispensable qualification for all offices and positions of trust and authority in the islands must be absolute and unconditional loyalty to the United States, and absolute and unhampered authority and power, to remove and punish any officer deviating from that standard, must at all times be retained in the hands of the central authority of the islands.

In all the forms of government and administrative provisions which they are authorized to prescribe, the Commission should bear in mind that the government which they are establishing is designed not for our satisfaction, or for the expression of our theoretical views, but for the happiness, peace and prosperity of the people of the Philippine Islands, and the measures adopted should be made to conform to their customs, their habits, and even their prejudices, to the fullest extent consistent with the accomplishment of the indispensable requisites of just and effective government. At the same time the Commission should bear in mind, and the people of the islands should be made plainly to understand, that there are certain great principles of government which have been made the basis of our governmental system, which we deem essential to the rule of law and the maintenance of individual freedom, and of which they have, unfortunately, been denied the experience possessed by us; that there are also certain practical rules of government which we have found to be essential to the preservation of these great principles of liberty and law; and that these principles and these rules of government must be established and maintained in their islands for the sake of their liberty and happiness, however much they may conflict with the customs or laws of procedure with which they are familiar. It is evident that the most enlightened thought of the Philippine Islands fully appreciates the importance of these principles and rules, and they will inevitably within a short time command universal assent. Upon every division and branch of the government of the Philippines, therefore, must be imposed these inviolable rules:

That no person shall be deprived of life, liberty or

property without due process of law; that private property shall not be taken for public use without just compensation; that in all criminal prosecutions the accused shall enjoy the right to a speedy and public trial; to be informed of the nature and cause of the accusation, to be confronted with the witnesses against him, to have compulsory process for obtaining witnesses in his favor, and to have the assistance of counsel for his defence; that excessive bail shall not be required, nor excessive fines imposed, nor cruel and unusual punishment inflicted; that no person shall be put twice in jeopardy for the same offence, or be compelled in any criminal case to be a witness against himself; that the right to be secure against unreasonable searches and seizures shall not be violated; that neither slavery nor involuntary servitude shall exist except as a punishment for crime; that no bill of attainder, or ex-post-facto law shall be passed; that no law shall be passed abridging the freedom of speech or of the press, or the rights of the people to peaceably assemble and petition the government for a redress of grievances; that no law shall be made respecting an establishment of religion, or prohibiting the free exercise thereof, and that the free exercise and enjoyment of religious profession and worship without discrimination or preference shall forever be allowed.

It will be the duty of the Commission to make a thorough investigation into the titles to the large tracts of land held or claimed by individuals or by religious orders; into the justice of the claims and complaints made against such land-holders by the people of the island, or any part of the people, and to seek by wise and peaceable measures a just settlement of the controversies and redress of the wrongs which have caused strife and bloodshed in the past. In the performance of this duty the Commission is enjoined to see that no injustice is done; to have regard for substantial right and equity, disregarding technicalities so far as substantial right permits, and to observe the following rules: That the provision of the Treaty of Paris, pledging the United States to the protection of all rights of property in the islands, and as well the principle of our own Government, which prohibits the taking of private property without due process of law, shall not be violated; that the welfare of the people of the islands, which should be a paramount consideration, shall be attained consistently with this rule of property right; that if it becomes necessary for the public interest of the people of the island to dispose of claims to property, which the Commission finds to be not lawfully acquired and held, disposition shall be made thereof by due legal procedure, in which there shall be full opportunity for fair and impartial hearing and judgment; that if the same public interests require the extinguishment of property rights lawfully acquired and held, due compensation shall be made out of the public treasury therefor; that no form of religion

and no minister of religion shall be forced upon any community or upon any citizen of the island; that upon the other hand no minister of religion shall be interfered with or molested in following his calling; and that the separation between State and Church shall be real, entire and absolute.

It will be the duty of the Commission to promote and extend, and, as they find occasion, to improve, the system of education already inaugurated by the military authorities. In doing this they should regard as of first importance the extension of a system of primary education which shall be free to all, and which shall tend to fit the people for the duties of citizenship, and for the ordinary avocations of a civilized community. This instruction should be given, in the first instance, in every part of the islands in the language of the people. In view of the great number of languages spoken by the different tribes, it is especially important to the prosperity of the islands that a common medium of communication may be established, and it is obviously desirable that this medium should be the English language. Especial attention should be at once given to affording full opportunity to all the people of the islands to acquire the use of the English language.

It may well be that the main changes which should be made in the system of taxation, and in the body of the laws under which the people are governed, except such changes as have already been made by the Military Government, should be relegated to the Civil Government which is to be established under the auspices of the Commission. It will, however, be the duty of the Commission to inquire diligently as to whether there are any further changes which ought not to be delayed, and, if so, they are authorized to make such changes subject to your approval. In doing so they are to bear in mind that taxes which tend to penalize or repress industry and enterprise are to be avoided, that provisions for taxation should be simple so that they may be understood by the people, that they should affect the fewest practicable subjects of taxation which will serve for the general distribution of the burden. The main body of the laws which regulate the rights and obligations of the people should be maintained with as little interference as possible. Changes made should be mainly in procedure, and in the criminal laws to secure speedy and impartial trials, and at the same time effective administration and respect for individual rights.

In dealing with the uncivilized tribes of the islands, the Commission should adopt the same course followed by Congress in permitting the tribes of our North American Indians to maintain their tribal organization and government, and under which many of those tribes are now living in peace and contentment, surrounded by a civilization to which they are unable or unwilling to conform. Such tribal governments should, however, be subjected to wise and firm regulation; and, without undue or petty interference, constant and active effort should be exercised to prevent barbarous practices and introduce civilized customs.

Upon all officers and employes of the United States, both civil and military, should be impressed a sense of the duty to observe not merely the material but the personal and social rights of the people of the islands, and to treat them with the same courtesy and respect for their personal dignity which the people of the United States are accustomed to require from each other.

The articles of capitulation of the City of Manila on the 13th of August, 1898, concluded with these words:

"This city, its inhabitants, its churches and religious worship, its educational establishments and its private property of all descriptions, are placed under the special safeguard of the faith and honor of the American Army."

I believe that this pledge has been faithfully kept. As high and sacred an obligation rests upon the Government of the United States to give protection for property and life, civil and religious freedom, and wise, firm and unselfish guidance in the paths of peace and prosperity, to all the people of the Philippine Islands. I charge this Commission to labor for the full performance of this obligation, which concerns the honor and conscience of their country, in the firm hope that through their labors all the inhabitants of the Philippine Islands may come to look back with gratitude to the day when God gave victory to American arms at Manila and set their land under the sovereignty and the protection of the people of the United States.

60. President Truman Proclaims the Independence of the Philippines

B Y this proclamation, dated so appropriately on the one hundred and seventieth anniversary of the Declaration of Independence, President Truman withdrew and surrendered "all rights of possession, supervision, jurisdiction, control or sovereignty" then existing and exercised in the Philippine Islands by the United States of America.

Here is an act, without parallel in world history, of a powerful nation freely granting independence to a colonial possession. In taking this step the United States has been impelled, not by the force of a revolution beyond her power to resist, nor by the coercion of a conquering country, but rather by the necessity of remaining true to her destiny as a democratic nation founded on principles of freedom and self-government.

President Truman's proclamation is the fitting climax of a long series of measures designed to prepare the people of the Philippine Islands for the arduous task of governing themselves. After more than thirty years of preliminary guidance by the United States, the framing of a Philippine Constitution and the gradual decrease of American control was provided for by Congress in the Philippine Islands Independence Act of March 24, 1934. The Act directed the President of the United States to proclaim Philippine Independence ten years after the inauguration of the new government set up under the constitution whose framing the act called for.

In spite of the conquest of the Islands by Japan in 1942 and the devastation and confusion wrought by the occupation and bitter fighting of the subsequent liberation, the time-table of independence was maintained. In accordance with the repeated declarations of the United States that full independence would be granted as soon as the people of the Islands were ready to assume that obligation, President Truman, finding that "They have clearly demonstrated their capacity for self-government," formally recognized the independence of the Philippines as a separate and self-governing nation.

The original of this proclamation, signed by President Truman, is lent to the Freedom Train exhibit by the National Archives.

61. President Theodore Roosevelt Reaffirms Our Determination to Withdraw from Cuba (1907)

W HEN Congress in 1898 demanded the withdrawal of Spain from Cuba, it declared that the United States had no intention of controlling or dominating Cuba and that American forces would leave when peace was restored. In spite of the opportunity presented by our victory in the Spanish-American War to annex conquered territory and the opportunities for annexation on subsequent occasions in which we deemed it necessary to intervene in Cuban affairs, the United States had refused to compromise Cuba's basic independence.

This original letter by Theodore Roosevelt, emphasizing to Secretary of War William Howard Taft certain aspects of American policy toward Cuba, was written during a period of American intervention which arose from the refusal of a major political party defeated in an election to participate in the government. After urgent appeals by the President of Cuba for the dispatch of American forces to the island to prevent the forcible overthrow of the government, President Roosevelt sent an investigating mission under Secretary of War Taft in an attempt to resolve the conflict. When the Cuban President resigned and the newly assembled Congress failed to command a quorum, Taft was made provisional governor and 7,500 Marines were landed to act as "a background to give confidence" that law and order would be maintained.

THE WHITE HOUSE

WASHINGTON

Personal.

January 22, 1907.

My dear Mr. Secretary:

In reference to Magoon's two letters of the 13th and
16th, which are returned herewith, I need hardly add to
what I said this morning.   There can be no talk of a
protectorate by us.   Our business is to establish peace
and order on a satisfactory basis, start the new government,
and then leave the Island; the Cuban Government taking
the reins into its own hands; tho of course it might be
advisable for some little time that some of our troops
should stay in the Islands to steady things.   I will not
even consider the plan of a protectorate, or any plan which
would imply our breaking our explicit promise because of
which we were able to prevent a war of devastation last
fall.   The good faith of the United States is a mighty
valuable asset and must not be impaired.

Sincerely yours,

Theodore Roosevelt

Hon. Wm. H. Taft,
    Secretary of War.

Theodore Roosevelt's Letter to Secretary of War Taft Regarding Our Promise to Withdraw from Cuba (See No. 61)

President Roosevelt had intervened with reluctance. In his message to Congress he made it abundantly clear that while the United States had no desire to annex Cuba, it was "absolutely out of the question that the island should continue independent" if the "insurrectionary habit" became confirmed. His solution, however, was to restore civil government and not to substitute American for Cuban rule.

On January 22, 1907, the President declared in this letter to Secretary Taft that "there can be no talk of a protectorate by us." He regarded it to be the American purpose "to establish peace and order on a satisfactory basis, start the government, and then leave the island . . ." A protectorate would break America's explicit promise to the contrary. "The good faith of the United States is a mighty valuable asset and must not be impaired."

This original signed letter is from the records of the Division of Territories and Island Territories now in the custody of the National Archives.

62. The U. S. Proclaims the End of Slavery and Peonage on the Island of Guam

CONTROL of the island of Guam of the Marianas group in the Western Pacific was acquired by the United States as a result of the treaty which ended the Spanish-American War of 1898. By order of President McKinley the administration of the government was entrusted to the United States Navy Department. The natives of Guam were so politically immature that it was not possible to extend to them immediately the rights enjoyed by citizens of the United States. But the ideal and ultimate goal has seldom been obscured. Captain Leary, first governor of Guam, found that a system of peonage which had been a basic practice under Spanish rule, persisted. It was clear that many natives continued to be the victims of a system of exploitation which amounted to virtual slavery. Within several months of assuming his administrative duties as governor Captain Leary issued this printed proclamation, lent to the Freedom Train by the National Archives.

PROCLAMATION!

To the Inhabitants of Guam:

In issuing this decree the Government desires and earnestly invokes Divine blessing and guidance in its official action and in the daily pursuits and occupations of the citizens of Guam.

By the cession of the Isle of Guam to the United States of America, all of the authority, power and responsibilities of sovereignty were transferred to this Government, and in transforming and organizing the new political power the surest and speediest route to success, prosperity and happiness for the inhabitants of this island is by benevolent assimilation to the fundamental principles that constitute the basis of Free American Government.

Honest labor with just compensation, dignified by faithful consideration of the mutual interests and welfare of all persons concerned, should insure prosperity to this community; whereas, the existing labor-degrading system of human bondage and unjust, indefinite servitude or Peonage, permitted during the late Spanish control in this island, is, in fact, a system of Slavery, and as such, is subversive of good government, is an obstacle to progressive civilization, a menace to popular liberty, and a violation of the sacred privileges guaranteed by the Constitution of the United States.

Now, therefore, by virtue of the authority vested in me by his Excellency, the President of the United States, I, Richard P. Leary, Captain, United States Navy, Governor of the Isle of Guam, do hereby announce and publicly proclaim absolute prohibition and total abolition of Human Slavery or Peonage in the Isle of Guam on and after the Twenty-second day of February, A. D. 1900, and all persons are hereby commanded to comply with the requirements of this proclamation.

IN WITNESS WHEREOF, I have hereunto set my hand and have caused the seal of the United States Naval Station, Isle of Guam, to be affixed.

Done at Agana, Isle of Guam, this First day of January, in the year of our Lord, One Thousand Nine Hundred, and of the Independence of the United States of America, the One Hundred and Twenty-fourth.

Richard P. Leary, U.S.N.
Governor

63. Lafayette Finds the Proposed Constitution to be "A Bold, Large and Solid Frame" for the New Government

THIS original manuscript letter, lent by the Lafayette College Library from the Collection of the American Friends of Lafayette, is fully reproduced below. It is a double reminder: that a great leader in the French Revolution remained so intensely interested in the progress of the new American government; and that he received his education in the principles of liberty while he was fighting, as a youthful general in the American army, to achieve something which he did not quite understand. But in America he came to know liberty and most of his future years were spent in trying to transplant it to France.

The letter speaks for itself, but with one note of caution. Lafayette dates it January 1, 1787, when it should really have been dated 1788.

My dear General

I am fortunate in this opportunity to wish you a Happy New Year, and to devote the first moments of this day to the heartfelt pleasure to remind you, my beloved General, of your adoptive son and most affectionate, devoted friend. I beg you will present my best respects to Mrs. Washington. Mde de Lafayette joins in the most tender compliments to you and to her and I hope, my dear General, that you will be so kind as to mention me very affectionately to all the family and friends.

It is needless for me to tell you that I read the new proposed constitution with an unspeackable eagerness and attention. I have admired it, and find it is a bold, large and solid frame for the Confederation. The electionneering principles with respect to the two Houses of Congress are most happily calculated. I am only affraid of two things—1st the want of a Declaration of Rights 2dly the great powers and possible continuance of the President, who may one day or other become a State Holder. Should my observations be well founded, I still am easy on two accounts. The first that a Bill of Rights may be made if wished for by the people before they accept the Constitution, my other comfort is that you cannot refuse being elected President, and that if you think the public vessel can stir without such powers, you will be able to lessen them, or propose measures respecting the permanence, which cannot fail to insure a greater perfection in the Constitution, and a new crop of glory to yourself. But in the name of America, of mankind at large, and your own fame, I beseech you, my dear General, not to deny your acceptance of the office of President for the first years. You only can settle that political machine, and I foresee it will furnish an admirable chapter in your history.

I am returned from the Provincial Assembly of Auvergne wherein I had the happiness to please the people and the misfortune to displease government to a very great degree. The Ministry asked for an encrease of revenue. Our province was among the few who gave nothing, and she expressed herself in a manner which has been taken very much amiss. The internal situation of France is very extraordinary. The dispositions of the people of which I gave you a picture are working themselves into a great degree of fermentation, but not without a mixture of levity and love of ease. The Parliaments are every day passing the boundaries of their Constitution, but are sure to be approuved by the Nation, when, among many unrational things, they have the good policy to call for a General Assembly. Governement see that the power of the crown is declining, and now want to retrieve it by an ill timed and dangerous severity. They have monney enough for this year, so at least they think, for my part, I am heartily wishing for a Constitution, and

a Bill of Rights, and wish it may be effected with as much tranquillity and mutual satisfaction as it is possible.

The Emperor has made a foolish attempt on Belgrade, but cannot fail to take it an other time, and at the entrance of the spring the two imperial courts will oppen a vigourous and no doubt successfull campaign against the Turks. These have been led into a war by Great Britain, and should France take a decisive part, it is more probable she will side with Russia. But this Governement will avoid being committed in the affair, and perhaps will not be the better for it. The King of Prussia is now courting France, and proposes, I think, to withdraw his regiments from Holland. But this is a very insufficient, and probably a very useless reparation.

Enclosed, my dear General, are an Arret of the Council, and a letter to Mr. Jefferson both of which after long negotiations we have had the satisfaction to obtain. I expected it might be finished before my journey to Auvergne, but new difficulties have arose and Mr. Jefferson and myself have but lately ended the business. I am more and more pleased with Mr. Jefferson. His abilities, his virtues, his temper, every thing of him commands respect and attracts affection. He enjoys universal regard, and does the affairs of America to perfection. It is the happiest choice that could be made.

Adieu, my dear General, with filial love and respect I have the honour to be

Your devoted and affectionate friend

Lafayette

64. Kosciuszko, "the George Washington of Poland," Declares His Partiality for the United States and Its Inhabitants (1786)

IN his native Poland and in France Kosciuszko had received an excellent training in military engineering. The outbreak of hostilities in America stirred his imagination. He was poor, but he was eager. He borrowed enough money to bring him to Philadelphia, where he offered his services to the Continental Congress. He was given a commission as colonel on October 18, 1776, and a stipend of 60 dollars a month. He was most active and highly ingenious. The failure of his superior officers to act upon his recommendations was probably the reason for the loss of Ticonderoga. But later, acting upon his advice, we achieved the momentous victory at Saratoga. That victory was a determining factor in persuading France to enter into an alliance with the United States. That alliance proved to be the determining factor in the final victory.

Kosciuszko recommended and drew up the plans for the fortification of West Point. He later served under

General Nathanael Greene in the southern campaigns; during General Greene's masterly retreat before the battalions of Lord Cornwallis in 1781 he was the officer in charge of the difficult problem of transportation.

Of him General Greene said: "Colonel Kosciuszko belonged to the number of my most useful and dearest comrades in arms. I can liken to nothing his zeal in the public service, and in the solution of important problems, nothing could have been more helpful than his judgment, vigilance and diligence. He was fearless of every danger. He never manifested desires or claims for himself, and never let any opportunity pass of calling attention and recommending the merits of others."

Kosciuszko's career after the achievement of American independence became a distinguished chapter in the world-wide struggle for freedom.

The original manuscript letter exhibited on the Freedom Train is from the collections of the Museum of the Polish Roman Catholic Union of America. The text of the letter is reproduced exactly as Kosciuszko wrote it. Although the grammar may be quaint and the spelling somewhat unorthodox there can be no disguising of the animating spirit.

New York 14.th July 1784

My Dear General

The events are uncertain, a Parson amidst the most glaring prospects; may find at Last nothing. but a fantom, or only a Sight Like in Looking glace, which will never be a possesion for injoyement.

Drawing the tickets in the lottery of chance for so many years, I am too well acquainted to depend upon probabilities where even certainties are So often doubtfull.

To put myself upon less precarious footing, I must contaract all possible accidents, that can befal me, and this by over sight am capable of.

I am going to embark tomorrow for france I beg you hoever if Congress should adopt a Peace establishement, you will please to interest yourself in the apointement as a chief Ingenieer with the rank of Brygadier General if it possible, this will be a proviso in case I should be bafled in my expectation at home.

The principle of propriety inculcated in my early age, have so strong hold of my feelings, that, to act against inward Conviction, make me very unhappy indeed.

As I must part, give me Leave to present my Sinsier thanks to you both, for so generous hospitality I experienced in your house, for so much interesting yourself in my favor, and for your friendship for me, your delicat feelings forbids me to express of my Greatitude, and the wishes of my heart—I leave to the strogle of my inward emotion; and the practice, to time; whenever uportunity will presents its self without knowkledge to you.

The seperation must be very sensible to a Person of susceptible mind and more so, when the affection with Esteem Link's to the persons of Merit—

I expect hoever that you will do me the honour to write me, it will be the only satisfaction I may yet enjoy by absence, and sure you will not deny me that.

In your Litters I hope you will not forget of your and your familly's health, in which I am so much interested; as to the information of public nature here, you will be pleased to give me very minutely in account, as by Long staying here I have forme a partiality for this country and for its Inhabitents, and would equally withem where ever I should be feel the Sentyment of good Patriot upon every occasion. fare well my dear General once more fare well —be as happy in my bosom will augur for you, Let me Shook here you by the hand by my delusive Imagination, as you should be present in Person, and Seal our friendship for each other for ever.

Yours,
Thad. Kosciuszko.

Pleas to inclose the Letters for me a Monsiew Monsieur Grand, banquier a Paris. He will send to me where ever I should be.

65. Tom Paine, Ambassador of Freedom to Two Worlds, Writes from Paris of "My Much Loved America" (1790)

LITTLE annotation is required to explain this letter written to the celebrated Dr. Benjamin Rush of Philadelphia by Thomas Paine from Paris, March 16, 1790. Having served as a voice of freedom during the American War for Independence (see items Nos. 14 and 15) he went back to one of his chief interests: the design and construction of iron bridges. To promote this project he went to Europe in 1787 and for the next few years he alternated between England and France. His ingenious, prefabricated bridge provoked wide commendation; it was the most cherished of his several inventions.

The beginnings of the French Revolution immediately commanded his interest and his participation, for he was the self-appointed missionary of the world revolution for freedom. There is a story (of which the details may not be highly authentic, but the spirit is correct) that Dr. Franklin once said: "Where freedom is, there is my country." To this Paine replied: "Where freedom is *not*, there is mine." Paine saw in the French Revolution the promise of a new birth of freedom for France, in spite of the fact that, as he quaintly phrases it, "little inconveniences, the necessary consequence of pulling down and building up, may arise." Few men knew better than Paine the extent to which the American example had influenced the thoughts and the actions of the men who first brought about the revolutionary upheaval in France. But, in the midst of the exhilarating ferment of change, Paine took time to express to his Philadelphia friend that he wished "most anxiously to see my much-loved America—it is the Country from whence all reformations must originally spring."

The present original signed letter, all in the hand-writing of Paine, is lent to the Freedom Train exhibit by the Library of Congress.

Doctr. Benjamin Rush, M. D.
Philadelphia
N. America

Paris March 16th 1790—

My Dear Friend

As I do not expect this letter will come to hand of a considerable time I shall not enter into any details of news or circumstances. My principal intention in writing it is to introduce a friend of mine and yourself, to the corresponding acquaintance of each other. Among the few intimates I have made on this side of the water, I have met with none more congenial than the Gentleman I am writing of, Mr. Christie, and it is by his desire that I undertake this office. As it is probable your future acquaintance, with the Atlantic between you, may continue a long time, I will leave you, in the outset, nothing to guess at that may be convenient to know in any acquaintance of this kind. Mr. Christie's Father is a Banker at Montrose, Scotland,—he Junr. has studied Physic as if he were to practice it, —but his intention is to settle in London in the Banking line. He is passing some at Paris as a man of observation, before he undertakes, Atlas-like, the world on his own shoulders. He has made himself acquainted with as many subjects, and as many literary characters ancient and modern as any one I have met with of his age—and is in confidence with several of our friends Drs. Price, Priestly, and your friend Dr. Purcival of Manchester—by whom he was introduced a few days ago, by letter, to Mrs. Neckar—and I have taken him with me to the Duke de la Rochefoucaut, the Marquis de la Fayette and others of my friends here.—

I leave this place in company with Mr. Rutlege tomorrow for London—I go expressly for the purpose of erecting an Iron Bridge which Mssrs. Walker's Rothesham, Yorkshire, and I have already constructed, and is now ready for putting together. It is an Arch of 110 feet span, and five feet high, from the land line—It is as portable as common Bars of Iron, and can be put up and taken down at pleasure and is in fact rendering Bridges a portable manufacture. Sir Joseph Banks, after paying me some compliments by letter on this novel construction, says—"I expect many similar improvements from your Countrymen, who think with vigour, and are in a great measure free from those shackles of Theory which are imposed on the Minds of our people even before they are capable of exerting their mental faculties to advantage."

With respect to the french Revolution be assured that every thing is going on right—little inconveniences, the necessary consequence of pulling down and building up, may arise, but even those are much less than ought to have been expected. Our friend the Marquis is, like his great Patron and Master, General Washington acting a great Part. I take over with me to London the Key of the Bastile which the Marquis entrusts to my Care as his present to General Washington, and which I shall send by the first American Vessel to N. York. It will be yet some months before the New Constitution will be completed at which time there is to be procession, and I am engaged to return to Paris to carry the American flag.

In England, the Ministerial party oppose every Iota of Reformation—the high Benificed Clergy and Bishops, cry out that the Church is in danger, and all those who are interested in the remains of the feudal System join the Clamour. I see very clearly that the conduct of the British Government, by opposing reformations will detach great Numbers from the Political interest of that Country, and that France thro the influence of principles and the divine right of Man to freedom will have a stronger party in England, than she ever had thro the Jacobite bug-bear of the divine right of Kings in the Stuart line

I see by the papers that you have had a convention to remodel the Constitution. I very soon saw that the Constitutionalists would overthrow the Constitution by rashly using that power which was entrusted to their moderation. The spirit of the Constitution required prudence, and the Actors substituted temper and party in the room of it and thereby subjected the legislation of every year to the caprice of an election day.

I wish most anxiously to see my much-loved America—it is the Country from whence all reformations must originally spring—I despair of seeing an Abolition of the infernal trafic in Negroes—we must push that matter further on your Side the water—I wish that a few well instructed Negroes could be sent among their Brethern in Bondage, for until they are enabled to take their own part nothing will be done.

I hope this summer will terminate all my prospects in Europe—but at any rate I will not exceed the spring vessels of next year. Present me with much affection to all my friend—as I pride myself on having many I particularize none.

I am with many wishes for your happiness and your family & connections.

Your affectionate friend etc.

Thomas Paine.

66. Francisco de Miranda Appeals for the Aid of the United States in the Liberation of South America (1798)

AMERICA has long been an inspiration and a symbol to peoples who seek and cherish freedom. Some have tasted the fruits of liberty by a first-hand examination of the tree on which they flourish; others have glimpsed the vision from afar. Francisco de Miranda, often called "The Father of Freedom in South America," saw it for himself: as a colonel in the Spanish army during the American Revolution and later, in the 1780's, during a lengthy visit to the United States. Here he became imbued with the spirit of freedom; here he first began to formulate plans for the liberation of his native Venezuela from the yoke of Spanish tyranny. From the United States he went to Europe where he became perilously embroiled in the French Revolution. He then began an active campaign (which extended even to Turkey and Russia) to secure military assistance for the revolution to liberate the northern colonies of Spanish South America. In this he counted upon the support of the United States where certain Federalist leaders had encouraged him. Alexander Hamilton was enthusiastic and envisaged himself as the commanding general of any United States army that would participate in the invasion.

The present manuscript is a contemporary signed copy of a letter in French sent by Miranda from London, March 24, 1798, to President John Adams. This document exhibited on the Freedom Train is from the manuscript collections of Rufus King who, as a staunch Federalist and then American ambassador to Great Britain, was greatly interested in Miranda's ambitious project. [This document from the Rufus King Papers was lent to the Freedom Train exhibit by The New-York Historical Society. It is a verified and signed copy of four folio pages. The original cannot be located in the archives of the United States; it is probably in the manuscript collections of the Adams family.]

Mr. President:

In the name of the Spanish-American colonies, I have the honor to send to Your Excellency the attached proposals. They have also been presented to the Ministers of His Britannic Majesty who have received them very favorably, evincing much satisfaction at having to deal in such a matter with the United States of America, and it seems to me that the delay I have experienced (really serious at a time as pressing as this), results precisely from the fact that the English Government seems to be waiting to see whether North America will decide to break definitely with France through her desire to make common cause and to work together for the absolute independence of the whole continent of the new world.

As the spirit of justice, generosity and attachment of my compatriots for the United States is better expressed in the document which gives me authority as well as instructions, I would like to attach a complete copy, in the belief that this friendly and frank act will serve more effectively to accelerate your decision. Counting always on the indispensable reserve in connection with everything that does not directly concern the United States —if any article contained in the document (or any other connected with it) requires explanation, Don Pedro Josef Caro, one of my compatriots, also Commissioner of the Spanish-American Colonies, who is charged with transmitting this to you, will be able to give complete satisfaction on every matter. His mission, after having received Your Excellency's orders, is to go immediately to the Spanish-American continent for the purpose of instructing our agents and compatriots on the present state of the negotiations entrusted to us—as well as on the political situation in Europe—I beg you kindly to assist him in anything he may require for this important task as well as facilitating his travel back and forth to the province of Santa Fe of Bogota.

I do not conceal, Sir, my anxiety at the approaching entry of French troops into Spain; fear that upheavals in the mother country might produce anarchistic repercussions in the colonies; and that the abominable French system might be introduced into our country because prompt and effective measures to prevent it had not been taken. May it be averted! Anyhow, I hope that the small assistance which we need to begin with and which amounts only to six or eight vessels of the line and four or five thousand troops, we will find as easily in England as in America. My desire is that the marine be English and the land troops American. Hoping that the United States will do for its compatriots of the South in 1798 what the King of France did for it in 1778!

I am always delighted to see at the head of the American executive branch that distinguished man, who, by his courage made his country independent, and who, by his wisdom gave it afterwards a well-balanced government, thus preserving its liberty. We will profit without doubt from your wise lessons and I am happy to tell you in advance that the proposed form of government is mixed, with a hereditary head holding the executive power under the name of Ynca, and what I like more—from the same family; a Senate composed of members of the nobility, but not hereditary, and a House of Commons elected from among all citizens who have requisite property qualifications. That is a sketch of the form of government which appears to unite the majority of the voters on the Spanish-American continent and which will doubtless prevent the fatal consequences of the French-Republican system that Montesquieu calls *extreme liberty*.

In addressing these proposals directly to you I thought to put all the required reserve into an affair as extraordinary as it is important—I also have the honor to attach here a population count, products of export and rate of consumption of Spanish-America, which, based on the most exact information as well as the most recent appeared to me to merit your attention.

With sentiments of the highest consideration and esteem, I have the honor to remain, the very humble servant of Your Excellency,

(Signed) Francisco de Miranda

London 24 March 1798   Verified.

Miranda.

To His Excellency John Adams—President of the United States of America

67. Louis Kossuth Calls the United States "This Glorious Home of Liberty" (1852)

Louis kossuth early attained prominence in liberal circles in Hungary. He became so prominent that he was arrested on a charge of high treason and thrown into prison. Popular opinion finally compelled the government to commute his sentence. Upon his release he became the leader of the extreme liberals who sought to sweep away the feudal débris which cluttered and stifled Hungary's political and economic life. When the news of the Revolution in Paris in early 1848 reached him he at once went into action. In April he issued his famous declaration of independence for Hungary and became virtual dictator of the nation. But the pressure of foreign intervention continued to mount; in August Hungarian arms collapsed and Kossuth fled to Turkey where he was interned.

Louis Kossuth's letter to President Fillmore presents not only a noteworthy eulogy of the principles of freedom and democracy as Kossuth had found them applied in America, but it reminds us of the great outburst of enthusiasm and sympathy with which the American people received news of the Hungarian revolution of 1848 and the subsequent visit of its popular leader.

When the President sent to the Senate the documents relating to a secret mission to Hungary investigating the grounds of possible United States recognition of the revolutionary government there, the Austrian government protested our action as unfriendly. In a widely publicized response, Secretary of State Daniel Webster set forth in positive fashion a lengthy review of the principles governing the United States in recognizing government founded on revolution and popular will. America, stirred by the revolution of 1848 almost as much as by the first French Revolution and firmly convinced of the universal applicability of its political system, never gave a State Department paper more widespread approval.

In September 1851, the fame of Kossuth as an heroic patriot reached such proportions that, in accordance with a resolution of Congress, an American warship was sent to bring the Hungarian leader from his exile in Turkey. Kossuth was given a tremendous reception in America. He was praised in the President's annual message to Congress; he was presented to the President by the Secretary of State; he was received with much ceremony by both Houses of Congress; and his tour through the nation was marked by enthusiastic and exuberant demonstrations.

The idolized Kossuth could not have failed to be impressed. On the eve of his departure he wrote this eloquent letter to President Fillmore expressing his gratitude. He regarded America as a living example of democracy at work. In the President's statement that "the United States cannot remain indifferent in a case in which the strong arm of a foreign power is involved to stifle public sentiment, and to oppress the spirit of freedom in any country," Kossuth found a true interpretation of the people's sentiments.

Such a magnanimous declaration, he wrote, "will be recorded in the history of mankind as a protestation on behalf of the everlasting principles of the law of nations against their infraction by violence."

This original letter is lent to the Freedom Train exhibit by the National Archives.

Washington City Jan. 12th 1852.

President,

The most generous invitation contained in an act of the Congress of the U. S. approved and officially transmitted to me by Your Excellency having afforded me the distinguished honor of being acceptably presented by the illustrious Secretary of State to the chief Magistrate of the Republic:

Having been upon subsequent resolutions of Congress received with almost unprecedented honors by the Senate and by the House of Representatives.

Having been entertained with unsurpassed kindness by the Senators and Representatives of the U. S. obliged with courtesies far excelling my aspirations by the heads of the various departments of the Executive Government, and favoured by marks of kind attention and sympathy by the Honorable Members of Congress in numbers which almost equalled the aggregate of the two illustrious legislative bodies of this great Republic: the time has come when the exigencies of my countrys affairs require me to depart from the City of Washington, and fulfill the agreeable duty of acknowledging personally that protective sympathy which many towns, cities and States of this glorious Confederation continue to manifest in favour of the just cause of my countrys downtrodden independence, and the freedom of the Europeen Continent so intimately connected with it.

This my departure becoming the more urgent, as according to the present condition of Europe every moments accident may call on me to answer those duties which in obedient compliance with my nations sovereign will I assumed when as unanimously elected Governor of the State of Hungary I took oath to God and the people to maintain that national independence which my nation has asserted so heroically, and had declared so legitimately; it is a matter of deep regret to me, not to be able individually to express my everlasting warm gratitude.

But though my mind be mournfully impressed with unconsolable grief, at the melancholy intelligence, connected with the last moments of my staying here, that the heart of my beloved and venerable mother has broken under the renewed cruel persecution inflicted upon my family by the House of Austria, still I cannot take my departure from the Capital without leaving a formal but sincere acknowledgement of all those memorable favours generously bestowed upon me.

Conscious as I am that this honors were neither deserved by, nor intended to me personally, who an humble exile never could consent to see myself aggrandised, while my country lies in ruins and in chains, I have them all the more thankfully received as manifestations of the respect for everlasting principles of national law and of the lively sympathy, which this great and generous country entertains for my beloved and never for a moment to be forgotten fatherland, now a temporary victim of the violation of those principles.

The oppressed nations of the European Continent so highly interested in those principles will look with consolation at these memorable favours I was honored with, as to a practical proof that the chief Magistrate of this great Republic was indeed a true interpreter of its peoples sentiments, and met with the dial concurrence of the enlightened Legislature of his glorious Country, when he officially declared that "the U. States cannot remain indifferent in a case in which the strong arm of a foreign power is invoked to stifle public sentiment, and to oppress the spirit of freedom in any country."

This magnanimous declaration followed by such generous manifestation will be recorded in the history of mankind as a protestation on behalf of the everlasting principles of the law of nations against their infraction by violence.

And the millions of my people will revive with hope and confidence when they shall come to know what favours were bestowed upon their exiled chief by the great Republic of the West, in acknowledgement of the justice of Hungarys cause.

In her name, and as her representative I have received them, and they have sunk into the very heart of my heart,—in her name, and as her representative I feel the duty of expressing my thanks for them, and desire Your Excellency as well as the Executive Officers, the Senate

and the House of Representatives collectively, and individually to receive the assurances of my, and my countrys eternal gratitude.

Sad and solemn is the hour of parting from a presence so consoling and so august, but I carry with me in my further wanderings the hope that the U. States will continue kindly to remember always my unhappy but most well deserving fatherland.

Neither the pangs of exile nor the egotisme of my patriotic feelings, or the interests of all those nations whose common rights and wrongs I plead before the mighty tribunal of publicity, will ever induce me to desire that the U. S. should for our sake put in jeopardy the own welfare and prosperity of this glorious home of liberty; but as the present condition of Europe, and the coming events on that Continent which cast already their shadow before them, cannot fail to attract the attention, and invite the consideration of such a power on earth as the U. S. are, I cannot forbear to hope that the very consciousness of that security which the U. States enjoy, while the greatest part of Europe quakes, will but more impres upon their true republican generosity the sentiments of supreme urgency to pronounce in respect to the law of nations and international duties and rights, as also in respect to the undisturbed safety of commercial intercourse, in favour of such principles, which founded upon the laws of nature, and of Natures God, are equally consistent with the fundamental principles of this great Republic and indispensable to the peace and contentement on earth.

Humanity would hail such a pronunciation from such a place with inexpressible joy, and it was the violation of those principles by armed foreign interference in Hungary which opened the door to a system of overwhelming despotism on the European Continent, the very fact that Hungary forced by the most treacherous oppression ever seen in the history of mankind, has in declaring its independence but exercised that right and followed that principle upon which stands so gloriously the very political existence of the U. States, and the fact that this legitimate independence was overthrown by the most cruel violation of international laws, makes me confidently hope that "the deep interest which the people of the U. S. feel in the spread of liberal principles, and the establishment of free governments, the warm sympathy with which it witnesses every struggle against oppression" as well, as its profound sentiment of justice, and its congenial generosity will become a source of such consolation to my native land, as the supreme constitutional authorities of this glorious Republic will in their wisdom deem consistent with the paramount duties towards their own country welfare and prosperity.

It is with these sentiments of hope and thanks that I beg leave to reiterate the assurance of my everlasting respect and gratitude, and humbly entreat Your Excellency to be pleased to communicate this my respectful farewell to the Senate and House of Representatives.

Mr. President

Your Excellencys
most humble and obedient servant
L. Kossuth

68. The First Woman to Serve in the Armed Forces of the United States Applies for a Pension

To have a woman serve in the armed forces of the United States is not a recent innovation. Pension records in the National Archives indicate that during the Revolutionary War a woman served in the Continental Army for over two years. In April 1781, Deborah Sampson of Middleboro, Massachusetts, enlisted as a private in Captain George Webb's Company of the Fourth Massachusetts Regiment. With considerable ingenuity, she concealed the fact that she was a woman and served with honor under the name of Robert Shurtleff for more than two years. She received a body wound by a musket ball in the Battle of Tarrytown; she recovered and was present at the capture of Lord Cornwallis at Yorktown in October 1781. While serving as an aide-de-camp to General Paterson at Philadelphia, "Private Shurtleff" fell ill with a fever and was hospitalized. What a musket ball had not earlier disclosed a fever now did; the audacious masquerade was at an end. In November 1783 Deborah Sampson received an honorable discharge. According to some accounts (not of the highest authenticity) this adventurous female was accorded the honor of parading down the ranks of her fellow soldiers before leaving the army.

On April 7, 1784, Deborah Sampson married Benjamin Gannett of Sharon, Massachusetts, and settled down to the somewhat more normal life of a wife and of a mother. She died in 1827. In her later years she gave several lectures in New England and New York recounting her wartime experiences and going through the Manual of Arms.

From January 1803 until 1818 Deborah Gannett received a disability pension from the State of Massachusetts for the wound received at the Battle of Tarrytown; but in September 1818, she exchanged this for a service pension of $96 a year from the Federal government. (The earliest provision for disability pensions was made by an act in 1790; in 1808 the United States assumed the Revolutionary pension obligations of the states. In 1818 a special provision was made for those who had served for nine months or more and were in indigent circumstances.)

Upon the death of Deborah Gannett, John Quincy Adams presented Congress with a petition in behalf of her husband, Benjamin, for a continuation of her pension during his lifetime. This was a most unusual request, and some discussion arose as to the propriety of such action, especially since there was no record of Benjamin Gannett having offered his services to the nation during the Revolution. After solemn deliberation it was declared that the American Revolution had furnished "no other similar example of female heroism, fidelity and courage" than that of Deborah Gannett and that a woman of her patriotism would never have married a traitor. With this conclusion, the House of Representatives on December 22, 1837, reported a bill granting a pension of $80 per annum from March 4, 1831, until the end of Gannett's natural life. During these lengthy and momentous deliberations Gannett died. Later, on July 7, 1838, Congress passed a special act granting the heirs of Deborah Gannett the monies that her husband would have received from the time of her death until his own.

Correspondence of this period between the Congressman from Massachusetts and the Pension Bureau gives the information that all the papers relative to Deborah Gannett's pension were destroyed when the British soldiers burned several government buildings in Washington in 1814. Fortunately, the original manuscript deposition, signed by Deborah Gannett in her claim for a pension, was preserved as a part of her pension file among the Veterans' Administration records now in the custody of the National Archives which has lent it to the Freedom Train exhibit.

United States

Massachusetts District—

Deborah Gannett, of Sharon, in the county of Norfolk, and District of Massachusetts, as resident and native of the United States, and applicant for a pension from the United States, under an Act of Congress entitled an Act to provide for certain persons engaged in the land and Naval Service of the United States, in the revolutionary war, maketh oath, That she served as a private soldier, under the name of Robert Shurtleff — in the war of the revolution, upwards of two years in manner following, Viz. — Enlisted in April 1781 in the company commanded by Captain George Webb in the Massachusetts Regiment commanded then by Colonel Shepherd — and afterwards by Colonel Henry Jackson — and served in said corps, in Massachusetts, and New York — until November 1783 — when she was honorably discharged in writing, which discharge is lost — During the time of her service, she was at the capture of Lord Cornwallis — was wounded at Tarrytown — and now received a pension from the United States, which pension she hereby relinquishes — She is in such reduced circumstances, as to require the aid of her country, — For her support —

Deborah Gannett

Massts. Dis. Sept. 14, 1818
Sworn to before Me.
Jno. Davis Dis. Judge Mass. Dist.

69. Governor Patrick Henry Instructs George Rogers Clark to Spread "Equal Liberty and Happiness" in the Illinois Country (1778)

IN several of the early colonial charters the Crown granted vague title to vast stretches of land westward to the ocean. Virginia, one of the colonies possessing such a claim, was notable for taking steps to make it *de facto* as well as *de jure*. Patrick Henry, Governor of Virginia during the American Revolution, was persuaded by a daring young surveyor, George Rogers Clark, to approve an expedition into the Illinois country north of the Ohio River. Clark was to capture any French towns or villages in that region that might be used by the British as focal points for Indian forays against the Americans. Although political strategists such as George Mason, Thomas Jefferson, and George Wythe approved the expedition, military security decreed high secrecy for the plans if they were to have any success.

Assent from the Virginia Assembly for outfitting Clark's expedition was secured on the plea for aid in defending Kentucky settlements. The Governor sent Clark an open letter of instructions on January 2, 1778, commissioning him a lieutenant colonel and directing him to go to Kentucky. On the same day, however, a private letter from the Governor instructed him specifically to capture the British post at Kaskaskia. In May, Clark set out for Illinois with 150 frontiersmen and a handful of hardy souls who planned to settle in the Northwest. On July 4, 1778, Kaskaskia was captured.

Communication between Illinois and Virginia was made difficult by the hazards of travelling through hostile Indian country and the rigors of winter weather, so on December 12, 1778, Governor Henry and the Virginia Council sent Clark further instructions. These are the orders, signed by Patrick Henry, that are displayed on the Freedom Train.

Large discretionary powers were given Clark by the Virginia Council, and he was requested to adopt such policies as would obtain the good will and friendship of the French and Indians along the frontier. A copy of Virginia's bill of rights and of the treaty of alliance between the American colonies and France was enclosed for the French settlers so they could learn the advantages of being "fellow-citizens & free men" along with the

Americans. Clark and his men were unofficial ambassadors of American democracy in this territory. Following instructions of the Virginia Council and his own fair-minded nature, Clark assured the French inhabitants that it was not the American custom to enslave those whom they conquered, and that all who chose to become loyal citizens would share the privileges and liberties of other Americans. These statements, together with Clark's toleration and generous treatment of their church, won over the hesitant French. In Kaskaskia, all the inhabitants took the oath of allegiance to the United States and were thenceforth considered as citizens of Virginia.

This Illinois country was ceded by Virginia to the Continental Congress in 1781 and formed a large portion of the territory organized by that Congress under the Ordinance of 1787. As a result of Clark's occupation of Kaskaskia, Vincennes, Cahokia and other posts along this northwestern frontier, the American peace commissioners at Paris were better able to negotiate with the British and to confirm, in the Treaty of 1783, the right of the United States to that territory.

These original signed instructions from Henry to Clark are from the pension file of James Meriwether, which is among records of the Veterans' Administration in the National Archives. They were submitted as evidence of George Rogers Clark's authority to grant commissions in the field and to substantiate thereby the claim of Meriwether, a member of his troops, for an officer's pension.

W[illia]msburg December 1778

Instructions to George Rogers Clark Esqr. Colonel & Commander in Chief of the Virginia Troops in the County of Illinois—

Sir,

You are to retain the Command of the troops now at the several posts in the county of Illinois and on the Wabash, which fall within the limits of the County now erected and called Illinois County, which troops marched out with, and have been embodied by you. You are also to take the Command of five other Companies, raised under the act of Assembly which I send herewith, and which if completed, as I hope they will be speedily, will have orders to join you without loss of time, and are likewise to be under your command; With your whole force you are to protect the Inhabitants of the County, & as occasions may serve, annoy the enemy.

It is thought that the Indian Nations may be overawed and inclined to peace with us, by the Adoption of proper measures with you. Or if that cannot be effected, that such of them as send out parties towards our Frontiers on this side of the Ohio, may be chastised by detachments from your quarter. For this purpose it will behove you to watch their motions, and to consider, that one great advantage expected from your situation is to prevent the Indians from warring on this side of Ohio.

In order more effectually to prevent this, you are to establish such posts in different parts of the Country as you judge best for your troops to occupy.

I consider your further success as depending upon the goodwill and friendship of the Frenchmen and Indians who inhabit your part of the Commonwealth. With their concurrence great things may be accomplished. But their animosity will spoil the fair prospect which your past successes have opened. You will therefore spare no pains to conciliate the affections of the French and Indians. Let them see and feel the advantages of being fellow citizens and freemen. Guard most carefully against every infringement of their property, particularly with respect to land, as our enemies have alarmed them as to that. Strict, and even severe, discipline with your soldiers may be essential, to preserve from injury those whom they were sent to protect and conciliate. This is a great and capital matter, and I confide that you will never lose sight of it, or suffer your troops to injure any person without feeling the punishment due to the offense. The honor and interest of the state are deeply concerned in this, and the attachment of the French and Indians depends upon a due observance of it.

John Todd Esquire being appointed County Lieutenant according to law, during pleasure, with ample powers chiefly confined to the Civil Department, will have directions to act in concert with you wherever it can be done. On your part, you will omit no opportunity to give him the necessary co-operation of the troops, where the case necessarily requires it. Much will depend upon the mutual assistances you may occasionally afford each other in your respective departments, and I trust that a sincere cordiality will subsist between you. The contrary will prove highly detrimental. Some measures will be fallen on for carrying on a trade to supply goods for the inhabitants of your County. You will afford the agents such aid or protection from time to time as affairs require, and your circumstances will permit.

I send you herewith some copies of the act of Government and Bill of Rights, together with the French alliance. These will serve to show our new friends the ground upon which they are to stand, and the support to be expected from their countrymen of France. Equal liberty and happiness are the objects to a participation of which we invite them.

Upon a fair presumption that the people about Detroit have similar inclinations with those at Illinois and Wabash, I think it possible that they may be brought to expel their British Masters, and become fellow citizens of a free State. I recommend this to your serious consideration, and to consult with some confidential persons on the subject. Perhaps Mr. Gibault, the Priest (to whom this country owes many thanks for his zeal and services,) may promote this affair. But I refer it to you to select the proper persons to advise with, and to act as occasion offers. But you are to push at any favourable occurrences which Fortune may present to you. For our peace and safety are not secure while the enemy are so near as Detroit.

I wish you to testify to all the subjects of Spain upon every occasion, the high regard and sincere friendship of this Commonwealth towards them. And I hope it will soon be manifest, that mutual advantages will derive from the Neighbourhood of the Virginians and the subjects of his Catholic Majesty.

I must observe to you that your situation is critical.

Far detached from the body of your country, placed among French, Spaniards, and Indian Nations, strangers to our people, anxiously watching your actions and behaviour, and ready to receive impressions favourable, or not so, of our Commonwealth and its Government, which impressions will be hard to remove, and will produce lasting good or ill effects to your country. These considerations will make you cautious and circumspect. I feel the delicacy and difficulty of your situation, but I doubt not your virtue will accomplish the arduous work with honor to yourself, and advantage to the Commonwealth. The advice and assistance of discreet good men will be highly necessary. For at the distance of your country, I cannot be consulted. General discretionary powers therefore are given you, to act for the best in all cases where these instructions are silent and the law has made no provision.

I desire your particular attention to Mrs. Rocheblave and her children, and that you suffer them to want for nothing. Let Mr. Rocheblave's property, which was taken, be restored to his lady so far as it can be done. You have the sum of sixty pounds sent for her use, in case you can't find her husband's effects to restore.

Prudence requires that provisions be laid in to subsist the Troops you have, & those to be expected to arrive with you. Colonel Bowman has contracted to deliver 35,000 lbs. Bear Bacon at Kentucky. But bread must be had at Illinois.

You will provide it, if possible, before the arrival of the Troops, or the necessity to buy it becomes general known, as perhaps advantages may be taken by raising the price. Lay up also a good stock of powder and Lead &c.

There is a cargo of goods at a Spanish post near you, belonging either to the Continent or this state. Rather than let your troops be naked, you are to take a supply for them out of these goods. But this is not to be done but in case of absolute necessity. Let an exact account be kept of what is used, and let me receive it.

In your negotiations or treatys with the Indians, you will be assisted by Mr. Todd. Let the treatys be confined to the subject of amity and peace with our people, and not to touch the subject of lands. You may accept of any services they offer for expelling the English from

Detroit or elsewhere. In case you find presents to the savages necessary, make them sparingly as possible, letting them know our stock of Goods is small at present, but by means of our trade with the French and other nations, we expect plenty of Goods before it is long.

Lieutenant Colonel Montgomery will convey to you ten thousand pounds for payment of the troops, and for other matters requiring money. In the distribution of the money you will be careful to keep exact accounts from time to time, and take security where it is proper.

Yours &c.

P. Henry

70. John Paul Jones Declares That, if the War Should Continue, He Wishes to Have "the Most Active Part in It" (1782)

FEW words are needed to bring back again the memories evoked by the mention of the name of John Paul Jones. His name is reverently enshrined in the naval annals of the United States; nor does it fail to find an esteemed place in the world history of war on the high seas. His career is one of the most dramatic of the many strange persons who served mightily in the War of Independence.

The outbreak of war found him in the American colonies—a fugitive from British justice and a sailor unemployed, or as more elegant and evasive language has put it, he "was forced to live upon the bounty of strangers." Five years later he was the toast of Paris and one of the great heroes of the American Revolution.

He had well earned his reputation. On December 7, 1775, he was made a lieutenant in the Continental Navy and, within a short time, was recognized as probably the ablest of all our naval officers. He was sent to Europe with the rank of captain and, with inferior ships and personnel, staged a series of commando raids upon the British coasts. The engagement between his *Bonhomme Richard* and the British *Serapis* was only one of his numerous triumphs, but it has become famous in world history. Jones himself said that "the scene was dreadful beyond the reach of language." Competent historians have declared that the brilliant and unexpected victory was "wholly and solely due to the immovable courage of Paul Jones." It was during this battle that Jones is said to have replied to the question of the British Captain Pearson, "Have you struck?", with his answer: "I've just begun to fight."

In April 1780 Jones went to Paris, where he was lionized. He was not a man to refuse the fruits of such popularity and for almost a year he was busy repaying the charming ladies of Paris for their accolades and hospitality. He returned to the United States in early

1781 and Congress, on April 14, gave him an official vote of gratitude. This was an inexpensive and simple gesture. But Jones was not entirely satisfied with such a gesture and he brought up the question of his rank. While Jones had been winning spectacular victories on the high seas many of the older officers, some of whom would have had difficulty in navigating a canoe, had chiefly exhausted themselves in maneuvers in political waters. They were easily able to block his promotion. Jones was able to demonstrate that he had not received a dollar from the United States during five years of service. This fact, coupled with his great and merited prestige, made too many politicos feel sheepish. So a compromise was reached. He was given command of the *America,* which was then being built at Portsmouth, New Hampshire. The *America* was the first and only 74-gun ship in the Continental Navy. Jones went to Portsmouth to supervise the construction of the vessel. It was a year of frustrations, for he could find neither the materials nor the trained personnel.

Then Congress determined to turn the *America* over to France to compensate for the loss of the *Magnifique* at Boston. Jones probably remembered the incident of earlier years when he was sent to Europe to command the *Indien,* which was being built at Amsterdam for the Continental Navy and which was turned over to the King of France before Jones could ever hoist his flag, but he does not mention it in this original signed letter lent to the Freedom Train by the United States Naval Academy Museum.

At the end of the War of Independence Congress abolished the Navy and Jones was without either commission or job. He went to Russia where he became an admiral, but as the result of several misunderstandings, he returned to Paris where he died in 1792. He was buried in a leaden casket, filled with alcohol to preserve the body in the event that the United States might ever wish to reclaim it. After many difficulties the casket was finally found and the body returned, with proper pomp and ceremony, in 1905: the belated tribute to a great American naval hero.

71. Sergeant Lee Claims a Pension for Services on the First American Submarine

SUBMARINES did not become an effective instrument of warfare until World War I and World War II. Thus we usually think of the submarine as a relatively modern invention. In 1776, however, an underwater attack was launched by American forces against British ships in New York harbor. No ship was destroyed and no lives were lost, but the machine in which the attempt was

Portsmouth, New Hampshire Sepr. 2d.
1782.

Your kind letter, my dear Morris, of the 13th.
Ult. and the public one of the same date are
as welcome favors and as necessary to me
as fresh Air and the saving hand of Friendship to a drowning Man. — I know your
ability and am convinced your friendship
for our Country will manifest itself so
effectually that we may avail of the loss of
the Magnifique at Boston — I know it
has been proposed by some wise Heads to offer
the America as a present to replace that
Ship. Are we in a condition to make
presents? If we were I should be against
offering to give a friend an empty Egg shell. —

The Honble
Gouverneur Morris Esqr. Assistant Minister of Finance &c &c

John Paul Jones' Letter to Gouverneur Morris, September 2, 1782 (See No. 70)

You know me I find, since "you are sure I
will rejoice at the present appearances of
Peace". An honorable Peace is and always
was my first wish. I can take no delight
in the effusion of human Blood, but if this
War should continue, I wish to have the
most active part in it. — With the
highest sense of your kind attentions and
good Opinion, and with the most earnest
desire to deserve, by my conduct the delicate
praises of a Friend of your high worth and
public Spirit, I am, sincerely, and affectionately
Your most Obliged
Paul Jones

John Paul Jones' Letter, second page

made brought a reputation to its inventor, David Bushnell, as the "father of the submarine."

Bushnell's imagination seized upon the theory of shooting projectiles under water, and he designed and constructed a machine out of oak timber. Since its shape resembled two tortoise shells joined together it received the nickname of "Bushnell's Turtle." On the outside of the boat was fastened a torpedo containing gunpowder together with a clock mechanism. Because of space limitations, the crew of this strange craft consisted of only one person. The operator, by cranking the propeller, could achieve a speed up to three miles an hour in still waters.

The Governor and Council of Safety in Connecticut, having seen and approved the machine, sent the young inventor to General Washington, who was then engaged in the defense of Long Island. At this time in 1776, British ships in New York harbor and British land forces on Staten Island threatened the safety of the American army. Plans for the destruction of these ships by a surprise attack with Bushnell's submarine were approved and preparations were begun. Sergeant Ezra Lee of Lyme, Connecticut, was chosen from a group of volunteers to receive necessary training.

A favorable night in August was selected for the attack on the *Eagle,* a 64-gun British ship. Lee climbed inside the submarine and was towed down the river until cast loose to continue his way alone. Because of inexperience and mischance, he did not complete his mission. He could not discover a wooden portion of the ship on which to fasten the torpedo, and he also had difficulty in keeping the *Turtle* submerged. Fearing discovery and knowing that time was short, Lee turned back to shore.

During his return voyage British soldiers on Governor's Island sighted the machine, and several hundred gathered to watch its motions. At length a party went down to the beach, shoved off in a barge, and rowed toward Lee. "At that moment Sergeant Lee thought he saw his certain destruction, and as the last act of defence, let go the magazine, expecting that they would seize that likewise, and thus all would be blown to atoms together." The baffled enemy suspected a "Yankee-trick" and returned to the island in alarm. Shortly thereafter the torpedo exploded with great force to the surprise and mystification of the British. Lee's expedition was observed from the shore of New York City by General Israel Putnam, who had directed the plan, and boats were sent out to bring Lee to safety.

Later attempts to use the *Turtle* ended in failure and ridicule for Bushnell, and he was forced to cease his experiments through lack of money. His efforts did not go unappreciated by the authorities, however, as he was made captain-lieutenant in 1779 in a company of sappers and miners, and in 1783 he was stationed at West Point as a captain. Little is known of Bushnell's later career;

some accounts say that he finally became a schoolteacher in Georgia.

Bushnell's unusual submarine experiments provoked a variety of comment ranging from a humorous 22-stanza poem, "The Battle of the Kegs" by Francis Hopkinson, to a serious appreciation by George Washington. On September 26, 1785, Washington wrote Thomas Jefferson in Paris: "Bushnell is a man of great mechanical powers, fertile in inventions and master of execution. He came to me in 1776, recommended by Governor Trumbull and other respectable characters, who were converts to his plan. Although I wanted faith myself, I furnished him with money and other aids to carry his plan into execution. . . . I then thought, and still think, that it was an effort of genius."

Ezra Lee's original signed deposition of June 1820 for a pension from the Federal government for his Revolutionary War service is lent by the National Archives to the Freedom Train.

72. Webster and Ashburton Inaugurate an Enduring Friendship between the United States and Canada

GOOD-NEIGHBORLINESS and Pan-Americanism have been keystones of American foreign policy during the past few decades. They are not entirely new concepts, however, as our long-peaceful relations with Canada demonstrate. The longest unfortified border in the world is that between the United States and Canada. It has been open and unfortified for over 100 years, a symbol of an international friendship based on understanding and trust. In the development of these amicable relationships a major step was the treaty negotiated at Washington, D. C., in 1842 by Secretary of State Webster and Lord Ashburton, Special Minister to Washington from Great Britain. It is known both as the Treaty of Washington and as the Webster-Ashburton Treaty.

From the time the Treaty of Paris was signed in 1783, there had been disagreement over the boundary line between the United States and Britain's North American Provinces (Canada). The identity of the St. Croix River was a matter of dispute, and, as it marked the border for the northern limits of Maine and Massachusetts, the question of ownership of a large area was involved. As new settlers moved into the disputed territory, conflicts between authorities became more numerous and culminated in the "Aroostook War" of 1838.

Another area of disagreement between Great Britain and the United States arose from Britain's attempts to stamp out the African slave trade following her own abolition of slavery. This led to several brushes with

American shipping as in the *Creole* case of 1841, which involved matters of international maritime rights, as did also the case of the *Caroline*. Diplomatic negotiations had several times been proposed but these efforts came to nothing because of the inflexibility of those conducting the diplomacy. This was the situation that confronted Daniel Webster when he became Secretary of State in 1841.

Webster's decision to attempt settlement of outstanding differences with Great Britain was received with approval and optimism. He had acquired tremendous prestige through his oratorical gifts and political ability displayed in the halls of Congress and the Senate. He was appointed Secretary of State by President Harrison, who died within a month of taking office and was succeeded by Vice President Tyler. All of Harrison's Whig cabinet resigned except Webster, who did not feel that he would be handicapped in his activities by the President's defection from the Whig party.

Lord Aberdeen became Prime Minister in Great Britain when Webster assumed control of foreign affairs for the United States, and, being of a more gentle and conciliatory spirit than his predecessor, he met American offers with more than customary grace. He named Lord Ashburton as Special Minister to Washington with full powers to treat for the settlement of all outstanding questions. Lord Ashburton declared that he considered the maintenance of peace between the two countries as of "extreme importance."

On June 13, 1842, negotiations officially commenced in Washington and continued throughout the sweltering Washington summer until terms satisfactory to all parties were concluded and a treaty was signed on August 9, 1842. In addition to representatives of the national governments, the states of Massachusetts and of Maine were each represented by a three-man, nonpartisan commission. On October 13, an exchange of ratifications took place in London between Edward Everett, American Ambassador to Great Britain, and Lord Aberdeen. And on November 10, a presidential proclamation formally announced the treaty to the American people.

The original Treaty of Washington bearing the signatures and seals of Daniel Webster and Lord Ashburton is from the general records of the United States Government now in the custody of the National Archives. Inscribed on heavy treaty paper are twelve articles dealing with settlement of the northern boundary dispute, suppression of the slave trade, and the extradition of criminals. Far beyond the specific terms it contains, the treaty is important for its effect in establishing an atmosphere of cordial relations in international affairs. The treaty itself was a monument to tact and patience; that it has endured without impairment is a tribute to confidence and friendship.

73. Benjamin Franklin Writes His Epitaph

O N this fascinating manuscript little need be added by way of explanation. Dr. Carl Van Doren, an esteemed authority in the field, declares that it is the most famous epitaph in the English language. It was first written by Franklin in 1728, when he first set up shop as a printer. And to his first love of printing he remained loyal. Many years later, in writing his will, Franklin began: "I, Benjamin Franklin, Printer, late Minister Plenipotentiary from the United States of America to the Court of France . . ." etc.

During the course of his lengthy career Franklin was several times importuned by friends to write out for them an autograph copy of his celebrated epitaph. This manuscript, lent to the Freedom Train exhibit by Colonel Richard Gimbel, was written out for Samuel Morris in Philadelphia and presented to him on August 31, 1776. In the midst of the difficult weeks which followed the Declaration of Independence Franklin, often termed "the first civilized American," managed to find at least a few brief moments to indulge an old sense of humor and to oblige a friend.

74. The French Nation Renders Tribute to the Memory of Dr. Franklin

F IVE days after the death of Benjamin Franklin in Philadelphia on April 17, 1790, James Madison moved that the House of Representatives, then in session in New York, wear mourning for the period of a month. There was no discussion and the motion was unanimously approved. But the Senate refused. Thomas Jefferson then proposed to President Washington that the executive departments should wear mourning. Washington was reluctant to establish such a precedent. Jefferson argued with him "that the world had drawn so broad a line between him and Dr. Franklin, on the one side, and the residue of mankind, on the other, that we might wear mourning for them, and the question still remain new and undecided as to all others." The President remained unconvinced.

The French, however, acted differently. Mirabeau, the greatest orator of the French Revolution, rose in the National Convention on June 11 and declared that nations, too long given to taking formal note of the death of only those persons in whom courts were interested, should rather wear mourning for the benefactors and heroes of humanity. "Would it not become us, gentlemen, to join in this religious act, to take a part in this homage, rendered, in the face of the world, both to the

The Body of

B. Franklin, Printer,

Like the Cover of an old Book,

Its Contents torn out,

And stript of its Lettering & Gilding,

Lies here, Food for Worms.

But the Work shall not be lost;

For it will, as he believ'd, appear once more

In a new and more elegant Edition

Corrected and improved

By the Author.———

Given by B Franklin to Saml Morris

August 31 1776 ————————

N.B. It is his own hand writing ————

Benjamin Franklin's Epitaph in His Own Hand (See No. 73)

rights of man and to the philosopher who has most contributed to extend their sway over the whole earth? Antiquity would have raised altars to this mighty genius who, to the advantage of mankind, compassing in his mind the heavens and the earth, was able to restrain alike both thunderbolts and tyrants. Europe, enlightened and free, owes at least a token of remembrance and regret to one of the greatest men who have ever been engaged in the service of philosophy and of liberty. I propose that it be decreed that the National Convention, during three days, shall wear mourning for Benjamin Franklin." The motion was carried by acclamation.

The first pamphlet printing of Mirabeau's address is from the Sterling Memorial Library of Yale University.

75. Congress Thanks the French Nation for the Tribute to the Memory of Dr. Franklin

IN VIEW of the sharp contrast between the official actions of the American and French governments in rendering tribute to the memory of Dr. Franklin this rare original broadside, from the collection of Mr. Frederic R. Kirkland, is a fitting companion for the Mirabeau speech which is carried on the Freedom Train. The period of mourning decreed by the French government was impressive; the tribute of Mirabeau was eloquent in the grand fashion. When these things drifted back to the United States even those who had been reluctant to decree a period of mourning for Dr. Franklin felt that something should be done. So, in this roundabout manner, something was done. Congress passed a resolution at its third session which President Washington approved on March 2, 1791, "That the President of the United States be requested to cause to be communicated to the National Assembly of France the peculiar sensibility of Congress to the tribute paid to the memory of Benjamin Franklin, by the enlightened and free representatives of a great nation, in their decree of June 11, 1790." Sensibility came at last, but came a little late.

76. Thomas Jefferson Writes from Paris in Praise of America (1785)

AFTER a period of strenuous service as Governor of Virginia during the closing years of the War of Independence and as a member of the Congress of the Confederation, Thomas Jefferson was sent abroad by Congress in May 1784 as a minister plenipotentiary to France. He arrived in Paris in August and worked with the dean of American statesmen, Dr. Benjamin Franklin, until July 1785, when the latter returned to America. At this time, Jefferson succeeded Franklin as minister to France. A distinguished Frenchman one day inquired of Jefferson: "C'est vous, Monsieur, qui remplace le Docteur Franklin?" ("It is you, sir, who replaces Dr. Franklin?") His humble reply was: "No one can replace him, sir: I only succeed him."

Paris presented many opportunities for Jefferson to satisfy his varied scientific and artistic interests. Although he was quite happy during his five years in France, he was not oblivious to the lot of the common man under the monarchies of the Old World. What his critical eye saw only served to intensify his deep love of America and the democratic principles for which it stood.

It was not until December 1789 that Jefferson was able to return to his own country, where, upon the insistence of President Washington, he became the first Secretary of State.

In this letter of June 17, 1785, to James Monroe, a fellow Virginian and lifelong friend, Jefferson discusses at some length the state of affairs in Europe and certain matters pertaining to the Confederation Congress of which Monroe was a member. It is in the concluding paragraph of his letter that Jefferson gives eloquent expression to his feeling about America. The letter was lent to the Freedom Train by Mr. Lawrence Gouverneur Hoes.

Paris, June 17, 1785.

Dear Sir,

I received three days ago your favor of April the 12th. You therein speak of a former letter to me, but it has not come to hand, nor any other of later date than the 14th of December. My last to you was of the 11th of May by Mr. Adams, who went in the packet of that month. These conveyances are now becoming deranged. We have had expectations of their coming to Havre, which would infinitely facilitate the communication between Paris and Congress; but their deliberations on the subject seem to be taking another turn. They complain of the expense, and that their commerce with us is too small to justify it. They therefore talk of sending a packet every six weeks only. The present one, therefore, which should have sailed about this time, will not sail till the 1st of July. However, the whole matter is as yet undecided. I have hopes that when Mr. St. John arrives from New York, he will get them replaced on their monthly system. By-the-bye, what is the meaning of a very angry resolution of Congress on this subject? I have it not by me, and therefore cannot cite it by date, but you will remember it, and oblige me by explaining its foundation. This will be handed you by Mr. Otto, who comes to America as Chargé des Affaires, in the room of Mr. Marbois, promoted to the Intendancy of Hispaniola, which office is next to that of Governor. He becomes the head of the civil, as the Governor is, of the military department.

I am much pleased with Otto's appointment; he is good-humored, affectionate to America, will see things in a friendly light when they admit of it, in a rational one always, and will not pique himself on writing every trifling circumstance of irritation to his court. I wish you to be acquainted with him as a friendly intercourse between individuals who do business together produces a mutual spirit of accommodation useful to both parties. It is very much our interest to keep up the affection of this country for us, which is considerable. A court has no affections; but those of the people whom they govern influence their decisions, even in the most arbitrary governments.

The negotiations between the Emperor and Dutch are spun out to an amazing length. At present there is no apprehension but that they will terminate in peace. This court seems to press it with ardor, and the Dutch are averse, considering the terms cruel and unjust, as they evidently are. The present delays, therefore, are imputed to their coldness and to their forms. In the meantime, the Turk is delaying the demarcation of limits between him and the Emperor, is making the most vigorous preparations for war, and has composed his ministry of warlike characters, deemed personally hostile to the Emperor. Thus time seems to be spinning out, both by the Dutch and Turks, and time is wanting for France. Every year's delay is a great thing for her. It is not impossible, therefore, but that she may secretly encourage the delays of the Dutch, and hasten the preparations of the Porte, while she is recovering vigor herself, also, in order to be able to present such a combination to the Emperor as may dictate to him to be quiet. But the designs of these courts are unsearchable. It is our interest to pray that this country may have no continental war till our peace with England is perfectly settled. The merchants of this country continue as loud and furious as ever against the Arret of August, 1784, permitting our commerce with their islands to a certain degree. Many of them have actually abandoned their trade. The ministry are disposed to be firm; but there is a point at which they will give way, that is, if the clamors should become such as to endanger their places. It is evident that nothing can be done by us at this time, if we may hope it hereafter. I like your removal to New York, and hope Congress will continue there, and never execute the idea of building their Federal town. Before it could be finished, a change of members in Congress, or the admission of new States, would remove them somewhere else. It is evident that when a sufficient number of the western States come in, they will remove it to Georgetown. In the meantime, it is our interest that it should remain where it is, and give no new pretensions to any other place. I am also much pleased with the proposition to the States to invest Congress with the regulation of their trade, reserving its revenue to the States. I think it a happy idea, removing the only objection which could have been justly made to the proposition. The time, too, is the present, before the admission of the western States. I am very differently affected towards the new plan of opening our land office, by dividing the lands among the States, and selling them at vendue. It separates still more the interests of the States, which ought to be made joint in every possible instance, in order to cultivate the idea of our being one nation, and to multiply the instances in which the people shall look up to Congress as their head. And when the States get their portions, they will either fool them away, or make a job of it to serve individuals. Proofs of both these practices have been furnished, and by either of them that invaluable fund is lost, which ought to pay our public debt. To sell them at vendue, is to give them to the bidders of the day, be they many or few. It is ripping up the hen which lays golden eggs. If sold in lots at a fixed price, at first proposed, the best lots will be sold first; as these become occupied, it gives a value to the interjacent ones, and raises them, though of inferior quality, to the price of the first. I send you by Mr. Otto a copy of my book. Be so good as to apologize to Mr. Thompson for my not sending him one by this conveyance. I could not burthen Mr. Otto with more on so long a road as that from here to L'Orient. I will send him one by a Mr. Williams, who will go ere long. I have taken measures to prevent its publication. My reason is, that I fear the terms in which I speak of slavery, and of our constitution, may produce an irritation which will revolt the minds of our countrymen against reformation in these two articles, and thus do more harm than good. I have asked of Mr. Madison to sound this matter as far as he can, and, if he thinks it will not produce that effect, I have then copies enough printed to give one to each of the young men at the College, and to my friends in the country.

I am sorry to see a possibility of * * * being put into the Treasury. He has no talents for the office, and what he has, will be employed in rummaging old accounts to involve you in eternal war with * * * and he will, in a short time, introduce such dissensions into the commission, as to break it up. If he goes on the other appointment to Kaskaskia, he will produce a revolt of that settlement from the United States. I thank you for your attention to my outfit. For the articles of household furniture, clothes, and a carriage, I have already paid twenty-eight thousand livres, and have still more to pay. For the greatest part of this, I have been obliged to anticipate my salary, from which, however, I shall never be able to repay it. I find, that by a rigid economy, bordering however on meanness, I can save perhaps five hundred livres a month, at least in the summer. The residue goes for expenses so much of course and of necessity, that I cannot avoid them without abandoning all respect to my public character. Yet I will pray you to touch this string, which I know to be a tender one with Congress, with the utmost delicacy. I had rather be ruined in my fortune than in their esteem. If they allow me half a year's salary as an outfit, I can get through my debts in time. If they raise the salary to what it was, or even pay our house rent and taxes, I can live with more decency. I trust that Mr. Adams' house at the Hague, and Dr. Franklin's at Passy, the rent of which has been always allowed him, will give just expectations of the same allowance to me. Mr. Jay, however, did not charge it, but he lived economically and laid up money.

I will take the liberty of hazarding to you some thoughts on the policy of entering into treaties with the European nations, and the nature of them. I am not wedded to these ideas, and, therefore, shall relinquish them cheerfully when Congress shall adopt others, and zealously endeavor to carry theirs into effect. First, as to the policy and making treaties. Congress, by the Confederation, have no original and inherent power over the commerce of the States. But, by the 9th article, we are authorized to enter into treaties of commerce. The moment these treaties are concluded, the jurisdiction of Congress over the commerce of the States springs into existence, and that of the particular States is superseded so far as the articles of the treaty may have taken up the subject. There are two restrictions only, on the exercise of the power of treaty by Congress. 1st. That they shall not, by such treaty, restrain the legislatures of the States from imposing such duties on foreigners, as their own people are subject to; nor 2dly, from prohibiting the exportation or importation of any particular species of goods. Leaving these two points free, Congress may, by treaty, establish any system of commerce they please; but, as I before observed, it is by treaty alone they can do it. Though they may exercise their other powers by resolution or ordinance, those over commerce can only be exercised by forming a treaty, and this probably by an accidental wording of our Confederation. If, therefore, it is better for the States that Congress should regulate their commerce, it is proper that they should form treaties with all nations with whom they may possibly trade. You see that my primary object in the formation of treaties is to take the commerce of the States out of the hands of the States, and to place it under the superintendence of Congress, so far as the imperfect provisions of our constitutions will admit, and until the States shall, by new compact, make them more perfect. I would say, then, to every nation on earth, *by treaty,* your people shall trade freely with us, and ours with you, paying no more than the most favored nation, in order to put an end to the right of individual States, acting by fits and starts, to interrupt our commerce, or to embroil us with any nation. As to the terms of these treaties, the question becomes more difficult. I will mention three differ-

ent plans. 1. That no duty shall be laid by either party on the productions of the other. 2. That each may be permitted to equalize their duties to those laid by the other. 3. That each shall pay in the ports of the other, such duties only as the most favored nations pay.

1. Were the nations of Europe as free and unembarrassed of established systems as we are, I do verily believe they would concur with us in the first plan. But it is impossible. These establishments are fixed upon them; they are interwoven with the body of their laws and the organization of their government, and they make a great part of their revenue; they cannot then, get rid of them.

2. The plan of equal imposts presents difficulties insurmountable. For how are the equal imposts to be effected? Is it by laying, in the ports of A, an equal per cent. on the goods of B, with that which B has laid in his ports on the goods of A? But how are we to find what is that percent.? For this is not the usual form of imposts. They generally pay by the ton, by the measure, by the weight, and not by the value. Besides, if A sends a million's worth of goods to B, and takes back but the half of that, and each pays the same per cent., it is evident that A pays the double of what he recovers in the same way from B: this would be our case with Spain. Shall we endeavor to effect equality, then, by saying A may levy so much on the sum of B's importations into his ports, as B does on the sum of A's importations into the ports of B? But how find out that sum? Will either party lay open their custom-house books candidly to evince this sum? Does either keep their books so exactly as to be able to do it? This proposition was started in Congress when our instructions were formed, as you may remember, and the impossibility of executing it occasioned it to be disapproved. Besides, who should have a right of deciding, when the imposts were equal? A would say to B, my imposts do not raise so much as yours: I raise them therefore. B would then say, you have made them greater than mine, I will raise mine; and thus a kind of auction would be carried on between them, and a mutual irritation, which would end in anything, sooner than equality and right.

3. I confess then to you, that I see no alternative left but that which Congress accepted, of each party placing the other on the footing of the most favored nation. If the nations of Europe, from their actual establishments, are not at liberty to say to America, that she shall trade in their ports duty free, they may say she may trade there paying no higher duties than the most favored nation; and this is valuable in many of these countries, where a very great difference is made between different nations. There is no difficulty in the execution of this contract, because there is not a merchant who does not know, or may not know, the duty paid by every nation on every article. This stipulation leaves each party at liberty to regulate their own commerce by general rules, while it

secures the other from partial and oppressive discriminations. The difficulty which arises in our case is, with the nations having American territory. Access to the West Indies is indispensably necessary to us. Yet how to gain it, when it is the established system of these nations to exclude all foreigners from their colonies. The only chance seems to be this: our commerce to the mother country is valuable to them. We must endeavor, then, to make this the price of an admission into their West Indies, and to those who refuse the admission, we must refuse our commerce, or load theirs by odious discriminations in our ports. We have this circumstance in our favor too, that what one grants us in their islands, the others will not find it worth their while to refuse. The misfortune is, that with this country we gave this price for their aid in the war, and we have now nothing more to offer. She, being withdrawn from the competition, leaves Great Britain much more at liberty to hold out against us. This is the difficult part of the business of treaty, and I own it does not hold out the most flattering prospects.

I wish you would consider this subject, and write me your thoughts on it. Mr. Gerry wrote me on the same subject. Will you give me leave to impose on you the trouble of communicating this to him? It is long, and will save me much labor in copying. I hope he will be so indulgent as to consider it as an answer to that part of his letter, and will give me his further thoughts on it.

Shall I send you so much of the Encyclopedia as is already published, or reserve it here till you come? It is about forty volumes, which probably is about half the work. Give yourself no uneasiness about the money; perhaps I may find it convenient to ask you to pay trifles occasionally for me in America. I sincerely wish you may find it convenient to come here; the pleasure of the trip will be less than you expect, but the utility greater. It will make you adore your own country, its soil, its climate, its equality, liberty, laws, people, and manners. My God! how little do my countrymen know what precious blessings they are in possession of, and which no other people on earth enjoy. I confess I had no idea of it myself. While we shall see multiplied instances of Europeans going to live in America, I will venture to say, no man now living will ever see an instance of an American removing to settle in Europe, and continuing there. Come, then, and see the proofs of this, and on your return add your testimony to that of every thinking American, in order to satisfy our countrymen how much it is their interest to preserve, uninfected by contagion, those peculiarities in their governments and manners, to which they are indebted for those blessings. Adieu, my dear friend; present me affectionately to your colleagues. If any of them think me worth writing to, they may be assured that in the epistolary account I will keep the debit side against them. Once more, adieu.

Yours affectionately.

P.S. June 19. Since writing the above, we have received the following account: Monsieur Pilatre de Roziere, who had been waiting for some months at Boulogne for a fair wind to cross the channel, at length took his ascent with a companion. The wind changed after awhile, and brought him back on the French coast. Being at a height of about six thousand feet, some accident happened to his balloon of inflammable air; it burst, they fell from that height, and were crushed to atoms. There was a Montgolfier combined with the balloon of inflammable air. It is suspected the heat of the Montgolfier rarefied too much the inflammable air of the other, and occasioned it to burst. The Montgolfier came down in good order.

77. Governor John Jay of New York Coins the Word "Americanize"

WHEN John Jay, the first Chief Justice of the Supreme Court, returned to the United States in 1795 from his mission of arranging a partial settlement of differences with Great Britain, he found himself elected Governor of New York. Jay resigned as Chief Justice and accepted the office. The New York legislature had fixed on Albany for the State capital and there Jay wrote the present letter, in which the word "Americanize" is used for the first time.

The conditions that led to Jay's coining of the word were partly the result of the treaty he had negotiated with England, for it involved the United States in difficulties with France, where the treaty was regarded as evidence of belligerent intentions. Both countries had their ardent supporters in the United States. The Federalists, of which Jay was a leader, were generally sympathetic to the British while the Antifederalists, or Republicans, were pro-French. Jay's Treaty was regarded by the Republicans of that period as an appeasement of Great Britain, and when one of the leading Federalists, Alexander Hamilton, spoke in its defense, he was stoned. France became increasingly belligerent toward the United States and by June 1797, the Secretary of State reported that over three hundred American ships had been seized by the French.

Affairs thus stood when on October 27, 1797, Jay wrote this letter to his friend Colonel John Trumbull, soldier, poet and lawyer. After encouraging the Colonel to continue in the legal negotiations which then engaged him, Jay turned to one of his favorite themes. The following is from the letter lent by Mr. William Jay Iselin:

"As to politics, we are in a better state than we were; but we are not yet in a sound state. I think that nation is not in a sound state whose parties are excited by objects interesting only to a foreign power. I wish to see our people more Americanized, if I may use that expression; until we feel and act as an independent nation, we shall always suffer from foreign intrigues."

What Jay meant by his newly-coined word is clear from its context. He had spent the summer of 1794 in England negotiating a treaty that promised to guarantee peace and financial stability at a time when both were necessary for the establishment of American nationality under a new Constitution. He was afraid that minds too much concerned with foreign quarrels might needlessly and recklessly squander America's hard-won independence.

78. The King of Siam Offers a Gift of Elephants to President Lincoln

EVER since receiving a package of 192 volumes of United States Government publications as a gift from the United States Government, the King of Siam, Somdetch Phra Paramender Maha Mongkut, had tried to think of a way in which to express his appreciation. Learning that in traveling menageries which toured the United States the elephant was looked upon as the most remarkable of all the animals, King Mongkut believed that he had come upon a means of being of great service. Opening with a salutation to "his most respected excellent presidency, the President of the United States of America," the King of Siam offered, if the President and Congress saw "fit to approve," to "procure young male and female elephants, and forward them one or two pairs at a time" to the United States. Then if these elephants could be:

". . . turned loose in forest where there was abundance of water and grass, in any region under the sun's declination both north and south, called by the English the torrid zone, and all were forbidden to molest them, to attempt to raise them would be well, and if the climate there should prove favorable to elephants, we are of the opinion that after a while they will increase until they become large herds, as there are here on the continent of Asia, until the inhabitants of America will be able to catch and tame and use them as beasts of burthen, making them of great benefit to the country, since elephants, being animals of great size and strength, can bear burdens and travel through uncleared woods and matted jungles, where no carriage and cart roads have yet been made."

In February 1862 President Lincoln filched a little time from his pressing duties as a war president to write a courteous reply to the oriental potentate:

"I appreciate most highly your Majesty's tender of good offices in forwarding to this government a stock

from which a supply of elephants might be raised on our own soil. This government would not hesitate to avail itself of so generous an offer if the object were one which could be made practically useful in the present condition of the United States. Our political jurisdiction, however, does not reach a latitude so low as to favor the multiplication of the elephant, and steam on land, as well as on water, has been our best and most efficient agent of transportation in internal commerce. I shall have occasion at no distant day to transmit to your Majesty some token or indication of the high sense which this government entertains of your Majesty's friendship."

In conclusion, the President, wished his Majesty "a long and happy life" and signed his letter, "Your good friend, Abraham Lincoln."

The King of Siam's letter, lent by the National Archives, is written in Siamese on beautifully embossed stationery and accompanied by the properly magnificent seals.

79. General Andrew Jackson Reports the Victorious Battle of New Orleans (1815)

THE War of 1812 ended officially on December 24, 1814, with the signing of the Treaty of Ghent. Slow means of communication and travel, however, prevented knowledge of this event from reaching America until after the Battle of New Orleans was fought and won in early January 1815.

Andrew Jackson, hero of that bloody struggle, was a tempestuous Tennessee planter known as "Old Hickory." Experienced as a statesman in the House of Representatives and the Senate of the United States, he won lasting military honor in the War of 1812 and became the seventh President of the United States in 1829. As major-general in command of the 7th military district of Florida, Alabama and Louisiana, Jackson was informed in December 1814 that veteran British troops under General Sir Edward Pakenham were making ready to attack New Orleans, the key to the entire Mississippi Valley. The lean and hawk-eyed general arrived in New Orleans on December 1, 1814, to assume personal command of its neglected defenses. Both sides appear to have been confident of victory. Wives of the British officers accompanied their husbands on board ship in anticipation of enjoying the balmy winter at New Orleans; and General Jackson wrote his own beloved Rachel to make ready to join him.

The superior British fleet defeated a small American force at Lake Borgne and began to disembark the invasion troops. Jackson's motley forces included Tennessee frontiersmen, French and Creole settlers of Louisiana, a battalion of black freedmen from the isle of Santo Domingo, and a crew of hardened buccaneers under Jean Laffitte. The British advanced farther than expected, but Jackson, instead of retreating, stood ground and parried. After numerous skirmishes the main battle was joined on the morning of January 8, 1815, and was settled in less than half an hour. The British suffered decisive defeat. General Pakenham and many of his officers were among the 289 British dead; some 2,000 others were casualties or prisoners. American losses totalled 71, including 13 dead.

The news of victory at New Orleans reached Washington at a time when the position of the Federal government was most delicate. Representatives of the disgruntled New England States were criticizing President Madison's conduct of the war; the Hartford Convention had adjourned on January 5, 1815, after publishing its recommendation that each state be allowed to conduct the war in its own fashion. This was an implied threat of secession. But word of Jackson's smashing victory at New Orleans and the announcement of the peace treaty at Ghent shifted the mood of the nation "from gloom to glory" and in the noisy exultation the threatening voice of disunion was stilled. The victory at New Orleans also started Andrew Jackson on the high road to the White House.

In this original signed letter of January 9, 1815, displayed on the Freedom Train, the weary but triumphant Jackson made his report of the battle to Secretary of War Monroe. The document is from the War Department collection in the custody of the National Archives.

Camp 4 miles below New Orleans, January 9, 1815.

Sir:

During the days of the 6th and 7th, the enemy had been actively employed in making preparations for an attack on my lines. With infinite labor they had succeeded on the night of the 7th in getting their boats across from the lake to the river, by widening and deepening the canal on which they had effected their disembarkation. It had not been in my power to impede these operations by a general attack: added to other reasons, the nature of the troops under my command, mostly militia, rendered it too hazardous to attempt extensive *offensive* movements in an open country, against a numerous and well disciplined army. Although my forces, as to number, had been increased by the arrival of the Kentucky division, my strength had received very little addition; a small portion only of that detachment being provided with arms. Compelled thus to wait the attack of the enemy, I took every measure to repel it when it should be made, and to defeat the object he had in view. General Morgan, with the New Orleans contingent, the Louisiana militia and a strong detachment of the Kentucky troops, occupied an entrenched camp on the opposite side of the river, protected by strong bat-

teries on the bank, erected and superintended by commodore Patterson.

In *my* encampment everything was ready for action, when, early on the morning of the 8th, the enemy after throwing a heavy shower of bombs and Congreve rockets, advanced their columns on my right and left, to storm my entrenchments. I cannot speak sufficiently in praise of the firmness and deliberation with which my whole line received their approach—*more* could not have been expected from veterans inured to war. For an hour the fire of the small arms was as incessant and severe as can be imagined. The artillery, too, directed by officers who displayed equal skill and courage, did great execution. Yet the columns of the enemy continued to advance with a firmness which reflects upon them the greatest credit. Twice the column which approached me on my left, was repulsed by the troops of General Carroll, those of General Coffee, and a division of the Kentucky militia, and twice they formed again and renewed the assault. At length, however, cut to pieces, they fled in confusion from the field, leaving it covered with their dead and wounded. The loss which the enemy sustained on this occasion, cannot be estimated at less that 1500 in killed, wounded and prisoners. Upwards of three hundred have already been delivered over for burial; and my men are still engaged in picking them up within my lines and carrying them to the point where the enemy are to receive them. This is in addition to the dead and wounded whom the enemy have been enabled to carry from the field, during and since the action, and to those who have since died of the wounds they have received. We have taken about 500 prisoners, upwards of 300 of whom are wounded, and a great part of them mortally. My loss has not exceeded, and I believe has not amounted to ten killed and as many wounded.

The entire destruction of the enemy's army was now inevitable, had it not been for an unfortunate occurrence which at this moment took place on the other side of the river. Simultaneously with his advance, upon my lines, he had thrown over in his boats a considerable force to the other side of the river. *These* having landed were hardy enough to advance against the works of General Morgan; and what is strange and difficult to account for, at the very moment when their entire discomfiture was looked for with a confidence approaching to certainty, the Kentucky reinforcements, ingloriously fled, drawing after them, by their example, the remainder of the forces; and thus yielding to the enemy that most fortunate position. The batteries which had rendered me, for many days, the most important service, though bravely defended, were of course now abandoned; not however, until the guns had been spiked.

This unfortunate route had totally changed the aspect of affairs. The enemy now occupied a position from which they might annoy us without hazard, and by means of which they might have been enabled to defeat, in a great measure, the effects of our success on this side the river. It became therefore an object of the first consequence to dislodge him as soon as possible. For this object, all the means in my power, which I could with safety use, were immediately put in preparation. Perhaps, however, it was somewhat owing to another cause that I succeeded beyond my expectations, In negociating the terms of a temporary suspension of hostilities to enable the enemy to bury their dead and provide for their wounded, I had required certain propositions to be acceded to as a basis; among which was this one—that although hostilities should cease on *this* side the river until 12 o'clock of this day, yet it was not to be understood that they should cease on the *other* side; but that no reinforcements should be sent across by *either* army until the expiration of that day. His excellency major-general Lambert begged time to consider of these propositions until 10 o'clock of today, and in the meantime recrossed his troops. I need not tell you with how much eagerness I immediately regained possession of the position he had thus hastily quitted.

The enemy having concentered his forces, may again attempt to drive me from my position by storm. Whenever he *does,* I have no doubt my men will act with their usual firmness, and sustain a character now become dear to them.

I have the honor to be, with great respect,

Your obedient servant,
Andrew Jackson
Major-General Comdg.

80. The News of Peace Comes Belatedly to the U. S. Frigate "Constitution" while on the High Seas

"First part fresh breezes with squally and cloudy.
"Middle part like weather.
"Latter part battling variable winds. At 7h 30m A.M. spoke and boarded the barque *Julia* under Hamburg colours from Cork bound to Lisbon out 15 days, informed us that the news at Cork when they left was, that peace had been signed at Ghent between the British and American commissioners...."

Thus the logbook of the U. S. frigate *Constitution* exhibited on the Freedom Train records for Wednesday, February 8, 1815, where and how knowledge of the Treaty concluding the War of 1812 with Britain was received by this valiant ship of the U. S. Navy. Not knowing that peace had been declared she had been in several engagements and had captured some ships as prizes.

This and other logbooks of the *Constitution* are now among the records of the Navy Department in the custody of the National Archives. At the conclusion of the War of Independence, every ship in the American Navy was sold. This was true disarmament. But the depredations of Barbary pirates and tense relations with France and England led Congress in 1794 to provide for the building of six frigates that were designed to be superior to those of any navy in Europe. The first of these to be completed were the *United States,* the *Constellation* and the *Constitution.*

In October 1797, the *Constitution* was launched at Boston and commissioned with a complement of 400 officers and men. It cost $302,917; was 204 feet in length; 43½ feet in the beam; had a displacement of 2,200 tons; and mounted from 38 to 55 guns, mostly 42-pounders. The copper fittings and bolts that held its great oak beams together were made by Paul Revere; and its original design was by Joshua Humphrey of Philadelphia.

The war with England in 1812 was primarily a naval one in contrast with the Revolution 36 years earlier, although the Battle at New Orleans was a rousing victory for General Andrew Jackson and American land forces. After many futile protests, it was apparent that only an appeal to arms would force the countries of the Old World to realize and recognize the rights of the American flag on the high seas. When the war broke out the United States Navy possessed only 18 seagoing vessels, of which seven were frigates. The logs of the *Constitution* record its victorious actions in the war against the British ships *Guerriere, Java, Picton, Cyane, Levant,* and others. Captain Isaac Hull won fame as commander of the frigate in its battle with the *Guerriere.* In this affray, it is said that when a large shot struck the hard oak sides of the *Constitution* and fell into the water without damaging the ship a sailor exclaimed in wonder that its sides must be made of iron. The idea caught the popular imagination and the affectionate name of "Old Ironsides" has been applied to the ship ever since. Because the ship came to personify America's sturdy strength it occupies a special place in the hearts of all its citizens.

For a while after the Peace of Ghent, the *Constitution* became flagship of the Mediterranean squadron. On September 14, 1830, however, the *Boston Advertiser* printed the news that the Secretary of Navy had recommended that the *Constitution* be disposed of as unfit for service. Two days later there appeared in a Boston paper a poem, "Old Ironsides," by Oliver Wendell Holmes. The poem stirred the nation; schoolboys throughout the land soon declaimed those lines beginning:

"Ay, Tear her tattered ensign down!
Long has it waved on high."

Protests prevented any destructive action and she was rebuilt in 1833.

In the same year great excitement was again aroused when a statue of President Andrew Jackson was used for a figurehead on "Old Ironsides." Violent arguments of a partisan character followed, and one audacious spirit, Samuel Dewey (cousin of George "Manila Bay" Dewey) climbed aboard the frigate one dark night and sawed off the statue's head. Consternation and confusion increased until Dewey traveled to the nation's Capital with the head and admitted his prank. The mutilated figurehead was replaced with another likeness of Jackson, and since then several other figureheads have been used on the ship.

At one time the U. S. Naval Academy used the *Constitution* as a training ship, and the young midshipmen at Annapolis joined the ranks of other navy heroes who had served on the ship in peace and war. This roster included Samuel Barron, John Barry, William Bainbridge, Stephen Decatur, Jr., George Dewey, Isaac Hull, James Lawrence, and Oliver Hazard Perry. In 1897, the centennial year of its launching, the *Constitution* was towed to Boston Harbor for an impressive celebration. For lack of funds the famous ship fell into disrepair. In 1925 Congress authorized the Navy to restore the ship, and through nation-wide contributions from the highest and the humblest sufficient funds were finally collected to repair and preserve the ship. Since then it has been a U. S. Naval Museum afloat.

81. The United States Returns a Part of the Boxer Indemnity Funds to China

WHEN the Sino-Japanese War of 1894–1895 revealed the weakness of China to the world, European powers hastened to obtain for themselves special concessions and spheres of influence. "The various powers," said the Dowager Empress of China, "cast upon us looks of tiger-like voracity, hustling each other in their endeavors to be the first to seize upon our innermost territories."

John Hay, McKinley's Secretary of State, was much concerned at the possible consequences of this carving up of China, and in September 1899, with the support of the British Foreign Office, he announced what has come to be known as the "Open Door" policy. In a note addressed to the major European nations, Hay recognized the existence of spheres of influence, but requested from each nation a declaration that each, in its sphere, would maintain the Chinese customs tariff and levy equal harbor dues and railway rates on the ships and merchandise of all nations.

Antipathy to foreigners had developed to such an extent, however, that a secret organization called the Boxers tried to drive the "foreign devils" out. In June 1900 they massacred over two hundred foreigners, mostly missionaries and their families, and besieged the foreign lega-

tions in Peking, including that of the United States. Anxious for the safety of its citizens in the legation, our government joined with Great Britain, Russia, Germany, France and Japan in sending a military expedition for the relief of all the legations. The international force assembled at Taku and marched to Peking, where it quickly raised the siege.

When John Hay had originally announced the "Open Door" policy, he was chiefly concerned with safeguarding American commercial interests in China. At the time of the joint intervention to put down the Boxers, however, he addressed a note to all powers concerned, in which he boldly announced that the objectives of the joint intervention were ". . . to seek a solution which may bring about permanent safety and peace to China, preserve Chinese territorial administrative entity . . . and safeguard for the world the principle of equal and impartial trade with all parts of the Chinese Empire." The other powers perforce agreed, and thus the danger of a general war was averted and the integrity of China preserved.

Despite the best efforts of the American representatives to keep the indemnity for damages at a reasonable figure, the only sum at which the powers concerned could agree was approximately 333 million dollars. Of this, some 24 million was allotted to the United States. Since American losses were estimated at approximately half that amount, President Theodore Roosevelt, Secretary of State Elihu Root, and the Congress determined to return the difference to the Chinese. Grateful for this extraordinary action, the Chinese decided to spend the money for the education of students in the United States. Curiously, the Boxer Rebellion, which was intended to separate China from the world, became the means whereby the Chinese learned Western methods and ideas in the United States. The return of a part of the Boxer indemnity funds and Hay's friendship at the time of the intervention both encouraged the excellent relations that have since existed between the peoples of China and the United States.

The original letter from Secretary of State Elihu Root to President Theodore Roosevelt is from the collections of the National Archives.

The President:

I send to you herewith for your signature, if it meets your approval, a draft of an Executive Order in execution of the Joint Resolution of Congress "To provide for the remission of a portion of the Chinese indemnity," approved May 25, 1908.

The Resolution provides that "the remission shall be at such times and in such manner as the President shall deem just."

The plan embodied in this Order provides for annual remissions as the payments under the original indemnity bond become due, beginning with the remission of $483,094.90 in the year 1909 and gradually increasing as the payments under the original bond increase until the remission becomes $1,383,785.36 in the year 1940. The draft has been submitted to Mr. Tang Shao Yi, the Special Ambassador of China, and meets his approval.

I send also the following explanatory papers:

1. A copy of a letter from the State Department to the Chinese Minister at Washington, dated June 15, 1907, announcing the purpose of the President to ask Congress for authority to remit a portion of the indemnity and explaining the basis of the proposed remission.

2. An extract from the President's Annual Message to Congress of December 3, 1907, asking for such authority, and also including the paragraph of the Message relating to the education of Chinese students in the United States.

3. A copy of the Joint Resolution of May 25, 1908.

4. A copy of a letter, dated July 11, 1908, from the American Minister in China to the President of the Board of Foreign Affairs of China announcing the action of Congress.

5. The translation of a letter from the President of the Board of Foreign Affairs of China to the American Minister, dated July 14, 1908, and a supplemental letter of the same date signed by the members of the Board of Foreign Affairs announcing the purpose of the Chinese Government to send and maintain for education in the United States Chinese students, one hundred each year for four years until the number in America amounts to four hundred, and thereafter a minimum of fifty each year, proposing to confer with the American Minister regarding the plan and asking the assistance of the American Government in carrying out the plan.

6. A copy of a cable despatch from the State Department to the American Minister in China, dated August 3, 1908, in response to the Minister's cable communication of the substance of the above-mentioned letters from the Foreign Office.

7. The translation of a draft of proposed regulations for the students to be sent to America to be supported out of the indemnity fund remitted by the United States, submitted by the Foreign Office of China to the American Minister. The Minister has been authorized by the State Department to approve this draft and he reports that he has done so with some slight amendments.

I respectfully suggest that a copy of the Executive Order be transmitted to the Treasury Department with instructions to comply with the provisions thereof regarding the remission of indemnity:—that a copy of all these papers be transmitted to the Commissioner of Education of the United States with instructions to aid in all appropriate ways within his power in the carrying out of the plan of the Chinese Government for the edu-

cation of students in America, and that a copy be laid before Congress for its information.

Respectfully submitted,

December 28, 1908. Elihu Root

82. President Theodore Roosevelt Informs Congress of the Action to Remit a Portion of the Boxer Indemnity Funds

THE background of this original signed letter has already been explained (see document No. 81). The text of President Roosevelt's letter explains itself. The document is lent to the Freedom Train exhibit by the National Archives.

TO THE SENATE AND HOUSE OF REPRESENTATIVES:

I transmit herewith for the information of Congress a copy of an Executive Order signed by me on the 28th day of December, 1908, in execution of the Joint Resolution of May 25, 1908, "To provide for the remission of a portion of the Chinese Indemnity," together with a letter from the Secretary of State and various documents explanatory thereof and explanatory also of a plan for the education of Chinese students in the United States, to which the Government of China proposes to devote a large part of the remitted indemnity. Copies of these papers have also been transmitted to the Commissioner of Education of the United States with instructions to aid in all appropriate ways within his power in the carrying out of the plans of the Chinese Government for the eudcation [sic] of students in America.

Theodore Roosevelt

January 4, 1909.

83. Congress Acts to Provide the First Important Measure to Aid Higher Education in the United States (1862)

AMERICANS have, since early colonial times, been generous in granting lands for the support of common school education, but the extension of this principle to aid a democratic and practical education on a higher level did not occur until the middle of the nineteenth century.

This was a result of long and persistent agitation from some of the western states where educational needs differed sharply from the training provided by many older, private institutions in the East. Many efforts were fruitless and it was not until Jonathan Baldwin Turner, a farmer and a former professor in the Illinois College at

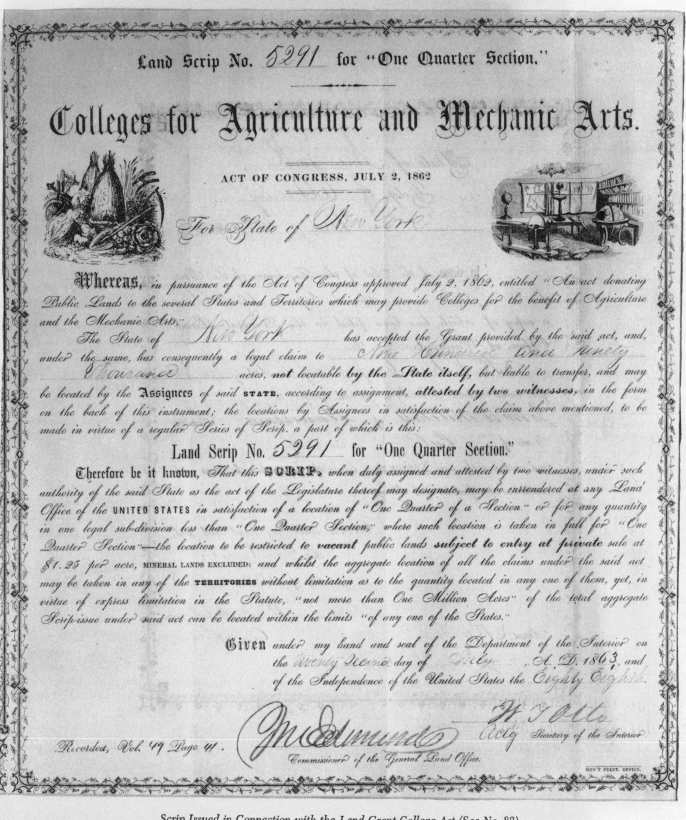

Land Scrip No. *5291* for "One Quarter Section."

Colleges for Agriculture and Mechanic Arts.

ACT OF CONGRESS, JULY 2, 1862

For State of *New York*

Whereas, in pursuance of the Act of Congress approved July 2, 1862, entitled "An act donating Public Lands to the several States and Territories which may provide Colleges for the benefit of Agriculture and the Mechanic Arts;" *New York* has accepted the Grant provided by the said act, and, under the same, has consequently a legal claim to *Nine Hundred and Ninety Thousand* acres, **not locatable by the State itself**, but liable to transfer, and may be located by the **Assignees** of said **STATE**, according to assignment, **attested by two witnesses**, in the form on the back of this instrument; the locations by Assignees in satisfaction of the claim above mentioned, to be made in virtue of a regular Series of Scrip, a part of which is this:

Land Scrip No. *5291* for "One Quarter Section."

Therefore be it known, That this **SCRIP**, when duly assigned and attested by two witnesses, under such authority of the said State as the act of the Legislature thereof may designate, may be surrendered at any Land Office of the **UNITED STATES** in satisfaction of a location of "One Quarter of a Section" or for any quantity in one legal sub-division less than "One Quarter Section," where such location is taken in full for "One Quarter Section"—the location to be restricted to **vacant** public lands **subject to entry** at **private** sale at $1.25 per acre, **MINERAL LANDS EXCLUDED:** and whilst the aggregate location of all the claims under the said act may be taken in any of the **TERRITORIES** without limitation as to the quantity located in any one of them, yet, in virtue of express limitation in the Statute, "not more than One Million Acres" of the total aggregate Scrip-issue under said act can be located within the limits "of any one of the States."

Given under my hand and seal of the Department of the Interior on the *Twenty Second* day of *July*, A. D. 186*3*, and of the Independence of the United States the *Eighty Eighth*.

W T Otto
Actg Secretary of the Interior.

Jn Edmunds
Commissioner of the General Land Office.

Recorded, Vol. 49 Page 41.

GOV'T PRINT. OFFICE.

Scrip Issued in Connection with the Land-Grant College Act (See No. 83)

Jacksonville, Illinois, took the lead in the movement that tangible results were produced.

Turner succeeded in interesting Justin Smith Morrill, a United States Senator from Vermont. In 1857 he introduced in Congress a bill donating Federal lands for the establishment of colleges for instruction in agriculture and the mechanic arts. This bill was approved by Congress in 1858, but was vetoed by President Buchanan in

1859. But a similar bill was approved by President Lincoln in July 1862.

By the Land-Grant College Act, popularly known as the Morrill Land-Grant Act, the Federal government donated to each state 30,000 acres of public lands for each Congressman and Senator the state was entitled to send to Washington.

Latest figures indicate that the Federal government has, for this purpose, granted a total of 118,000,000 acres —an area four times the size of the state of New York. The Land-Grant College Act led directly to the establishment of a most important system of state educational institutions aided by the Federal government. This was most important because it was begun at a time when many of the states were themselves unable to provide funds for such purposes.

The Morrill Act was probably the most important piece of educational legislation ever passed in the United States. A prominent agriculturist, L. H. Bailey, wrote of it: "It recognizes the principle that every citizen is entitled to receive educational aid from the government and that the common affairs of life are proper subjects with which to educate or train men."

Under its generous provisions sixty-nine land-grant colleges have been established. Many of the western state universities sprang from the Act, and others received a decided impetus from its provisions. Cornell University, at Ithaca, New York, was the principal beneficiary of the piece of scrip exhibited on the Freedom Train.

This document, lent by the National Archives, is the original land scrip issued to the State of New York and which authorized that state to receive 900,090 acres of land still in the public domain.

84. John Peter Zenger Provokes Governor Cosby to a Test of Freedom of the Press (1734)

ZENGER was born in Germany and came to New York at the age of thirteen. His father died while still on the ship which brought them to the new world. Young Zenger was then apprenticed to William Bradford, one of the foremost of colonial printers, for a period of eight years. Here he learned something of the art of printing and of publishing. Having served his apprenticeship he contracted an unfortunate marriage, spent a brief time of residence in Kent County, Maryland, and then returned to New York City. In 1722 he married a second time and this time his spouse was Anna Catherina Maulin. After four years of vicissitudes Zenger finally set up a printing shop for himself. But in this venture he enjoyed no special prosperity.

It was only after he became embroiled in the political struggles of the 1730's that he became conspicuous. The arbitrary and tyrannical acts of Governor Cosby reached a climax in the removal of Lewis Morris from the chief justiceship of the province. The leaders of the opposition to the governor decided that the best way to wage battle would be to establish a newspaper. Cosby and his friends had their own newspaper in Bradford's *New-York Gazette*. Lewis Morris, James Alexander, William Smith and others selected Zenger and established him as the publisher of a new paper, the *New-York Weekly Journal*. With the first issue of the *Journal* it was clear that the fight was on. Zenger's sponsors wrote many of the articles, for Zenger himself was not too facile with a quill. But whether he wrote little or much he was legally responsible for all that he printed.

That responsibility was soon to be tested. In the fall of 1734 the Council, in response to the prompting of the governor, ordered that numbers 7, 47, 48 and 49, alleged to contain certain unsavory doggerel rhymes, be publicly burned. But there was a problem in finding some authorized person to perform this burning. One after another turned down the opportunity; it was finally done by a Negro slave of the sheriff. At the same time Zenger was charged with libel, and bail of £400 was fixed for himself and £200 for his sureties. This has ever been a favorite device of those who exercise arbitrary power. The sum demanded represented a small fortune. Zenger was unable to post the bond and went to jail. But from his cell he continued to assist in the publication of the paper. It was only in the April term of 1735 that his trial for criminal libel came up.

By yet another high-handed gesture Zenger's attorneys were disbarred and the trial was postponed and the defendant was taken back to jail. Meanwhile, Zenger's supporters were active. It was true that the court and the governor had succeeded in intimidating those lawyers who might otherwise have come to his defense. So they went to Philadelphia and secretly enlisted the aid of Andrew Hamilton, former attorney general of the province of Pennsylvania. Hamilton's sudden appearance in the August trials provided a stir. He pleaded for the right of the jury to inquire into the truth or falsity of the alleged libel. When his plea was denied by the judges he appealed to the jury itself to take the matter into its hands. The jury itself was in peril by assuming such a responsibility. And Hamilton's arguments were full of "bad law."

The jury quickly returned with an acquittal for Zenger. In their decision, inspired by Hamilton's eloquence, they established a precedent which later became a part of recognized law. Freedom of the press achieved a notable victory.

This original copy is lent to the Freedom Train exhibit by the Library of Congress.

85. John Peter Zenger Continues to Edit His "New-York Weekly Journal" while in Jail and Awaiting Trial (November 25, 1734)

AFTER his indictment, bail for Zenger was fixed at £400 and £200 for his sureties (see document No. 84). This proved exorbitant and Zenger was thrown into jail. Meanwhile his newspaper continued publication. His sponsors may have continued to provide both the copy and the finances. Kent Cooper, in a recent novelized biography, maintains that it was Anna Zenger, his wife, who carried on during his imprisonment. The facts are difficult to establish.

The excerpt here reproduced from an original copy of number 55, November 25, 1734, is lent to the Freedom Train by the Library of Congress. It would indicate that Zenger, rather than his sponsors, was writing the copy. No exact verification can be had of the "Hole of the Door of the Prison," although it would seem to carry a measure of authenticity.

To all my Subscribers and Benefactors who take my weekly Journall.

Gentlemen, Ladies and Others;

As you last week were Disappointed of my Journall, I think it Incumbent upon me, to publish my Apoligy which is this. On the Lords Day, the Seventeenth of this Instant, I was Arrested, taken and Imprisoned in the common Goal of this Citty, by Virtue of a Warrant from the *Governour,* and the Honorable *Franciss Harrison,* Esq; and others in Councill of which (God willing) yo'l have a Coppy, whereupon I was put under such Restraint that I had not the Liberty of Pen, Ink, or Paper, or to see, or speak with People, till upon my Complaint to the Honourable the Chief Justice, at my appearing before him upon my *Habias Corpus* on the *Wednesday* following. Who discountenanced that Proceeding, and therefore I have had since that Time, the Liberty of Speaking through the Hole of the Door, to my Wife and Servants by which I doubt not yo'l think me sufficiently Excused for not sending my last week's *Journall,* and I hope for the future by the Liberty of Speaking to my Servants thro' the Hole of the Door of the Prison, to entertain you with my Weekly *Journal* as formerly.

And am your obliged
Humble Servant
J. Peter Zenger

John Peter Zenger's "New-York Weekly Journal" announces Vindication of a Free Press (See Nos. 85-87)

86. John Peter Zenger Publishes the Account of the Vindication of a Free Press

AFTER Andrew Hamilton's stirring appeal to the jury in the trial of Zenger it did not take much time for them to declare him innocent of the charges (see Nos. 84 and 85). The Freedom Train displays, through the courtesy of the Library of Congress, an original copy of issue number 93 (August 18, 1735) in which he announces his vindication.

87. Benjamin Franklin Defends Freedom of the Press

THE editorial "On Freedom of Speech and of the Press" published by Benjamin Franklin in his *Pennsylvania Gazette* for November 10-17, 1737, is an expression of his view that without a free press a free society is impossible. In his youth, Franklin's journalism had involved him in trouble with the Massachusetts authorities and at the time of this editorial he was publishing a paper as well as political pamphlets. When John Peter Zenger, a New York printer and publisher, was tried in a libel suit, Franklin followed the case with interest. The verdict of "not guilty" enlarged the freedom of the press and Franklin, in his editorial, supported the precedent it established.

Zenger was the publisher of the *New-York Weekly Journal,* a newspaper set up by the provincial leaders opposed to the arbitrary actions of the royal governor. In the fall of 1734, the governor became so irritated by the vigorous attacks against him that he had Zenger arrested and thrown in jail. Zenger languished there ten months before he was tried; meanwhile, from his prison cell, he gave instructions for publishing the paper.

At the trial Andrew Hamilton, Zenger's lawyer, an extraordinarily able and vigorous figure, argued for a new interpretation of the law for seditious libel. The British had come to accept the doctrine that in such a suit it was only necessary for the prosecuting authorities to establish the fact that the defendant had actually published the objectionable passages. Zenger's lawyer insisted that it was also necessary for the prosecution to establish that the passages objected to were false—in other words, he set up the principle that one could not libel the government merely by telling the truth about it. When the judge declined to accept this interpretation, the attorney turned and appealed to the jury, who brought in a verdict of not guilty. In time, the new interpretation of the law came to be the accepted one.

The editorial published in Franklin's newspaper was probably from his own pen. It certainly has many marks of his homely and forceful style. And it does express the publisher's views on the subject, from the opening sentence: "Freedom of speech is a principal pillar of a free government; when this support is taken away, the constitution of a free society is disolved, and tyranny is erected on its ruins. . . ."

This original printing is lent to the Freedom Train by the Library of Congress.

88. John Wilkes Attacks the Policies of George III

ONE of the most famous issues of a periodical that has involved freedom of the press is No. 45 of the *North Briton.* This magazine, published by John Wilkes, was devoted to attacking the ministers of George III, the autocratic monarch against whom the American patriots later rebelled. Issue No. 45, which criticized the King's speech closing Parliament on April 19, 1763, repre-

sented the King as the victim of dishonest ministers, who had put lies in his mouth. Since the King had actually been dictating his ministers' policies, both became furious and proceeded against the anonymous *North Briton* under a general warrant, by which forty-nine persons were arrested. Although Wilkes escaped the first prosecution under a technicality, he became involved in a bitter controversy. When he was finally tried, sentenced, and imprisoned, his popularity was immense—crowds of supporters regularly assembled outside the prison gates. On his release, he began a turbulent career in politics, championing freedom of the press, freedom of choice for voters, and the protection of individual liberty.

An ugly, witty man, Wilkes was the English representative of the Boston Sons of Liberty, and during the American Revolution actively championed the Colonial cause in Parliament. Wilkes-Barre, Pennsylvania, is named for him and another English defender of America.

This original printing of No. 45 of the *North Briton* is from the collections of the Library of Congress.

89. Elijah Lovejoy Dies Defending Freedom of the Press

THIS is a contemporary account of the trial of rioters whose lawless action caused the death of a courageous man, a man described by one of his contemporaries as "the first martyr in America to the great principles of the freedom of speech and of the press."

Elijah Parish Lovejoy was a young Presbyterian clergyman who served as editor of the Presbyterian weekly for the West, the *St. Louis Observer.* By 1836 his growing sympathy for the anti-slavery cause forced him to leave St. Louis. He journeyed twenty-five miles up the Mississippi to Alton, Illinois, at that time one of the most prosperous cities in the state. Alton was populated by emigrants from New England and other eastern states and thus was quite sympathetic to Lovejoy's belief in the doctrine of gradual emancipation of the slaves. Gradually, however, he came to advocate immediate emancipation of the slaves in his *Alton Observer.* Soon the young preacher found himself in bitter conflict with the citizens of Alton, who proceeded to destroy his printing press. The Ohio Anti-Slavery Society, which Lovejoy had been instrumental in organizing, promptly forwarded new presses, but as soon as they arrived various groups assembled and destroyed them. Early in November 1837 another press arrived in Alton and this time a group of sixty young abolitionists from nearby towns gathered to defend the press which was stored in a warehouse. On the night of November 7 a mob attacked the warehouse and, when repulsed by the abolitionists, attempted to set it on fire. When Lovejoy stepped outside the warehouse in an effort to dissuade the incendiaries he was shot and killed.

Lovejoy's death aroused much interest but little sympathy—even in the North. The attorney general of Massachusetts, before a large crowd in Fanueil Hall, described Lovejoy as a "presumptuous and imprudent" man who had "died as the fool dieth."

Fool? Martyr? Hero? In his own day Lovejoy was given these and many other descriptive terms. What word conveyed the greatest measure of exactitude is not so important today. What is important is that he so strongly believed in certain principles and in his constitutional right to voice them freely that he was willing to die for them. The grim fact of history is that he did die in attempting to express them.

The printed account of the Alton Trials, published in New York in 1838, is lent to the Freedom Train exhibit by the Library of Congress.

90. George Hay Defends Freedom of the Press from Legislative Control

PARTISAN fury ran high in the new American republic at the close of the century. In the presidential election of 1796, the Federalists had managed to win by an extremely close margin. It was so close, in fact, that the successful candidate, John Adams, was constantly taunted by the opposing Republicans that he was "President by three votes."

At about this time the Federalist administration was having increasing difficulties with France. French naval vessels and privateers were violating America's "freedom of the sea" by making indiscriminate seizures of American merchantmen.

Goaded on by the incessant political attacks of the Republicans and fearful of disunity in the event of war with France, the Federalists resolved in 1798 to crush the Republican opposition, if possible, with a series of repressive measures. Among these was the Sedition Act which was designed to silence derogatory criticism, both oral and printed, of the government and public officers. It prescribed fine and imprisonment for such criticism and gave Federalist judges the means of enforcing the statute against offenders. The Sedition Act was vigorously enforced and several editors of Republican papers found themselves imprisoned or ruined by heavy fines.

Some of the leading Federalists, however, saw the dangers inherent in such a law. John Marshall, the future great justice of the Supreme Court, was one of these. Another was the financial genius, Alexander Hamilton, who warned his colleagues: "Let us not establish a tyranny, Energy is a very different thing from violence." These warnings were in vain and Republican resentment burst forth like a flood. In printed word and fervent speeches the Republicans described the Sedition Act as despotic. They denounced the Act as despotic and the Federalists as tyrants. They denounced the Act as contrary to the First Amendment to the Constitution. "Congress shall make no law . . . abridging the freedom of speech, or of the press. . . ."

One of the best protests was an essay which appeared in 1799 by "Hortensius," a regular contributor to the *Richmond Examiner*. This pen name concealed George Hay, son of the keeper of the famous Raleigh Tavern at Williamsburg, Virginia, and an able attorney whom Thomas Jefferson, as President, later made United States Attorney for the District of Virginia. In his brilliant legal essay Hay arrived at the conclusion that "the freedom of the press . . . means the total exemption of the press from any kind of legislative control."

Thomas Jefferson was the leading Republican figure in the campaign against the Sedition Act and other repressive Federalist measures. Consequently, when he became President in 1801, Jefferson issued pardons to all persons who had been convicted under the Act and Congress eventually repaid all the fines.

The exhibited first edition, printed in Philadelphia in 1799, is from the collections of the Library of Congress.

91. John Milton Defends the Liberty of Printing (1644)

"As good almost kill a Man as kill a good Book; who kills a Man kills a reasonable creature, Gods Image; but he who destroys a good Book, kills reason it self. . . ." Opened for exhibit on the Freedom Train is the page to show this oft-quoted phrase from the *Areopagitica*, John Milton's eloquent argument against censorship of the press.

It was the poet's ringing rebuttal to the outcry raised against him because of his controversial pamphlets on divorce. Milton wished to divorce his young wife because she was "stupid." He proposed a sweeping reform of the marriage laws which would "wipe away ten thousand tears out of the life of men." Milton's opponents had hoped to silence him through a technicality. The law of Great Britain required all books and pamphlets to be licensed and registered with the Stationers' Company, but Milton's pamphlets had been neither licensed nor registered. The Stationers complained against him in a petition to Parliament.

Instead of yielding ground, Milton wrote the *Areopagitica*, deliberately unlicensed and unregistered, in which he called for the repeal of the licensing law and attacked the whole system of licensing and censorship of the press.

Though repeal of the law did not immediately follow, the pamphlet accomplished its purpose. The licensing system had received a death blow. His words will long remain at a high level of lofty eloquence in behalf of the freedom of the press.

This copy of the original edition, published in London in 1644, is lent to the Freedom Train exhibit by the Library of Congress.

92. Thomas Jefferson Declares That an Honest Press is "Equally the Friend of Science and Civil Liberty" (1807)

Few men in American public life have been attacked more savagely by the press than was Jefferson, especially during his two terms as President. Yet freedom of the press remained one of his cherished subjects and no American has more consistently reached the heights of eloquence in its defense.

This particular letter was written to Thomas Seymour of Hartford, Connecticut. Seymour was one of the most distinguished men of public affairs in Connecticut. He was five times speaker of the General Assembly and from 1793 to 1803 he was a member of the State Senate, then called the House of Assistants. He was chief judge of the Court of Common Pleas of Hartford County. From 1784 to 1812 he served as the first mayor of the incorporated city of Hartford.

Jefferson's letter was written in reply to a letter dated December 20, 1806, and signed by Thomas Seymour and six other gentlemen. They wished to explain to Jefferson the background of several cases of libel that were about to come to trial. They, being Republicans (not, of course, to be confused with the present Republican Party), heartily damned the Federalists who, in their words, had been pouring forth "a continued torrent of abuse, not only copious and uninterrupted, but irresistable" against the government in Washington and all its officers. In presenting the Republican point of view they also give their opinions of the freedom of the press:

"The Press we consider as essential to *our* Liberties; *its* liberty inviolable. In the liberty of the Press we include, the right to publish our sentiments on every measure of the Government; to examine it freely in all its tendencies; but not to charge its authors, with motives subversive of the liberties & happiness of the nation."

Jefferson, in a real sense, rebukes the partisan attitude of his Connecticut followers and restates his belief that the press should and must remain free.

The present document, lent to the Freedom Train exhibit by the Library of Congress, is what is known as a "polygraph" copy—one created by the aid of a mechanical device in which another pen, linked with the one held in the hand of the writer, simultaneously produced a second copy.

Washington, February 11, 1807.

Sir,
The mass of business which occurs during a session of the Legislature, renders me necessarily unpunctual in acknowledging the receipt of letters, and in answering those which will admit of delay. This must be my apology for being so late in noticing the receipt of the letter of December 20th, addressed to me by yourself, and several other republican characters of your State of high respectability. I have seen with deep concern the afflicting oppression under which the republican citizens of Connecticut suffer from an unjust majority. The truths expressed in your letter have been long exposed to the nation through the channel of the public papers, and are the more readily believed because most of the States during the momentary ascendancy of kindred majorities, in them have seen the same spirit of opposition prevail.

With respect to the countervailing prosecutions now instituted in the Court of the United States in Connecticut, I had heard but little, and certainly, I believe, never expressed a sentiment on them. That a spirit of indignation and retaliation should arise when an opportunity should present itself, was too much within the human constitution to excite either surprise or censure, and confined to an appeal to truth only, it cannot lessen the useful freedom of the press.

As to myself, conscious that there was not a *truth* on earth which I feared should be known, I have lent myself willingly as the subject of a great experiment, which was to prove that an administration, conducting itself with integrity and common understanding, cannot be battered down, even by the falsehoods of a licentious press, and consequently still less by the press, as restrained within the legal and wholesome limits of truth. This experiment was wanting for the world to demonstrate the falsehood of the pretext that freedom of the press is incompatible with orderly government. I have never therefore even contradicted the thousands of calumnies so industriously propagated against myself. But the fact being once established, that the press is impotent when it abandons itself to falsehood, I leave to others to restore it to its strength, by recalling it within the pale of truth. Within that it is a noble institution, equally the friend of science and of civil liberty. If this can once be effected in your State, I trust we shall soon see its citizens rally to the republican principles of our Constitution, which unite their sister-States into one family. It would seem impossible that an intelligent people, with the faculty of reading and right of thinking, should continue much longer to slumber under the pupilage of an interested aristocracy of priests and lawyers, persuading them to distrust themselves, and to let them think for them. I sincerely wish that your efforts may awaken them from this voluntary degradation of mind, re-

[122]

store them to a due estimate of themselves and their fellow citizens, and a just abhorrence of the falsehoods and artifices which have seduced them. Experience of the use made by federalism of whatever comes from me, obliges me to suggest the caution of considering my letter as private. I pray you to present me respectfully to the other gentlemen who joined in the letter to me, and to whom this is equally addressed, and to accept yourself my salutations, and assurances of great esteem and consideration.

Th. Jefferson

93. Thomas Jefferson Declares That Newspapers are Indispensable since the Basis of Government is Public Opinion

THOMAS JEFFERSON'S convictions concerning a free press were strong and unchanging throughout his life. To Jefferson the press was an important and integral part of the whole democratic system. His whole doctrine was simply this: maintain a free press, see that the people get the facts, and the people will govern themselves wisely.

One of Jefferson's clearest statements of the importance of a free press in a democratic society is found in his letter of January 16, 1787, written to Edward Carrington, one of his friends and political associates in Virginia, while he was serving as Minister to France. If the press were free, the truth would reach the people, and the people could and would form correct judgments in matters of government. ". . . Were it left to me to decide whether we should have a government without newspapers, or newspapers without a government," wrote Jefferson, "I should not hesitate a moment to prefer the latter. . . ." The letter in the Freedom Train exhibit is a letter-press copy (the eighteenth-century equivalent of the modern carbon copy) made from the original and is lent by the Library of Congress.

Paris, January 16, 1787.

Dear Sir,

Uncertain whether you might be at New York at the moment of Colonel Franks' arrival, I have enclosed my private letters for Virginia under cover to our delegation in general, which otherwise I would have taken the liberty to enclose particularly to you, as best acquainted with the situation of the persons to whom they are addressed. Should this find you at New York, I will still ask your attention to them.

In my letter to Mr. Jay, I have mentioned the meeting of the Notables, appointed for the 29th instant. It is now put off to the 7th or 8th of next month. This event, which will hardly excite any attention in America, is deemed here the most important one which has taken place in their civil line during the present century. Some promise their country great things from it, some nothing. Our friend de La Fayette was placed on the list originally. Afterwards his name disappeared, but finally was reinstated. This shows that his character here is not considered as an indifferent one, and that it excites agitation. His education in our school has drawn on him a very jealous eye from a court whose principles are the most absolute despotism. But I hope he has nearly passed his crisis. The King, who is a good man, is favorably disposed towards him, and he is supported by powerful family connections and by the public good will. He is the youngest man of the Notables except one whose office placed him on the list.

The Count de Vergennes has within these ten days had a very severe attack of what is deemed an unfixed gout. He has been well enough, however, to do business today. But anxieties for him are not yet quieted. He is a great and good minister, and an accident to him might endanger the peace of Europe.

The tumults in America I expected would have produced in Europe an unfavorable opinion of our political state. But it has not. On the contrary, the small effect of these tumults seems to have given more confidence in the firmness of our governments. The interposition of the people themselves on the side of government has had a great effect on the opinion here. I am persuaded myself that the good sense of the people will always be found to be the best army. They may be led astray for a moment, but will soon correct themselves. The people are the only censors of their governors; and even their errors will tend to keep these to the true principles of their institution. To punish these errors too severely would be to suppress the only safeguard of the public liberty. The way to prevent these irregular interpositions of the people, is to give them full information of their affairs through the channel of the public papers, and to contrive that those papers should penetrate the whole mass of the people. The basis of our governments being the opinion of the people, the very first object should be to keep that right; and were it left to me to decide whether we should have a government without newspapers, or newspapers without a government, I should not hesitate a moment to prefer the latter. But I should mean that every man should receive those papers, and be capable of reading them. I am convinced that those societies (as the Indians) which live without government, enjoy in their general mass an infinitely greater degree of happiness than those who live under the European governments. Among the former, public opinion is in the place of law, and restrains morals as powerfully as laws ever did anywhere. Among the latter, under pretence of governing, they have divided their nations into two classes, wolves and sheep. I do not exaggerate. This is a true picture of Europe. Cherish, therefore, the spirit of our people, and keep alive their attention. Do not be too severe upon their errors, but reclaim them by enlightening them. If once they become inattentive to the public affairs, you and I, and Congress and Assemblies, Judges and Governors, shall all become wolves. It seems to be the law of our general nature, in spite of individual exceptions; and experience declares that man is the only animal which devours his own kind; for I can apply no milder term to the governments of Europe, and to the general prey of the rich on the poor. The want of news has led me into disquisition instead of narration, forgetting you have every day enough of that. I shall be happy to hear from you sometimes, only observing that whatever passes through the post is read, and that when you write what should be read by myself only, you must be so good as to confide your letter to some passenger, or officer of the packet. I will ask your permission to write to you sometimes, and to assure you of the esteem and respect with which I have honor to be, dear Sir, your most obedient, and most humble servant.

Th. Jefferson.

94. President Wilson Drafts a Covenant for the League of Nations (1918)

WOODROW WILSON, 28th President of the United States, was a moving spirit in the years-long struggle to establish international cooperation for the maintenance of peace. The great passion of his life was the League of Nations. He was not—and he would have been the first to say it—the originator of the idea. For centuries men had been seeking some means for preventing war, and various methods had been tried. Wilson was, in a sense, the compiler and editor of these many ideas and suggestions.

He brought together the best out of the past and then solicited from his contemporaries their most promising contributions. Working with all these, he contributed his own forceful thinking to the further development of the grand concept: the maintenance of peace through international cooperation.

Before typing out his first draft for a League of Nations Covenant, or constitution, Wilson had studied in detail a draft prepared at his suggestion by one of his advisers, Colonel Edward M. House. With this before him, he worked out his own first draft and later, after further conference and thought, revised it in his own clear handwriting. This was done in the summer of 1918, while World War I still convulsed Europe. But this was only the beginning.

On November 11, 1918, an armistice was signed; and in January of the following year, nations gathered at Paris to draw up a treaty of peace. President Wilson was there, as were others who had given serious thought to the idea of international organization. The French had their plan; the British theirs; and there were many others. Woodrow Wilson's draft was changed again as he took part in the deliberations of the League of Nations Commission set up by the Peace Conference; other drafts were presented for consideration and were partly incorporated in the ever-developing instrument.

Out of this hopeful ferment came the Covenant of the League of Nations which was incorporated in the Treaty of Versailles. Wilson's first draft did not, of course, appear as such in the final document; but many of his words remained—and his spirit permeated it.

The League of Nations never became exactly the body which Woodrow Wilson had envisioned, for the United States was there only as an "observer." Nevertheless, it promised to be "a living force devoted to the task of assisting the peoples of all countries in their desire for peace, prosperity, and happiness," as he described it in his "call" to the British, French, Italian and other governments to attend the first meeting on January 16, 1920.

The final Covenant represented the thinking and the hopes of many men and women from many nations. More than that, it represented Woodrow Wilson.

"There can be no question," said Herbert H. Asquith, addressing the National Liberal Club in London in the summer of 1918, at a time when thinking on the formation of an international peace organization was beginning to crystallize, "that President Wilson has done more than any statesman of the Entente to concentrate the minds, not only of his own people and of the Allies, but of neutral nations, and I will add, so far as they are allowed to hear and know the truth, of the enemy peoples themselves, upon this as our dominating and worldwide aim."

Six years later, Dr. Edwin Anderson Alderman, in a memorial address in honor of Woodrow Wilson before a joint session of the two Houses of Congress December 15, 1924, said:

"It is commonly said that the historic rank of Woodrow Wilson is wrapped up in the destiny of the Covenant . . . surely the fame of Woodrow Wilson does not rest upon an instrument the orderly growth of which into final usefulness may so change its structure and modify its form as to cause it to become another and an even better instrument. It depends upon an unconquerable idea, so greatly conceived and set forth that it must continue to grow. . . ."

The United Nations of today is the promise of the "better instrument" dimly foreseen so soon after Woodrow Wilson's death. Whether it be the final, or merely another, embodiment of that "unconquerable idea" to which he gave his thought and his life is a question which profoundly affects the future of civilized man.

Wilson's own typescript with his manuscript corrections was lent to the Freedom Train exhibit by the Library of Congress.

DECLARATION BY UNITED NATIONS:

A JOINT DECLARATION BY THE UNITED STATES OF AMERICA,
THE UNITED KINGDOM OF GREAT BRITAIN AND NORTHERN
IRELAND, THE UNION OF SOVIET SOCIALIST REPUBLICS,
CHINA, AUSTRALIA, BELGIUM, CANADA, COSTA RICA, CUBA,
CZECHOSLOVAKIA, DOMINICAN REPUBLIC, EL SALVADOR,
GREECE, GUATEMALA, HAITI, HONDURAS, INDIA, LUXEMBOURG,
NETHERLANDS, NEW ZEALAND, NICARAGUA, NORWAY, PANAMA,
POLAND, SOUTH AFRICA, YUGOSLAVIA.

The Governments signatory hereto,

Having subscribed to a common program of purposes
and principles embodied in the Joint Declaration of
the President of the United States of America and the
Prime Minister of the United Kingdom of Great Britain
and Northern Ireland dated August 14, 1941, known as
the Atlantic Charter.

Being convinced that complete victory over their
enemies is essential to defend life, liberty, independence
and religious freedom, and to preserve human rights and
justice in their own lands as well as in other lands,
and that they are now engaged in a common struggle
against savage and brutal forces seeking to subjugate
the world, DECLARE:

(1) Each Government pledges itself to employ its
full resources, military or economic, against those
members of the Tripartite Pact and its adherents with
which such government is at war.

Declaration by the United Nations (See No. 95)

(2) Each Government pledges itself to cooperate
with the Governments signatory hereto and not to make
a separate armistice or peace with the enemies.

The foregoing declaration may be adhered to by
other nations which are, or which may be, rendering
material assistance and contributions in the struggle
for victory over Hitlerism.

Done at Washington
January First, 1942

The United States of America
by Franklin D Roosevelt

The United Kingdom
of Northern Ireland & Great Britain
by Winston Churchill

On behalf of the Government
of the Union of Soviet Socialist
Republics
Maxim Litvinoff

National Government of the Republic of China
T. V. Soong
Minister for Foreign Affairs

The Commonwealth of Australia
by R.G. Casey.

The Kingdom of Belgium
by Cte. A. Straten

Canada
by Leighton McCarthy

Declaration by the United Nations, second page

The Republic of Costa Rica
by Mr. Fernandez

The Republic of Cuba
by Aurelio F. Concheso.

Czechoslovak Republic
by V. S. Hurban
The Dominican Republic
by J. M. Troncoso

The Republic of El Salvador
by C. A. Alfaro
The Kingdom of Greece
by Cimon G. Diamantopoulos.

The Republic of Guatemala
by Enrique Lopez Herrarte.

La République d'Haïti
par Fernand Dennis.

The Republic of Honduras
by Julián R. Cáceres

India by
Girja Shankar Bajpai.

The Grand Duchy of Luxembourg
by Hugues Le Gallais
The Kingdom of the Netherlands
Signed on behalf of
the Govt of the Dominion
of New Zealands
by Frank Langstone
The Republic of Nicaragua
by Frein De Bayle

The Kingdom of Norway
by W. Munthe Morgenstierne
The Republic of Panamá
by Alstvardo

The Republic of Poland
by Jan Ciechanowski.

The Union of South Africa
by Ralph W. Close

The Kingdom of Yugoslavia
by Constantin A. Fotitch

Declaration by the United Nations, third page

95. The United Nations Declare Themselves for a Great Common Purpose

IN his message to Congress of January 7, 1941, President Franklin Delano Roosevelt stated the broad principles upon which peace should be made after the defeat of the Axis powers and their satellites. The President said: "We look forward to a world founded upon four essential human freedoms . . . freedom of speech and expression . . . freedom of every person to worship God in his own way . . . freedom from want . . . freedom from fear."

These principles were elaborated in the Atlantic Charter which was announced on August 14, 1941, by President Roosevelt and Winston Churchill, the Prime Minister of the United Kingdom. This declaration was drafted during the meetings between Mr. Roosevelt and Mr. Churchill, and their advisers, aboard the United States cruiser *Augusta* and the British battleship *Prince of Wales* in the guarded secrecy of Newfoundland's Placentia Bay.

The meeting which resulted in the Atlantic Charter occurred at a time when the Axis was nearly at the peak of its powers. The Nazis and their European allies had occupied France, Belgium, the Netherlands, Denmark, Norway, Yugoslavia, and Greece. The exultant Wehrmacht was striking deep into the territory of the Soviet Union. The Afrika Korps and the Italians were massing for a drive on Egypt and the Suez Canal. In the Atlantic, German submarines were sending to the bottom vital cargoes needed by the British and Russians. In the Far East, Japan had extended her undeclared war far down the coast of China.

The Atlantic Charter established common principles on which the United States and the United Kingdom based their hopes for a better future for the world. These principles, declared to be inherent in the national policies of the two nations, were: (1) No aggrandizement out of the war; (2) No territorial changes, except those desired by the people concerned; (3) All people to have the right to choose their own form of government and all peoples who were forcibly deprived of sovereign rights and self-government to have those losses restored; (4) All nations to have access, on equal terms, to the world's trade and raw materials; (5) Fullest economic collaboration between all nations toward improved labor standards, economic adjustment, and social security; (6) A peace guaranteeing the safety of all nations and enabling the peoples of those nations to be free from fear and want; (7) Freedom of the seas; and (8) The abandonment of the use of force by all nations.

Approximately four months later, December 7, 1941, the Japanese navy struck at Pearl Harbor. By December 11, the United States was at war with Japan, Germany, and Italy, all of which first had declared war on the United States.

On January 1, 1942, some five months after the Atlantic Charter was issued, the principles of the Charter were subscribed to at Washington by twenty-four nations in addition to the United States and the United Kingdom in a document called Declaration by United Nations. The original signed document, which has been loaned by the Department of State for the Freedom Train exhibit, was signed by the following nations: The Union of Soviet Socialist Republics, China, Australia, Belgium, Canada, Costa Rica, Cuba, Czechoslovakia, Dominican Republic, El Salvador, Greece, Guatemala, Haiti, Honduras, India, Luxembourg, The Netherlands, New Zealand, Nicaragua, Norway, Panama, Poland, South Africa, and Yugoslavia.

During the course of the war, nineteen other nations signed the Declaration. They were: Mexico, the Philippine Commonwealth, Ethiopia, Iraq, Brazil, Bolivia, Iran, Colombia, Liberia, France, Ecuador, Peru, Chile, Paraguay, Uruguay, Turkey, Egypt, and Saudi Arabia.

These forty-five nations declared that "complete victory over their enemies is essential to defend life, liberty, independence and religious freedom, and to preserve human rights and justice in their own lands as well as in other lands, and that they are now engaged in a common struggle against savage and brutal forces seeking to subjugate the world." Each promised cooperation with the others and that it would not make a separate armistice or peace.

During the next year, the military fortunes of the Allies reached their lowest point in the war, and then began to rise. At Stalingrad, the Russian forces stood firm and began to drive the Nazis back. In Africa, the British defeated the Nazis at El Alamein, and Anglo-American forces successfully landed in northern Africa. In the Pacific, United States Marines established themselves on Guadalcanal. The strength of the United Nations steadily increased, bringing closer the complete victory essential for the defense of "life, liberty, independence and religious freedom."

96. The San Francisco Conference Formulates the Charter of the United Nations (1945)

THE United Nations Conference on International Organization met at San Francisco from April 25 through June 26, 1945 in order to create a body that would realize the ideals of the earlier Declaration by the United Nations. Approximately eleven hundred delegates from fifty nations attended to prepare a charter for a general international organization for the maintenance of peace and security.

The objectives of the resulting Charter, shown here, were, as stated in the Preamble, ". . . to save succeeding generations from the scourge of war, which twice in our lifetime has brought untold sorrow to mankind, and to reaffirm faith in fundamental human rights, in the dignity and worth of the human person, in the equal rights of men and women and of nations large and small, and to establish conditions under which justice and respect for the obligations arising from treaties and other sources of international law can be maintained, and to promote social progress and better standards of life in larger freedom."

Though it was called upon to undertake a task which no previous international meeting had ever accomplished, the San Francisco Conference met with high hopes for the success of the work which confronted it. The nations which thus met had already demonstrated their ability to work together. Not only in the prosecution of the war, but in the preparations for the organization which was meant to keep the post-war peace, the principal Allies had established a working collaboration without precedent. At Moscow in 1943, the United States, the United Kingdom, the Soviet Union, and China had pledged to continue their united action "for the organization and maintenance of peace and security." As a result of the conversations at Dumbarton Oaks, from August to October 1944, these four Allies had reached certain agreements upon proposals for a world security organization; later, at Yalta, the United States, the United Kingdom, and the Soviet Union had seemingly enlarged the area of their understanding. These proposals and understandings became the basis of the work at San Francisco.

The nature of the Conference itself gave reason to hope that more would be accomplished there than at any previous international meeting. The delegates deliberated under a double compulsion. Twin urgencies faced them. Every nation represented at the Conference was engaged in the war which was yet to be won. And many of the delegates realized that if another war came, it would probably bring with it the dismal conclusion of modern civilization. It was, therefore, the common determination of all those who participated that the Conference would have to reach a broad and firm agreement.

The present Charter in this exhibit is the result of the delegates' labors. With a declaration of united purpose to preserve the peace, it combines machinery to give practical effect to that purpose. The Charter commits the United Nations to: the maintenance of international peace and security; the development of friendly relations among nations based on respect for the principle of equal rights and self-determination of peoples; the achievement of international cooperation in solving international problems; and the promotion and encourage-ment of respect for human rights and for fundamental freedoms for all.

The Charter also states the principles which its members accept as binding. "Sovereign equality" of the member states is to be the foundation of their association. Fulfillment of the obligations of the member states is pledged. Members are to "settle their international disputes by peaceful means." Members are to "refrain in their international relations from the threat or use of force against the territorial integrity or political independence of any state, or in any other manner inconsistent with the Purpose of the United Nations." Finally, the Charter binds those of its members having responsibilities for administration of territories whose peoples have not yet attained the full measure of self-government, to recognize the principle "that the interests of the inhabitants of these territories are paramount" and to "accept as a sacred trust" the obligation to promote their well-being.

To implement the purposes of the Charter the delegates established, in addition to a Secretariat and a Trusteeship Council, four principal instruments: an enforcement agency, a forum for discussion and debate, a social and economic institute, and an international court. The first is called the Security Council; the second, the General Assembly; the third, the Economic and Social Council; the fourth, the International Court of Justice.

The Charter of the United Nations came into force as a fundamental law for the peoples of the world on October 24, 1945. The General Assembly convened for the first time in London in January 1946, elected a Secretary-General and created the three other instruments provided for in the Charter. In time, other bodies were established, like the Atomic Energy Commission and the International Refugee Organization. All the organizations of the United Nations, however, and all their accomplishments, stem from this Charter, drawn up at San Francisco in the spring of 1945.

The Charter that was written and signed in San Francisco was reproduced in exact facsimile by the Department of State and each signatory nation was supplied with a copy. The United States' official copy was lent to the Freedom Train exhibit by the Department of State. It is bound in gold-embossed blue morocco leather and bears on the cover the seal of the United Nations.

97. President Franklin D. Roosevelt Proclaims an Unlimited National Emergency (1941)

SEPTEMBER 1939 plunged Europe into the flames of war. With the new cataclysm came a mounting crisis throughout the world. On September 8, 1939, a few days after war was declared between Great Britain and Germany, the President of the United States proclaimed the existence of a "limited" national emergency and directed measures for strengthening national defenses "within the limits of peacetime authorizations." As a ruthless plan of the Nazi leaders to achieve world domination became all too obvious, the need of positive and immediate action to aid the embattled democratic nations was urgent. One European country after another collapsed and fell victim to Nazi hordes and their demented philosophy of the supreme State.

Within two years of the proclamation of a limited emergency, the world situation had greatly worsened. Passage by Congress in March 1941 of the first Lend-Lease Act had made the United States the "arsenal of democracy," yet France was on the verge of collapse and Great Britain ripped and flattened by incessant air attacks. Further measures were needed to protect the American hemisphere from the possibility of hostile encirclement, and to prevent the infiltration of foreign agents and "fifth Columnists." On May 27, 1941, the President of the United States proclaimed the existence of an unlimited national emergency. By this action, the President was authorized to use the reservoir of emergency military and economic powers that are delegated to him by statute.

Since the objectives of the Axis included the overthrow of the existing democratic order "and a world-wide domination of peoples and economies through the destruction of all resistance on land and sea and in the air," all military, naval, air and civilian defenses were placed in a state of readiness to repel any threats or acts of aggression directed against any part of the western hemisphere. Every loyal citizen was called upon to engage in production for defense "to the end that a system of government that makes private enterprise possible may survive" and "to insure the survival of the only kind of government which recognizes the rights of labor or capital."

The original proclamation of May 27, 1941, is part of the general records of the United States Government in the custody of the National Archives. It bears the seal of the United States and the signatures of Franklin Delano Roosevelt, President of the United States, and of Cordell Hull, Secretary of State.

98. General Eisenhower is Selected to Command the Invasion of Western Europe

THE Russians had long been clamoring for the opening of a "second front" against the Germans. This clamor continued long after the Allied invasion of Italy, which succeeded in pinning down many of the best Nazi

divisions. In the Soviet mind, this did not represent the desired "second front." It was highly appropriate, therefore, that when the decision was made to appoint General Eisenhower the supreme commander the news should first go immediately to Marshal Stalin.

The document exhibited on the Freedom Train is the original pencilled draft by General George Marshall stating that "the immediate appointment of General Eisenhower to command of OVERLORD OPERATION has been decided upon." It is signed by President Roosevelt and bears a note of explanation and gift from General Marshall to General Eisenhower.

It is lent to the Freedom Train exhibit by General Dwight D. Eisenhower.

99. The Invasion of Western Europe is Agreed Upon at Teheran (1943)

THE Freedom Train has in its exhibit one of the most significant policy-determining documents of World War II. On this unpretentious piece of paper is recorded the confidential agreement of the Anglo-American Combined Staffs to launch the greatest amphibious operation in the history of the world. It is the agreement to inform Premier Stalin that the invasion of Hitler's "Fortress Europe" would be definitely made through landings on the coast of Normandy in France.

Steps in the ideological and military warfare of the United Nations against the Axis were marked by meetings between the heads of the chief Allied nations and their military staffs at various times and places determined by civilian or military necessity. The principles of the Atlantic Charter and the four freedoms were reiterated by the Declaration of the United Nations on January 1, 1942. Twenty-six nations opposed to the Nazi-Fascist ideologies adopted the principles of the Charter and agreed not to conclude separate peace with the Axis. In October 1943, the foreign secretaries of the United States, the United Kingdom, the Union of Soviet Socialist Republics and China met for the first time to discuss policies. In the Moscow Declaration they recognized the necessity of continued post-armistice cooperation as well as the need for an international organization which would guarantee both peace and security.

More immediate military decisions were made at a meeting of the "Big Three" from November 28 to December 1, 1943. The first meeting between President Franklin D. Roosevelt and Premier Josef Stalin took place at Teheran, the capital of Iran, at a conference which Prime Minister Winston Churchill also attended. These three heads-of-states agreed on a united policy regarding postwar Germany and selected the date and the leader for the Anglo-American invasion of Europe. General Dwight

From the President to Marshal Stalin

The immediate appointment of General Eisenhower to command of Overlord operation has been decided upon.

Roosevelt

Cairo, Dec. 7. 43

Dear Eisenhower, I thought you might like to have this as a memento. It was written very hurriedly by me as the final meeting broke up yesterday, the President signing it immediately.

W.S.C.

The Appointment of General Eisenhower to Command the Invasion of Europe (See No. 98)

Agreed:-

To inform Stalin that we will launch OVERLORD ~~by June 1st~~ *during May*, ~~and will simultaneously make the biggest attack on Southern France that is permitted by the landing craft available at that time.~~ *and*

in ~~conjunction~~ ~~together~~ with a supporting operation in Southern France of the largest scale that is permitted by the landing craft available at that time

Agreement on Operations "Overlord" and "Anvil". President Roosevelt's Corrections are above, Admiral Leahy's below (See No. 99)

D. Eisenhower was selected as Supreme Allied Commander for the invasion.

The agreement displayed on the Freedom Train assured Stalin that the Anglo-American invasion to be made through Normandy, for which the code word was "Overlord," would be launched "by June 1st," which the President changed in red pencil to "during the month of May." (The "Overlord" operation had been decided upon at the Quebec meeting between Churchill and Roosevelt in August 1943. The Teheran Conference, however, decided upon the actual time of the invasion.) "Anvil," a supporting operation in southern France "of the largest scale that is permitted by the landing craft available at that time," was also agreed upon. Admiral Leahy, the President's Chief of Staff, made the changes in pencil; and on the back the President noted: "Tues. a. m. Nov. 30th 1943. This is the original."

The invasion of Normandy took place on June 6, 1944, followed by the landings in southern France in August. Few conferences of the Allied chiefs-of-state were held after Teheran, with the exception of one at Yalta in the Crimea in February 1945 and one at Potsdam, Germany, in July. Germany surrendered to the Allied powers at Rheims in May 1945, and Japan, having accepted the Potsdam Declaration on August 14, formally surrendered on September 2, 1945.

This document recording the invasion agreement is from the collections of the Franklin D. Roosevelt Library at Hyde Park, New York.

100. Secretary of War Henry L. Stimson Congratulates the Supreme Commander upon the Successful Invasion of Western Europe

THE Department of the Army has lent to the Freedom Train exhibit the original signed draft of a message of congratulations from the Secretary of War to the Supreme Allied Commander on the epochal success achieved during the first phases of the invasion of Western Europe.

June 27, 1944.

To General Eisenhower
Signed Stimson

The success in the attainment of the first major [OVERLORD: crossed out. Ed.] objective clearly reflects your able leadership. I am highly appreciative of this achievement and send warmest regards to you and to your staff.

Stimson

101. General Wainwright Attempts to Send a Last Message from Corregidor (1942)

CORREGIDOR will ever be known as one of the greatest defensive battles in military history. The Freedom Train exhibits, from the archives of the Department of the Army, the text of the first part of General Wainwright's interrupted message. After the hostilities were over the remainder of the text became available. It read:

"With many guns and anti-aircraft fire-control equipment destroyed, we are no longer able to prevent accurate bombardment from the air. With numerous batteries of heavy caliber emplaced on the shores of Bataan and Cavite, the enemy now brings devastating crossfire to bear on us, outranging our remaining guns.

"Most of my batteries, seacoast, anti-aircraft and field, have been put out of action by the enemy. I have ordered the others destroyed to prevent them from falling into enemy hands. In addition, we are now overwhelmingly assaulted by Japanese troops on Corregidor.

"There is a limit to human endurance, and that limit has long since been past. Without prospect of relief, I feel it is my duty to my country and to my gallant troops to end this useless effusion of blood and human sacrifice.

"If you agree, Mr. President, please say to the nation that my troops and I have accomplished all that is humanly possible and that we have upheld the best traditions of the United States and its Army.

"May God bless and preserve you and guide you and the nation in the effort of ultimate victory.

"With profound regret and with continued pride in my gallant troops I go to meet the Japanese commander. Good-by, Mr. President."

102. The Intelligence Officer of the Encircled Garrison at Bastogne Says, "Merry Christmas" to His Superiors While General McAuliffe Says "Nuts" to the Germans

ON Christmas Eve of 1944, the Intelligence Officer of the 101st Airborne Division was preparing his daily report on the enemy situation. The map as completed and displayed in the Freedom Train exhibit, through the courtesy of the Department of the Army, shows an unbroken ring of German units around the Division at Bastogne, Belgium. In the center of the ring of red symbols indicating enemy units, the Intelligence Officer, in a mood of defiance and unbroken spirit, wrote the words "Merry Christmas" and made the routine distribution of

WAR DEPARTMENT
CLASSIFIED MESSAGE CENTER
INCOMING CLASSIFIED MESSAGE

~~SECRET~~

ABL

CSWD
May 6
2:23 AM

URGENT

From: Fort Mills
To: Chief of Staff

No Number May 6, 1942

For the President of the United States. With broken heart and
head bowed in sadness but not in shame I report to your Excellency
that today I must arrange terms for the surrender of the fortified
islands of Manila Bay (Corregidor) (Fort Hughes) (Fort Drum) and——

NoSig

Note: Remainder of this message being serviced.

Action Copy: SGS

Info. Copies: File

OPD
White House
Comm. Room
G-2

CM-IN   (5/6/42)   AM 3:00

RECRADED UNCLASSIFIED
ORDER SEC WAR BY TAG/ 7F28

~~SECRET~~

COPY NO.

THE MAKING OF AN EXACT COPY OF THIS MESSAGE IS FORBIDDEN

General Wainwright's Last Message from Corregidor (See No. 101) the report. Even more challenging and inspiring to the men of the 101st Airborne Division was the Christmas message of their acting commander, Brigadier General Anthony C. McAuliffe. In it he reported the German commander's demand for the surrender of the garrison and reiterated his classic reply: "Nuts!"

103. Admiral Spruance Reports on the Victorious Operations at Iwo Jima

IT was necessary to acquire a series of strategic island bases in the Pacific to carry out American military strategy for the crushing of the Japanese empire. Liberation of the Philippines was followed by action in the Marianas and by the taking of Iwo Jima and Okinawa. In the Freedom Train exhibit is displayed the original signed report by Admiral R. A. Spruance, Commander of the Fifth Fleet, relating the part played by the Navy in the Iwo Jima operations. This report is from the archives of the Department of the Navy.

104. Admiral Halsey Describes American Naval Action in Philippine Waters (1944)

THE Freedom Train exhibits, through the courtesy of the Department of the Navy, Admiral William F. Halsey's signed official report of naval action in Philippine waters following the invasion of Leyte in October 1944.

The battle for Leyte Gulf was one of the most savage and dramatic of the entire war. The Japanese planned to annihilate the American invasion forces in a series of sudden blows. Three Japanese naval forces approached from three different directions. The enemy units totalled some 75 warships and included four carriers and nine battleships, supported by submarines and planes.

The battle was a lopsided and total victory for the Americans. We sank four carriers, three battleships, six heavy cruisers, two light cruisers and nine heavy destroyers. Heavy damage was inflicted upon the remainder of the fleet. As a result of the battle of Leyte Gulf Admiral Mitscher declared that Japan had been reduced to the level of a fifth-rate power.

105. Admiral Nimitz Reports the Victory of Midway (1942)

THE sneak attack on Pearl Harbor in December 1941 temporarily paralyzed the American Pacific Fleet. But within six months the United States had reassembled a powerful striking force and launched an offensive naval action. The battle of Midway in June 1942 was both a psychological and a tactical victory. President Franklin D. Roosevelt, in addressing Congress in January 1943, described Midway as America's most important victory in the Pacific in 1942.

The original battle report on Midway, signed by Admiral Chester William Nimitz, is lent to the Freedom Train exhibit by the Department of the Navy.

106. Secretary of the Navy Knox Praises the Marine Corps

THE United States Marine Corps was founded by an act of the Continental Congress on November 10, 1775. After a brilliant record during the American Revolution it succumbed to the economy axe wielded so indiscriminately after the Treaty of Paris in 1783. But the next great national emergency—the undeclared war with France, brought about its revival. The present Marine Corps was established by act of Congress on July 11, 1798. Throughout the years the Marines have fought everywhere and with the highest distinction. The present original signed document, lent by the United States Marine Corps, finds its place in the Freedom Train exhibit because of its felicitous phrasing of a tribute richly earned. The precious documents which comprise the Freedom Train exhibit are guarded by a special detachment of United States Marines.

My dear General Holcomb:

On this 1943 anniversary of the United States Marine Corps the men and women of the Navy and the Coast Guard proudly stand at salute in respect and admiration for one of the greatest fighting organizations the world has ever known.

The Marines launched this nation's first land offensive in the Pacific. Knowing the terrific odds, Americans everywhere awaited the outcome with hope and with prayer; but Americans everywhere also knew that the Marines would conduct themselves in keeping with their traditions of glory, remaining "Ever Faithful" even unto death itself. The Marines did not fail.

Today our offensive is growing. The Marines again are on the march, advancing with their brothers in arms of the other great fighting forces. They will not halt until they have pierced the heart of the enemy's homeland.

In this 168th year of its history, the Marine Corps daily adds shining new pages to a long and brilliant record, with the brightest chapters now about to unfold. The entire Naval Service is honored to call the Marine Corps its own.

Sincerely,
Frank Knox

107. General Stilwell Describes the Bravery of His Chinese Troops (1944)

IN this original manuscript of a penned personal letter for the attention of the Chief of Staff, General Joseph W. Stilwell praises the battle actions of his Chinese troops. He reports that in some twenty-three actions against tenacious and "tough" opposition they have been "uniformly successful except in three small attacks in which we bumped our noses . . . the men are keen and fearless . . . and they attack with dash . . . they now know they can lick the Japs and have their tails up."

This original document is lent to the Freedom Train exhibit by the Department of the Army.

108. President Franklin Delano Roosevelt Pays Tribute to an Early Hero of World War II

IN appreciation of and tribute to the courage and high devotion to duty exhibited by young Captain Colin P. Kelly, Jr., in attacking certain units of the Japanese forces in 1941, President Franklin D. Roosevelt wrote this letter to the President of the United States in 1956, requesting that favorable consideration be given to Colin Kelly III for appointment to the United States Military Academy at West Point. The letter was written "as an act of faith in the destiny of our country. I desire to make a request which I make in full confidence that we shall achieve a glorious victory in the war we now are waging to preserve our democratic way of life."

After the Japanese made their sneak attack at Pearl Harbor on December 7, 1941, twenty-six-year-old Kelly was among that gallant group of air pilots who carried the desperate fight to the enemy that swarmed in the Philippine Seas. In an attack on one of the Japanese battleships off northern Luzon, Kelly lost his life. A special order of the Army on December 12 mentioned the "brilliant performance of the American Army and Navy fliers and the fliers of the Philippine Commonwealth in attacking enemy units with total disregard for their own safety." One of the fliers who was mentioned by name was Captain Colin P. Kelly, Jr., of Madison, Florida. The young hero received many posthumous honors, among which this letter is unique. Written on official White House stationery, pale green in color, it was entrusted to the Archivist of the United States for delivery to the President of the United States in 1956. It is lent to the Freedom Train exhibit by the National Archives.

It should be added that the details of Kelly's alleged exploits against the enemy were not fully established at the time the letter was written. And there was a certain morale value in the wide publication of such a letter. Undeniable, however, is the fact that Kelly was among the first to lose his life in a great cause and under spectacular circumstances. And the simple eloquence of the letter remains undimmed.

December 17, 1941

To the President of the United States in 1956:

I am writing this letter as an act of faith in the destiny of our country. I desire to make a request which I make in full confidence that we shall achieve a glorious victory in the war we are now waging to preserve our democratic way of life.

My request is that you consider the merits of a young American youth of goodly heritage—Colin P. Kelly, III—for appointment as a Cadet in the United States Military Academy at West Point. I make this appeal in behalf of this youth as a token of the Nation's appreciation of the heroic services of his father who met death in line of duty at the very outset of the struggle which was thrust upon us by the perfidy of a professed friend.

In the conviction that the service and example of Colin P. Kelly, Jr. will be long remembered, I ask for this consideration in behalf of Colin P. Kelly, III.

Franklin D. Roosevelt

109. General Mark W. Clark Proclaims Final Victory of the Allied Forces in Italy

THERE has never been a proper appreciation of the contribution of Allied arms in the Italian campaign to the ultimate victory. Prime Minister Winston Churchill once spoke of Italy as part of the "soft under-belly of the Axis." This proved to be highly inaccurate. During many months of slugging, desperate warfare the Allies inched their way northward. By mid-April of 1945 the long-prepared and final offensive began. The concerted efforts of the British 8th Army and the American 5th Army broke the vaunted Gothic line of the enemy and Bologna was finally stormed. The loss of Bologna forced the Germans into a general retreat. On April 30 General Clark announced that "the German Army no longer exists in Italy as a military force." The final capitulation of the Germans turned over to the Allies more than a million prisoners. These were the bulk of the forces suspected of being prepared to make a final stand for Hitler in northern Italy and in southeastern Germany.

The original signed typescript of the victory proclamation is lent to the Freedom Train exhibit by General Mark W. Clark.

HEADQUARTERS 101ST AIRBORNE DIVISION
Office of the Division Commander

24 December 1944

What's Merry about all this, you ask? We're fighting - it's cold
we aren't home. All true but what has the proud Eagle Division accomplished
with its worthy comrades of the 10th Armored Division, the 705th Tank Destro
er Battalion and all the rest? Just this: We have stopped cold everything
that has been thrown at us from the North, East, South and West. We have
identifications from four German Panzer Divisions, two German Infantry
Divisions and one German Parachute Division. These units, spearheading the
last desperate German lunge, were headed straight west for key points when
the Eagle Division was hurriedly ordered to stem the advance. How effectively this was done will be written in history; not alone in our Division's
glorious history but in World history. The Germans actually did surround us
their radios blared our doom. Their Commander demanded our surrender in
the following impudent arrogance.

December 22nd 1944

"To the U. S. A. Commander of the encircled town of Bastogne.

The fortune of war is changing. This time the U. S. A. forces in
and near Bastogne have been encircled by strong German armored units. More
German armored units have crossed the river Ourthe near Ortheuville, have
taken Marche and reached St. Hubert by passing through Hombres-Sibret-Tillet
Libramont is in German hands.

There is only one possibility to save the encircled U. S. A. Troop
from total annihilation: that is the honorable surrender of the encircled
town. In order to think it over a term of two hours will be granted beginning with the presentation of this note.

If this proposal should be rejected one German Artillery Corps
and six heavy A. A. Battalions are ready to annihilate the U. S. A. Troops
in and near Bastogne. The order for firing will be given immediately after
this two hour's term.

All the serious civilian losses caused by this Artillery fire
would not correspond with the well known American humanity.

The German Commander

The German Commander received the following reply:

22 December 1944

"To the German Commander:

N U T S !

The American Commander

Allied Troops are counterattacking in force. We continue to hold
Bastogne. By holding Bastogne we assure the success of the Allied Armies.
We know that our Division Commander, General Taylor, will say: "Well Done!"

We are giving our country and our loved ones at home a worthy
Christmas present and being privileged to take part in this gallant feat of
arms are truly making for ourselves a Merry Christmas.

McAULIFFE,
Commanding.

"Merry Christmas" from the Encircled 101st Airborne Division at Bastogne in 1944 (See No. 102)

HEADQUARTERS 15TH ARMY GROUP
A.P.O. # 777, U. S. ARMY
To the Soldiers of the 15th Army Group

With a full and grateful heart I hail and congratulate you in this hour of complete victory over the German enemy, and join with you in thanks to Almighty God.

Yours has been a long, hard fight—the longest in this war of any Allied troops fighting on the Continent of Europe. You men of the Fifth and Eighth Armies have brought that fight to a successful conclusion by your recent brilliant offensive operations which shattered the German forces opposing you. His surrender was the inevitable course left to him; he had nothing more to fight with in Italy.

You have demonstrated something new and remarkable in the annals of organized warfare: you have shown that a huge fighting force composed of units from many countries with diverse languages and customs, inspired, as you have always been, with devotion to the cause of freedom, *can become an effective and harmonious fighting team.*

This teamwork which you have exemplified has included in full measure the supporting arms who have worked with us throughout the campaign. The magnificent support which we have always had from the Allied air and naval forces in this theater has written a new page in the history of cooperative combat action.

Our exultation in this moment is blended with sorrow as we pay tribute to the heroic Allied soldiers who have fallen in battle in order that this victory might be achieved. The entire world will forever revere their memory.

The war is not over. The German military machine has been completely crushed by the splendid campaigns which you and your colleagues of the Western and Russian fronts have just completed. There remains the all important task of inflicting a similar complete defeat on our remaining enemy—Japan. Each one of us in the 15th Army Group must continue without pause to give the full measure of effort to that task wherever we may be called upon to serve.

I am intensely proud of you all and of the honor which I have had of commanding such invincible troops. My thanks go to each of you for your capable, aggressive and loyal service which has produced this great victory.

Men of the 15th Army Group, I know you will face the task ahead with the same magnificent, generous and indomitable spirit you have shown in this long campaign. Forward, to final Victory. God bless you all.
May 1945

Mark W. Clark
General, USA Commanding

110. General Yamashita, "Tiger of Malaya," Surrenders to American Forces in the Philippines

ON September 3, 1945, the day after General MacArthur accepted the surrender of all Japanese armed forces and all armed forces under Japanese control, General Yamashita ("Tiger of Malaya") surrendered to Major General Leavey in the Philippines. General Jonathan Wainwright was present at the ceremony, although he did not sign the documents.

This original surrender document is lent to the Freedom Train exhibit by the National Archives.

111. The Frayed Remnant of Japanese Might Surrenders on Truk

TRUK was once an awesome bastion of Japanese naval power. But, with the rapid disintegration of the empire, its garrison joined the long series of surrenders (for the general background see descriptive material on item No. 115). Japanese forces on Truk Atoll surrendered to Vice Admiral Murray on September 2, 1945. In this official surrender document, lent to the Freedom Train exhibit by the National Archives, the signatures of the Japanese emissaries are in English rather than Japanese characters.

112. Germany Surrenders Unconditionally at Rheims

BEFORE the crushing might of Allied arms, Hitler's vaunted *Festung Europa* crumbled into final ruin in the spring of 1945 and its Nazi masters died ignominiously or slunk into precarious hiding, leaving substitute fuehrers to yield in unconditional surrender the frayed remnants of an empire. Thus the Nazi revolution against modern civilization came to an end. It came so close to succeeding, however, that the testimony of its failure, the surrender documents signed at Lüneburg, Rheims, and Berlin, will remain forever among the most significant records of our times.

Squirming under the heels of the victorious Allied Expeditionary Force and the conquering Red Army, the Germans, in the vain hope of obtaining a softer peace, sought to surrender only to the AEF. At Lüneburg, Field Marshal Sir Bernard Law Montgomery sternly rejected the bid for a surrender of the German armies in Holland, northwest Germany, and Denmark to the AEF alone.

Agwar, personal attention Gen. Marshall.

Reurad 4303. Since December twenty third, in three serious actions lasting two days each, and in some twenty smaller actions, Chinese have been uniformly successful except in three small attacks in which we bumped our noses. Opposition is eighteenth jap division, and they are tough. Only two prisoners so far. They have been well dug in, with heavy allotment of machine guns, and fight to the last. Terrain is dense jungle. We have used two regiments of three eight division and one of two two division. All performed very well indeed. At first there was much waste of ammunition. This has been corrected. The men are keen and fearless. Company officers lead them in, and they attack with dash. Numerous instances of men who deserve D.S.C. They now know they can lick the japs and have their tails up. Two batteries of seventy-fives have been in action. Performance excellent. Japs have been using about same amount of artillery. Three battalions of the jap fifty-fifth regiment have been well chewed up. Known jap casualties include one regimental commander and three battalion commanders, besides numerous company officers. In last action by sixty-fifth regiment of two two division our liaison officers report two hundred and fifty dead japs. The principal weak-

Jan 2800

General Stilwell's Personal Report to General Marshall (See No. 107)

nesses are patrolling and the high command. My opinion of the Chinese soldier is what it has always been. With good training, equipment, and leadership, he is as good as anybody. We hope to prove it, fully realizing that this is only a small show as yet. The foregoing is heartily concurred in by all liaison officers with whom I have talked. P.S. I will keep you informed of developments, since I suspect you will hear very little about us in S.E.A.C. communiqués.

Stilwell.

Secret - priority

General Stilwell's Report, second page

Trapped, General Admiral Hans Georg von Friedeburg, who had become head of the German Navy when Grand Admiral Karl Dönitz succeeded Hitler as Reichspräsident, consequently yielded those armies to all the Allies when he surrendered to Montgomery on Lüneburg Heath on May 4, 1945, three days before the general surrender at Rheims. Kinzel, G. Wagner, Poleck, and Friedel also signed this document.

On May 5, General Admiral von Friedeburg arrived at General Dwight D. Eisenhower's AEF Headquarters at Rheims. Final capitulation was expected at once, but again the Admiral tried to avoid surrendering to the Soviet High Command. He claimed he had no authority to do so. Lieutenant General Walter Bedell Smith, Chief of Staff to General Eisenhower, for whom he acted, refused to consider such a partial surrender, and finally von Friedeburg asked Reichspräsident Dönitz to authorize

him to accept the Allied terms or to send someone who could. Colonel General Alfred Jodl was so authorized and flew to Rheims.

It was nearly 3:00 A.M., (or 0241 hours, by military time keeping) on May 7 when the unconditional surrender of "all forces on land, sea, and in the air" under German control was signed by Jodl for the German High Command, by Smith for the Supreme Commander of the Allied Expeditionary Force, and by General Ivan Sousloparov for the Soviet High Command. General François Sevez of the French Army witnessed the signing. The document provided that military operations were to cease on May 8 at 2301 hours, (11:01 P.M.) central European time.

Orders were issued at Rheims for the carrying out of the surrender of the German Army and Air Forces on the Western Front, in Norway, and in the Channel

Islands, and, in a document signed by Admiral Sir Harold M. Burrough, the surrender of the German Naval Forces, including the U-Boat fleet, was provided for.

Besides the general surrender document, Jodl signed an agreement that representatives of the German High Command would meet later to execute a formal ratification of the surrender. For this purpose Dönitz designated General Field Marshal Keitel, Chief of Staff of the Armed Forces High Command and Commander in Chief of the Army, General Admiral von Friedeburg, Commander in Chief of the Navy, and Colonel General Hans Jurgen Stumpff, representative of the Commander in Chief of the Air Forces.

The ratification meeting took place on May 8 in Berlin. There another instrument of surrender, which except for one or two additions repeated the Rheims document, was signed by the German officers named by the Reichspräsident, by Air Chief Marshal Sir Arthur Tedder for the Supreme Commander of the Allied Expeditionary Force, and by Marshal Georgi Zhukov for the Supreme High Command of the Red Army. Carl Spaatz, Commanding General of the United States Strategic Air Forces, and F. de Lattre-Tassigny, Commanding General of the First French Army, were witnesses. The Berlin surrender was drawn up in English, Russian, and German, but it was specified that only the English and Russian texts were "authentic."

Victory in Europe became official in the United States on May 8, 1945. On that day President Truman proclaimed the end of the war in Europe and designated Sunday, May 13, as a day of prayer and thanksgiving.

The Rheims surrender document is lent to the Freedom Train exhibit by the National Archives, the custodian of this and other instruments of surrender.

113. Justice Returns to Wake Island

O N Wake Atoll, where a small band of civilians and United States Marines held out so valiantly in the early days of the war in the Pacific until they were forced to surrender, Brigadier General L. H. M. Sanderson, United States Marine Corps, accepted the surrender of the enemy on September 4, 1945. (For the general background see document No. 115.) The Freedom Train, through the courtesy of the National Archives, displays the original surrender document.

114. General Stilwell Accepts the Surrender of the Japanese Forces on the Ryukyus Islands

G ENERAL Joseph W. ("Vinegar Joe") Stilwell accepted the surrender of the Japanese forces on the Ryukyus Islands on September 7, 1945. For the general back-

ground see the descriptive material introducing document No. 115. The text of the original instrument of surrender was lent to the Freedom Train exhibit by the National Archives.

115. The Log of the USS "Missouri" Records the Formal Surrender of Japan

T HERE is a plate on the deck of the battleship *Missouri* marking the spot where General Douglas MacArthur, Supreme Commander for the Allied Powers, accepted the capitulation of the Japanese, the only remaining partner of the original Rome-Berlin-Tokyo Axis. The *Missouri* was anchored in Tokyo Bay; the time was 0908 hours (9:08 A.M.) on Sunday, September 2, 1945. The fighting had already ended, but this was the ceremony that formally ended the conflict. Only three months had elapsed after the surrender of Nazi Germany, but nearly four years had passed since Pearl Harbor. At first, the United States and her allies in the Pacific had resisted stubbornly but could fight only delaying actions as the Japanese swept through the Philippines, Malaya, and Java to stand, in New Guinea, at the very gates of Australia. There the enemy advance was finally stopped. In the battles of the Coral Sea in May and of Midway in June 1942, the Japanese fleet was severely damaged. On Guadalcanal and New Guinea, ground troops fought doggedly against the entrenched enemy through jungle hazards and withering sniper attacks.

At last the tide turned. Lae, Makin, Tarawa, Kwajalein, Eniwetok, Saipan, Guam and Tinian were taken, each with its toll. The Philippines were liberated by a brilliant campaign, and with the taking of Iwo Jima and Okinawa, in the spring of 1945, our forces were on the threshold of Japan. The original typewritten battle reports of naval action in the Battles of Midway, Iwo Jima, and Leyte Gulf are displayed on the Freedom Train and in terse language they describe these American victories.

Japan was doomed. Her air force was destroyed and her fleet annihilated. Although there were still millions of her troops in the field, Japan's masters felt that, cut off as the home islands were, they could not long maintain either forces or empire. On July 26, the Potsdam Declaration issued an ultimatum that called for unconditional surrender. On August 5, the first atomic bomb burst over Hiroshima. On August 8, the Soviet Union joined the struggle and, shortly afterward, a second atom bomb fell on Nagasaki.

On Friday morning, August 10, a Japanese broadcast was picked up saying that Japan was ready to surrender and to accept terms of the Potsdam Declaration if the Emperor's prerogatives were not prejudiced. That evening the fact that a peace proposal had been received was officially confirmed and the next day the United

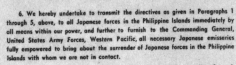

Instrument of Surrender

of the

Japanese and Japanese-Controlled Armed Forces in the Philippine Islands

to the

Commanding General

United States Army Forces, Western Pacific

Camp John Hay
Baguio, Mountain Province,
Luzon, Philippine Islands

3 September 1945

Pursuant to and in accordance with the proclamation of the Emperor of Japan accepting the terms set forth in the declaration issued by the heads of the Governments of the United States, Great Britain and China on 26 July 1945, at Potsdam and subsequently adhered to by the Union of Soviet Socialist Republics; and to the formal instrument of surrender of the Japanese Imperial Government and the Japanese Imperial General Headquarters signed at Tokyo Bay at 0908 on 2 September 1945:

1. Acting by command of and in behalf of the Emperor of Japan, the Japanese Imperial Government and the Japanese Imperial General Headquarters, We hereby surrender unconditionally to the Commanding General, United States Army Forces, Western Pacific, all Japanese and Japanese-controlled armed forces, air, sea, ground and auxiliary, in the Philippine Islands.

2. We hereby command all Japanese forces wherever situated in the Philippine Islands to cease hostilities forthwith, to preserve and save from damage all ships, aircraft and military and civil property, and to comply with all requirements which may be imposed by the Commanding General, United States Army Forces, Western Pacific, or his authorized representatives.

3. We hereby direct the commanders of all Japanese forces in the Philippine Islands to issue at once to all forces under their command to surrender unconditionally themselves and all forces under their control, as prisoners of war, to the nearest United States Army Force Commander.

4. We hereby direct the commanders of all Japanese forces in the Philippine Islands to surrender intact and in good order to the nearest United States Army Force Commander, at times and at places directed by him, all equipment and supplies of whatever nature under their control.

5. We hereby direct the commanders of all Japanese forces in the Philippine Islands at once to liberate all Allied prisoners of war and civilian internees under their control, and to provide for their protection, care, maintenance and immediate transportation to places as directed by the nearest United States Army Force Commander.

6. We hereby undertake to transmit the directives as given in Paragraphs 1 through 5, above, to all Japanese forces in the Philippine Islands immediately by all means within our power, and further to furnish to the Commanding General, United States Army Forces, Western Pacific, all necessary Japanese emissaries fully empowered to bring about the surrender of Japanese forces in the Philippine Islands with whom we are not in contact.

7. We hereby undertake to furnish immediately to the Commanding General, United States Army Forces, Western Pacific, a statement of the designation, numbers, location and commanders of all Japanese armed forces, ground, sea or air, in the Philippine Islands.

8. We hereby undertake faithfully to obey all further proclamation, orders and directives deemed by the Commanding General, United States Army Forces, Western Pacific, to be proper to effectuate this surrender.

Signed at Camp John Hay, Baguio, Mountain Province, Luzon, Philippine Islands, at 1210 hours 3 September 1945:

Tomoyuki Yamashita
TOMOYUKI YAMASHITA,
General, Imperial Japanese Army
Highest Commander, Imperial
Japanese Army in the Philippines.

Denhici Okochi
DENHICI OKOCHI,
Vice Admiral, Imperial Japanese Navy
Highest Commander, Imperial
Japanese Navy in the Philippines.

By command of and in behalf
of the Japanese Imperial
General Headquarters

Accepted at Camp John Hay, Baguio, Mountain Province, Luzon Philippine Islands, at 1210 hours 3 September 1945: For the Commander-in-Chief, United States Army Forces, Pacific:

Edmond H. Leavey
EDMOND H. LEAVEY,
Major General, USA
Deputy Commander, United States Army Forces,
Western Pacific.

General Yamashita's Surrender to General Leavey in the Philippines (See No. 110)

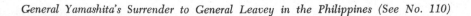

States, on behalf of itself, the United Kingdom, the Soviet Union and China, replied that the Emperor and Japanese people would be subject to the control of the Supreme Commander for the Allied Powers. Three days later authoritative word of Japan's acceptance was received, and at 7 P.M., August 14, President Truman announced the unconditional surrender of Japan.

In the preliminary negotiations that led up to the signing of the formal articles of surrender, the Japanese accepted the provision that the Emperor would be subject to the Supreme Commander for the Allied Powers, General Douglas MacArthur. Accordingly, the Emperor issued a proclamation, or rescript, calling on the people to cease hostilities. "We command all our people," the Emperor proclaimed, "forthwith to cease hostilities, to lay down their arms and faithfully to carry out all the provisions of Instrument of Surrender and the General Orders issued by the Japanese Imperial Government and the Japanese Imperial Headquarters hereunder." The Hirohito Rescript was issued the same day that the Tokyo Surrender was signed. It is dated, in the transla-

tion, "This second day of the ninth month of the twentieth year of Syowa," that is, September 2, at the twentieth year (1945) of the reign of Emperor Hirohito, the "era of Enlightened Peace."

In obedience to the imperial rescript, the general surrender at Tokyo Bay was followed by the capitulation of various Japanese armies in the field. Japanese forces in the outlying areas of the empire surrendered to the United States Army, Navy, or Marine Corps; in South East Asia the Supreme Allied Commander, Lord Louis Mountbatten, accepted their surrender. Separate instruments were signed for the Palau Islands, the Marianas, Wake, Truk, the Philippines, and the Ryukyus, in terms which followed rather closely the Tokyo Instrument.

Signatures on the Japanese instruments of surrender are a mixture of East and West, since some of the Japanese wrote their names in the orthodox characters of the Orient, in sharp contrast with the occidental script used by the Americans. The surrender instruments are not of uniform appearance; some consist of a single sheet and others are several pages in length. Some are printed on parchmentized paper, while others are typewritten on ordinary bond paper. However, the terms are all the same: unconditional surrender.

From the original instruments of surrender, which are among records of the War Department General Staff and of the Joint Chiefs of Staff in the National Archives, four have been lent by the National Archives for exhibit on the Freedom Train. Of these the document signed in the Philippines is the most formal in appearance. Printed on parchment-type paper, the unconditional surrender was signed in western style by General Tomoyuki Yamashita ("Tiger of Malaya"), Vice Admiral Denhici Okochi, and Major General Edmond H. Leavey, Deputy Commander of the U. S. Army Forces in the Western Pacific. General Jonathan Wainwright had been present at the signing of the formal surrender in Tokyo Bay and was flown from that ceremony to the Philippines to witness the ceremony on Luzon the following day. Thus the man who had directed the defense of the Philippines in the darkest days of Bataan and Corregidor and who had suffered imprisonment for five years by the enemy was present when that same enemy bowed to acknowledge complete defeat.

Japanese forces on Truk surrendered to Vice Admiral G. D. Murray, USN, on the same day that the principal Japanese surrender ceremonies took place on the *Missouri*. Two days later, on September 4, Brigadier General L. H. M. Sanderson, USMC, accepted the surrender of the Japanese on Wake Island, where 600 American Marines and civilians had fought valiantly against overpowering numbers in the dark days of December 1941. General Joseph W. Stilwell accepted the surrender of Japanese forces in the Ryukyus on September 7, 1945.

Through the courtesy of the Department of the Navy, the Freedom Train exhibits a portion of the log of the *Missouri* for September 2, 1945, the day of the surrender ceremonies.

116. General Eisenhower's Personal Flag

FIVE white stars in a circle on a field of red form the personal flag of General of the Army Dwight D. Eisenhower. [Lent by General Dwight D. Eisenhower]

117. Commodore Perry's Flag

THE original 31-star flag flown by Commodore Matthew C. Perry that was flown from his flagship at the time of the opening up of Japan, 1854. This flag was also displayed on the "USS Missouri" during the surrender ceremony at Tokyo Bay on September 2, 1945. [Lent by the U. S. Naval Academy Museum]

118. Iwo Jima Flag

ENSHRINED in the hearts of all Americans is the flag raised on Mount Suribachi by the U. S. Marines in the invasion of Iwo Jima. [Lent by the Navy Department]

119. Geruma Shima Flag

THIS is the flag that, on March 30, 1945, was raised by a battalion of the 306th Infantry over the heights of Geruma Shima, the first Japanese insular possession to be captured, liberated or occupied by the armed forces of the United States. [Lent by the U. S. Coast Guard]

120. Flag Flown from USS "Missouri" when the Japanese Surrendered

THE Ensign flown from the "Big Mo", the U. S. Battleship "Missouri" on September 2, 1945 when the Japanese signed the surrender in Tokyo Bay. [Lent by the U. S. Naval Academy Museum]

121. SHAEF Flag

AGAINST a field of solid white is emblazoned the shield of Supreme Headquarters Allied Expeditionary Forces. Its blazing sword symbolizes the liberation of the peoples of Europe enslaved by Nazi tyranny. [Lent by General Dwight D. Eisenhower]

122 - 132 Bonds of Freedom

FREEDOM and opportunity were the dreams and the achievements of the pioneers who laid the foundations of the United States of America. It required vision and courage and work to carve out of a wilderness a new nation based upon a new idea: government of the people, by the people and for the people.

It required vision, labor and thrift to provide the means to win our independence, put the new nation on a firm foundation, develop its vast natural resources, build its canals and railroads and farms and industries so that every American citizen might have an enlarged measure of freedom and opportunity to better himself in a land that offers the average man more incentives and more rewards than any other on earth.

The United States Treasury exhibits on the Freedom Train eleven original bonds of historic issues that helped to finance our wars for independence and the preserva-

Only this text in English is authoritative

ACT OF MILITARY SURRENDER

1. We the undersigned, acting by authority
of the German High Command, hereby surrender
unconditionally to the Supreme Commander, Allied
Expeditionary Force and simultaneously to the
Soviet High Command all forces on land, sea, and in
the air who are at this date under German control.

2. The German High Command will at once
issue orders to all German military, naval and
air authorities and to all forces under German
control to cease active operations at 2301 hours
Central European time on 8 May and to
remain in the positions occupied at that time. No
ship, vessel, or aircraft is to be scuttled, or any
damage done to their hull, machinery or equipment.

3. The German High Command will at once
issue to the appropriate commanders, and ensure
the carrying out of any further orders issued by
the Supreme Commander, Allied Expeditionary Force
and by the Soviet High Command.

4. This act of military surrender is without
prejudice to, and will be superseded by any
general instrument of surrender imposed by, or
on behalf of the United Nations and applicable
to GERMANY and the German armed forces as a whole.

- 1 -

5. In the event of the German High Command
or any of the forces under their control failing
to act in accordance with this Act of Surrender,
the Supreme Commander, Allied Expeditionary Force
and the Soviet High Command will take such punitive
or other action as they deem appropriate.

Signed at Rheims at 0241 on the 7th day of May, 1945.
France

On behalf of the German High Command.

Jodl

IN THE PRESENCE OF

On behalf of the Supreme Commander,   On behalf of the Soviet
Allied Expeditionary Force.   High Command.

W. B. Smith   *Sousloparov*

-2-

Major General, French Army
(Witness)

Germany's Unconditional Surrender at Rheims, May 7, 1945 (See No. 112)

tion of the Union as well as for the expansion and development of the nation in times of peace. The history
of these bonds contains much of the history of the American nation.

1779

6% loan certificate. This is one of the first securities
ever to bear the proud new name of the United States of
America; it was issued at a time when there was little
hope of winning the War of Independence. This bond
was one which could only be cashed in the bank of hope
and faith in the destiny of the new nation. That bank
remains solvent and in operation.

1803

6% Louisiana Domestic Stock. $11,250,000 worth, in
all, was issued to the government of France in partial
payment for the Louisiana Territory, bought by the
United States for $15,000,000, adding to this young na-
tion the land now embraced in the states of Louisiana,
Arkansas, Oklahoma, Kansas, Missouri, Iowa, Minnesota,
Nebraska, North and South Dakota, Montana and parts
of Colorado and Wyoming. This was one of the greatest
real estate bargains in all history. President Thomas
Jefferson thought it might take a possible hundred years
to settle this territory, but by 1846 the United States had
pushed beyond it to the Golden Gate of California.

1812

This 6%, 12-year Stock ($2,150,000 issued) helped finance the war which won us freedom of the seas.

1846

In "The Year of Decision" this 6%, 10-year loan ($4,-999,149 issued) raised funds to extend our frontiers to the Pacific Ocean and the Rio Grande and to begin the development and colonization of the vast area beyond the borders of the Louisiana Purchase.

1862

These "Five-Twenties" of 1862 were a 6% loan for 5 or 20 years ($514,771,600 issued). This bond helped finance the war that preserved the Union. On it is pictured the battle of the *Monitor* and the *Merrimac* which made wooden ships obsolete and started us on the way to becoming a great naval power.

1868

6% Consolidated Debt Consols of 1868 ($42,539,930 issued). Length of loan 5 or 20 years. $7,200,000 of these bonds paid for Alaska's 600,000 square miles, rich in furs, fish, forests, minerals, and of strategic importance. The Alaska purchase was long called "Seward's Folly," but by 1900 the gold found in Alaska had itself paid back more than the cost of the whole territory.

1898

3% loan to "provide ways and means to meet war expenditures" of the Spanish-American War ($198,678,720 issued). It was redeemable August 1908 and payable August 1918. Liberation for Cuba, Puerto Rico and the Philippines was won with the help of this bond.

1906

2% Panama Canal Loan ($54,631,980 issued). Authorized "to provide for the construction of a canal connecting the waters of the Atlantic and Pacific Oceans." It was redeemable after 10 years and payable 30 years from the date of issue. This peace bond raised the funds to purchase from the Republic of Panama the strip now called the Canal Zone and build one of the most important trade arteries in the world. A part of the money thus raised enabled heroic Walter Reed, General Gorgas, and others to conquer two of the great scourges of mankind: malaria and yellow fever.

1918

Victory Liberty Loan 4¾% Convertible Gold Note. Issued to make the world "free for democracy and forever guaranteeing to the people of the world the principles of government by the consent of the governed." Four Liberty Loans and a Victory Loan raised a total of more than $21 billion for World War I.

1941–1945

Defense and War Savings Bonds, Series E, Registered, 10 year appreciation bond. Sold to individuals only. More than 85,000,000 Americans invested $42 billion in these bonds during World War II.

1947

United States Savings Bonds, Series E. This is the same bond as the defense and war issues Series E. More than $14 billion has been invested in U.S. Savings Bonds, Series E, F and G, during 1946–1947.

ACKNOWLEDGMENTS

THE Freedom Train exhibit is a part of the educational program of the American Heritage Foundation. It received its first impetus from a proposal made by Attorney General Tom Clark. The idea took root and grew. Wide and enthusiastic support elaborated it into a citizens' movement for the purpose of developing a greater awareness of the heritage of freedom which we enjoy as Americans. Its program is "to persuade all Americans that only by *active personal participation* in the affairs of the nation can we safeguard and preserve our liberties and continue to demonstrate to ourselves and to the world that the way of free men is best."

The Freedom Train with its precious documents is a dramatic device to focus the attention of the American people on a re-examination of their heritage of freedom. Here are the documents of the Freedom Train—many of the most cherished documents of our American past. Here they are for all to read and ponder. The American Heritage Foundation, in cooperating with the publishers in making this book available, believe that it is rendering another and an important public service.

The present book was designed to provide an opportunity for a leisurely and serious reading of many of the basic documents of our history. For each document an attempt has been made to present the historical background and other remarks necessary or helpful to a better understanding of its significance. Where facsimiles present the full and legible contents of a document these materials are not reprinted in the text. Otherwise either the full text or the most significant passages are in most cases reproduced in type. In the case of books and pamphlets the contents are described and often quoted.

The chief responsibility for the selection of the materials comprising the Freedom Train exhibit fell to two committees of the American Heritage Foundation. The Documents Advisory Committee was made up of Julian P. Boyd, Solon J. Buck, Luther H. Evans, Frank Monaghan, A. S. W. Rosenbach, and S. K. Stevens. The Documents Approval Committee was composed of Winthrop W.

Aldrich, John W. Davis, John Foster Dulles, and Edwin L. Weisl. In the labors of both committees the work of Louis A. Novins, vice president and secretary of the American Heritage Foundation was ubiquitous and invaluable.

The books and manuscripts and other memorabilia of the American heritage are lent to the Freedom Train exhibit through the gracious cooperation of many institutions and individuals. To them the American public owes a vote of gratitude for their enlightened participation in a great educational effort. In the main text of *Heritage of Freedom* the source of each item is indicated. The list of donors of historical materials to the Freedom Train includes: American Philosophical Society; Mrs. Marshall Ludington Brown, Chicago; General Mark W. Clark, Presidio of San Francisco; Colonial Williamsburg and the Institute of Early American History and Culture; Department of the Army; Department of the Navy; General Dwight D. Eisenhower, Washington, D. C.; Franklin D. Roosevelt Library, Hyde Park, New York; Colonel Richard Gimbel, Philadelphia; Laurence Gouverneur Hoes, Washington, D. C.; William Jay Iselin, Katonah, New York; The John H. Scheide Library, Titusville, Pennsylvania; Frederic R. Kirkland, Philadelphia; Lafayette College Library and the American Friends of Lafayette; Library of Congress; Henry Bradley Martin, New York City; Howard L. Milkman, Long Island City, New York; Mrs. Frank Monaghan, Washington, D. C.; Museum of the Polish Roman Catholic Union of America, Chicago; National Archives; New-York Historical Society; New York State Library, Albany; Princeton University Library; Dr. A. S. W. Rosenbach, Philadelphia; Philip H. Rosenbach, Philadelphia; Sterling Memorial Library, Yale University; United States Coast Guard; United States Department of State; United States Naval Academy Museum; United States Treasury Department; Walters Art Gallery, Baltimore; Washington and Lee University.

Among those who contributed documents and advice and services to the Freedom Train exhibit two stand out most prominently. The enlightened and energetic cooperation of the National Archives and the Library of Congress was magnificent and indispensable. The National Archives had an additional and burdensome responsibility: the physical assembling of the materials and their preparation for exhibition. The Freedom Train exhibit is highly indebted to Dr. Solon J. Buck, Archivist of the United States, and to several members of the staff of the National Archives: Miss Bess Glenn, Mrs. Elizabeth H. Bukowsky, Florence Nichol, Mary Frances Handley and Peggy Mangum. The many services of Mrs. Elizabeth E. Hamer, Chief of the Division of Exhibits and Publications, were invaluable. The contributions of the Library of Congress were of the highest order. The assistance of Dr. Luther H. Evans, Librarian of Congress, and several members of his staff merit a special accolade: Verner

Clapp, Chief Assistant Librarian; Alvin C. Kremer; Donald H. Mugridge; Vincent L. Eaton; Dorothy S. Eaton; and Herbert J. Sanborn, Exhibits Officer.

So many persons have contributed so generously and effectively to the Freedom Train exhibit and to *Heritage of Freedom* that a detailed public acknowledgment of their services would be difficult to make. But no list could pretend to a partial measure of completeness without recording our gratitude to the following: Edward P. Alexander, Director of Education of Colonial Williamsburg; Louis Annin Ames, New York City; James T. Babb, Librarian of Yale University; Miss Dorothy Barck, Librarian of the New-York Historical Society; Dr. Carl Bridenbaugh, Director of the Institute of Early American History and Culture, Williamsburg; Fitz Stephen Burke, Assistant Librarian, Yale Club of New York City; L. H. Butterfield, Princeton University Library; William A. Coblenz, Department of Justice; Charles F. Gosnell, Librarian, New York State Library, Albany; Louis R. Gottschalk, University of Chicago; John F. Gough, Jersey City; Dr. Kent Greenfield, Chief Historian, Department of the Army; Colonel Stanley J. Grogan, Deputy Chief of Staff, Sixth Army; Miecislaus Haiman, Chicago; Miss Betty Herscher, Washington, D. C.; Mrs. Eleanor Iselin, Katonah, New York; Mrs. Esther Jablow, New York City; Miss Edna L. Jacobsen, Head, Manuscripts and History Section, New York State Library; Messmore Kendall, New York City; Joseph Lewis, New York City; Dr. William E. Lingelbach, Librarian, American Philosophical Society; Professor Allen W. Moger, Washington and Lee University; Professor Theodore E. Norton, Lafayette College; Commander W. C. Norvell, Officer in Charge, Security Review Section, Department of the Navy; Mrs. Richard V. Oulahan, Treasury Department; Giuseppe Prezzolini, Columbia University; William A. Scheide, Princeton, New Jersey; Edward Stanley, Department of Justice; and R. H. Williams, 2nd, Director of the Historical Society of Pennsylvania.

The unusual design of the exhibit cars of the Freedom Train was the work of Edward Burdick of the Diorama Corporation of America. The complicated and difficult supervision of the building and assembling of the Train was the responsibility of S. G. Somers, Exhibits Director for the Adjutant General of the Army. The manuscript of *Heritage of Freedom* has come under the fine scrutiny of Daniel C. Haskell and Sylvester Vigilante, two esteemed members of the staff of the New York Public Library. Photographs used in the facsimile pages are from the superb collection of all the documents of the Freedom Train exhibit made by Peter A. Juley of New York City. Miss Ruth Munro and Mrs. Frank Monaghan gave cheering and invaluable assistance in the preparation of the manuscript. John Fleming of the Rosenbach Company was especially helpful in the assembling of the documents. Julian P. Boyd, Librarian of Princeton

University, has given generously of his many talents in every phase of the work. The staff of Princeton University Press has given the book a fine impetus and much encouragement.

A special measure of praise goes to Winthrop W. Aldrich, Chairman of the Board of Trustees, and to Thomas D'A. Brophy, President of the American Heritage Foundation, for the determination and the fine vision they have infused into one of the greatest educational movements ever launched in America.

The admirably effective collaboration of Louis A. Novins, together with his energy and perspicacity, have provided a rare and cherished pleasure.

FRANK MONAGHAN

FOR FURTHER READING

THESE notes do not present a bibliography for the subjects involved. They represent suggestions for additional reading on sundry matters with which the public is not too well acquainted. They also give the opportunity of recording credits and appreciations which could not conveniently find their way into the main text.

1. The translation of the Columbus letter is by R. H. Major, in *Hakluyt Society Publications* XII (1847); see also Samuel Eliot Morison, *Admiral of the Ocean Sea: A Life of Christopher Columbus* (1942).

2. The description of this document is taken from Dr. Julian P. Boyd's history of the John H. Scheide Library; see also W. S. McKechnie, *Magna Carta* (1905, 1914); also Sidney Painter, "Magna Carta," *American Historical Review* LIII, 42-49 (Oct. 1947).

3. In addition to William Bradford's classic history, *Of Plimouth Plantation*, see George F. Williams' *Saints and Strangers* (1945).

4. W. S. Carpenter, *Development of American Political Thought* (1930); John Chester Miller, *Origins of the American Revolution* (1943).

6. In this bold statement of a theory of imperial relations which denied the authority of Parliament, and asserted that the colonies were, in effect, self-governing dominions linked to the British Empire only by a common allegiance to the Crown, Jefferson took an advanced position that only a few Americans in 1774—among them John Adams, Roger Sherman, Benjamin Franklin, and James Wilson—dared to support. See R. G. Adams, *The Political Ideas of the American Revolution* (1922).

7. T. J. Wertenbaker, *Torchbearer of the Revolution* (1940).

9. G. J. McRee, *Life and Correspondence of James Iredell* (1857-58).

10. This article is entirely from the pen of Dr. Julian

P. Boyd, Librarian of Princeton University and eminent authority on Jefferson; see his *The Declaration of Independence: The Evolution of the Text* (1945).

11. Sir G. O. Trevelyan, *The American Revolution* (1899-1907).

13. E. C. Burnett, *The Continental Congress* (1941); Merrill Jensen, *The Articles of Confederation* (1940).

14. Philip Fover, ed., *The Complete Writings of Thomas Paine* (1945); Moncure D. Conway, *The Life of Thomas Paine* (1892); Philip Davidson, *Propaganda and the American Revolution* (1941).

16. Esther Forbes' *Paul Revere & the World He Lived In* (1942) is a charming and scholarly biography.

17. E. C. Burnett, *The Continental Congress* (1941).

19. The full story is given by John H. Scheide in "The Lexington Alarm," *Proceedings of the American Antiquarian Society*, vol. 50, pp. 48-79 (April 1940).

20. Among many accounts of the Yorktown campaign, one of the best is still Benson J. Lossing's *Pictorial Field-Book of the Revolution* (1860).

21. Samuel Flagg Bemis, *The Diplomacy of the American Revolution* (1935).

22. Samuel H. Brockunier, *Roger Williams, the Irrepressible Democrat* (1940).

23. Jefferson himself has provided the best accounts of the reformation of the Virginia laws and of the objectives of the Statute for Religious Freedom. See his *Autobiography* and his *Notes on Virginia*. See also Sanford H. Cobb, *Rise of Religious Liberty in America* (1902); and H. R. McIlwaine, *Struggle of the Protestant Dissenters for Religious Toleration in Virginia* (1894).

24. See the introduction by Wilberforce Eames in the facsimile reprint of *The Bay Psalm Book* (1903); also George Parker Winship, *The Cambridge Press 1638-1692* (1945).

27. Frank Monaghan, *John Jay: Defender of Liberty* (1935).

28. A. C. McLaughlin, *The Confederation and the Constitution 1783-1790* (1905); Max Farrand, *The Records of the Federal Convention of 1787* (1911); Charles Warren, *The Making of the Constitution* (1928); and Carl Van Doren, *The Great Rehearsal* (1948).

29. There still remained in the country many patriotic leaders who could not accept the idea of nationality implied in the phrase "We, the People." Among the stubborn defenders of the States' Rights point of view was Patrick Henry who, in the Virginia ratifying convention, thundered: "What right had they to say, "We the People? . . . Who authorized them to speak the language of We the People, instead of We, the States?"

30. E. S. Corwin, *The Constitution and What it Means Today* (1947); David Hutchison, *The Foundations of the Constitution* (1928).

31. E. S. Corwin, *The Constitution and What it Means Today* (1947).

32. J. B. McMaster and F. D. Stone, *Pennsylvania and the Federal Constitution* (1888).

34. Helen Hill, *George Mason, Constitutionalist* (1938); Kate Mason Rowland, *The Life of George Mason* (1892).

35. E. S. Corwin, *The Constitution and What it Means Today* (1947).

39. Jefferson's letter is important on other grounds than its judgment of the proposed Federal Constitution. Expanding with his great subject, the American minister to France—where he stood on a vantage-point and could survey his country's course—set forth his philosophy of government in concise and memorable terms. He was less concerned than were most of the framers of the Constitution over popular disturbances like Shays' Rebellion, to which he refers. To those who were concerned he posed the question: "Say, finally, whether peace is best preserved by giving energy to the government, or information to the people. This last is the most certain. . . . Educate and inform the whole mass of the people. Enable them to see that it is their interest to preserve peace and order, and they will preserve them."

40. Edward M. Burns, *James Madison, Philosopher of the Constitution* (1938).

41. The best recent biography is: Nathan Schachner, *Alexander Hamilton* (1946); see also the excellent article on Hamilton by Allan Nevins in the *Dictionary of American Biography*.

43. V. H. Paltsits, *Washington's Farewell Address* (1935).

44. See "The Story of the American Flag" in the *National Geographic Magazine* XXXII, 286-303 (October 1917); a comprehensive account is George H. Preble's *Origin and History of the American Flag* (1917).

45. Oscar G. T. Sonneck's *Star Spangled Banner,* published by the Library of Congress (1914), is an exhaustive study.

47. S. F. Bemis, "Washington's Farewell Address: A Foreign Policy of Independence," *American Historical Review* XXXIX (1934), 250-268.

48. The quotation from Professor Randall's *Lincoln the President—Springfield to Gettysburg* (1945) is used by permission of Dodd, Mead & Company, the publishers.

51. F. Lauriston Bullard, "*A Few Appropriate Remarks*": Lincoln's Gettysburg Address (1944).

52. D. D. Wallace, *Life of Henry Laurens* (1915).

58. R. C. Downes, *Frontier Ohio, 1788–1803* (1935).

63. Louis Gottschalk has written a series of studies of Lafayette's career in America: *Lafayette Comes to America* (1935); *Lafayette Joins the American Army* (1937); and *Lafayette and the Close of the American Revolution* (1942).

64. Miecislaus Haiman, *Kosciuszko in the American Revolution* (1943).

68. Elizabeth F. Ellet, *The Women of the American Revolution* (1850).

69. C. W. Alvord, *The Illinois Country* (1920); James A. James, *The Life of George Rogers Clark* (1928).

70. Lincoln Lorenz, *John Paul Jones* (1943); John S. Barnes, ed., *The Logs of the Serapis-Alliance-Ariel, under the Command of John Paul Jones, 1779–1780* (1911); D. C. Seitz, ed., *Paul Jones: His Exploits in English Seas during 1778–1780: Contemporary Accounts Collected from English Newspapers* (1917).

71. Article on David Bushnell in the *Dictionary of American Biography;* Gardner W. Allen, *A Naval History of the American Revolution* (1913).

73. Franklin's printing career may be traced in Carl Van Doren's fine biography, *Benjamin Franklin* (1938); see also Franklin's own account in his unrivaled *Autobiography.*

76. Gilbert Chinard, *Thomas Jefferson* (1939); Claude Bowers, *The Young Jefferson* (1945); Karl Lehmann, *Thomas Jefferson: American Humanist* (1947).

77. Actually this view was held by the ablest men in both parties. It was the core of the foreign policy of Washington and Adams and of Jefferson as well. For background, see Frank Monaghan, *John Jay: Defender of Liberty* (1935).

79. Marquis James, *Andrew Jackson* (1938) chaps. 9-15, with excellent maps and plans.

80. I. N. Thomas, *The Frigate Constitution.*

87. There are good brief accounts of Zenger's career and trial in Frank L. Mott's *American Journalism* (1941); see also article on Zenger by R. B. Morris in the *Dictionary of American Biography.*

88. Commendable lives of Wilkes have been written by Horace Bleackley (1917) and by Raymond Postgate (1929), the latter bearing the title *That Devil Wilkes,* which was George III's term for him.

90. The Sedition Act and its counterpart, the Alien Act, are treated in all general histories of the United States. One of the best accounts, containing many quotations from the contemporary press, is in John Bach McMaster's *History of the People of the United States* II (1885), chap. 10, "The Quarrel with France."

92. James Edward Pollard, *The Presidents and the Press* (1947); Frank Luther Mott, *Jefferson and the Press* (1943).

93. Ralph Barton Perry, *Puritanism and Democracy* (1944); Zechariah Chafee, Jr., *Freedom of Speech* (1919); Frank L. Mott, *Jefferson and the Press* (1943).

112. This description follows closely the text of the excellent little pamphlet published by the National Archives in 1945 when the surrender documents were first exhibited to the public.

INDEX OF PRINCIPAL NAMES AND SUBJECTS

(The numbers refer to Documents, not pages)